DATE DUE

DEMCO 38-296

A GRAMMAR OF RESPONSIBILITY

A GRAMMAR
OF RESPONSIBILITY

by
Gabriel Moran

A Crossroad Book
The Crossroad Publishing Company
New York

1996
The Crossroad Publishing Company
370 Lexington Avenue, New York, NY 10017

Printed in the United States of America

Library of Congress Cataloging-in-Publication Data

Moran, Gabriel
    A grammar of responsibility / by Gabriel Moran.
        p.   cm.
    Includes bibliographical references and index.
    ISBN 0-8245-1554-4
    1. Responsibility.   I. Title.
BJ1451.M649   1996
170—dc20   95-54001
                                                CIP

To and For Maria

CONTENTS

INTRODUCTION

A writer has to be either audacious or naive to write a book that crosses as many academic divisions as this one does. I am fully aware that scholars rightfully protect the boundaries of their disciplines from presumptuous intruders. My only defense is that, having decided to track the term "responsibility," I followed where it led. I therefore draw my examples from a wide range of specialties, but my intention is the fairly modest one of suggesting how best to use a single word.

"Responsibility" is a word that now makes a frequent appearance in ordinary speech. It also shows up in discussions of politics, psychology, economics, religion, ecology, and numerous other areas. Everyone seems to like the idea of responsibility. At least there is no debate among politicians as to whether people should be responsible or not. The drawback to this consensus is that when an idea is acclaimed by everyone then no one is forced to examine the complex character of the idea.

I have been tracking the term "responsibility" for more than twenty-five years. It first caught my attention when I was teaching ethics in the late 1960s. It was just one of those markers that people inserted at the appropriate spot. And yet, there was something elusive about its meaning. While there was abundant literature on ideas such as freedom, rights, and law, there seemed to be less to say about responsibility. Perhaps that was because it was then a less commonly used term.

During the last two decades the use of the term "responsibility" has grown rapidly, and the frequency of its appearance continues to accelerate. The constant invocation of responsibility has now gone beyond a faddish season or two. Responsibility has become a talisman of the late twentieth century. In a world that often seems to be spinning out

1

of control, what is assumed to be needed is that "people take responsibility."

The number of books on the subject of responsibility has also
expanded in the last few decades. I acknowledge my debt to many of
these books in my footnotes. However, I have avoided much of the
language that has become standard in this literature. As happens in
many areas, controversies have developed between several schools of
thinking, each using a technical vocabulary. In this book I step back
from these debates to take notice of how people are using the term
responsibility, to speculate on its popularity, and to suggest a way of
speaking that might open a conversation across academic specialties.

I began with an impression that "responsibility" made its big
entrance in the nineteenth century, before it blossomed in the twentieth. Subsequent study largely confirmed my guess. Of course, the
word existed before the nineteenth century, but it was a somewhat
unusual term, not something people were constantly urged to take.
Perhaps more important, the meaning of the term was quite different
before the nineteenth century. Still, emergence of a new idea or a shift
in the meaning of a term would not necessarily be a story worth
telling.

What motivates this book is a suspicion that I have had from the
beginning, a suspicion that strengthened as I proceeded. Is it possible
that "responsibility," far from being the medicine to cure our problems
is expressive of the bind in which we find ourselves? The widespread
assumption is that too many people lack responsibility. Could it be
that very many people are trying to take too much responsibility, and
that one of the worst pieces of advice they can be given is "take responsibility for your life"?

Behind this question is an issue I immediately engage in chapter 1
but cannot answer without all of the chapters that follow. Is "responsibility" a nineteenth-century word whose moral lifespan did not out-
last Victoria? If that is the case, then responsibility in the twentieth
century would have become a clever instrument of manipulation, or
less deviously, a piece of confused rhetoric. In either case, responsibility would weigh heavily on the backs of the poor and those convicted
of crime. The hard-working middle class might also sink under the
burden of trying to be responsible.

One route to go would be to attack the very idea of responsibility;
ultimately, however, such an attack would be quixotic. I think that the

nineteenth century was not all wrong on the point; there is obviously some positive and desirable reality that people are trying to indicate with the term responsibility. But the situating of responsibility today is starkly different from what it was a century ago.

On the one side today the economic and political systems that surround the individual human being are massive; no one, even the people supposedly in charge, is certain how to move these systems. On the other side, people *feel* that they should be responsible for themselves. Nothing is held to be more important than making one's own decisions. These two sides of life have no obvious meeting point. Even powerful, rich, and smart people can be blind to how much they are caught within this conflict. Economists and politicians may be working on one side, psychologists and preachers on the other side; but the connecting links for these efforts are likely to be missing.

I locate the cross hairs of Western history in the paradoxical figure of Friedrich Nietzsche. With Nietzsche, the final exaltation of the human will is to be found. No one is above; "man" is the supreme power in the universe. Man and only man is responsible for himself. At the same time, Nietzsche represents the beginning of the end of the modern ideal of free, autonomous man. Several decades before Freud's investigations, Nietzsche revealed the dark underside from which human actions emerge. "Man" is a helpless pawn in forces beyond his imagination. Man is not in control and therefore not responsible for any of his actions.

A century after Nietzsche, the wildly contradictory picture of "man" is played out in the United Nations, the Internet, the congress, television talk shows, law courts, businesses, schools, environmental disputes, and almost any place one can name. Several decades of feminist criticism have taught most of us to be suspicious of pronouncements about "man." However, substituting the term "human" for "man" would only deal with part of the issue. Our linguistic problem, inherited from centuries past, is a set of dichotomies: "man versus nature," "man versus God," "man versus society." In this book I propose ways of speaking that can overcome these dichotomies. Only with such changes can responsibility be situated in a matrix of many relations, including that of women and men. In documenting the views of Nietzsche, Weber, Heidegger, Sartre, and many other writers, it is necessary to discuss what they say about "man," both for historical accuracy and to understand the problem still present in our language.

"Humans and nature" is a slight improvement over "man and nature," but "human and nonhuman natures" opens new possibilities. A reader struck by the use of "man," especially in chapter 2, should notice that it is the language I am criticizing not advocating. Every chapter of this book is about shaping a relational language to describe responsibility in the lives of women, men, children, and some nonhumans.

Aristotle's word for a solution to a problem means "to untie a knot." That is the most I am trying to do in the work that follows. I make no claim to offer political answers to questions of national policy, economic theories for improving the gross national product, theological formulations for church life, or ecological cures for the environmental crisis. I do, however, draw from these and other areas to explore how to employ the term responsibility. What I seek to lay out is a comprehensive and consistent way of speaking; comprehensive in referring both to ordinary speech and specialized uses; consistent in relation to the etymology and history of responsibility, while maintaining a cohesiveness in the meaning of the term.

The argument is mainly philosophical in trying to gather historical, logical, and empirical evidence to support the distinctions of language I propose. I would also add that religion is a major part of the story and cannot be avoided. We are still recovering from the modern rebellion against the Christian church and its theology, which had the effect of excluding from many studies a major element in human experience. Outside of moral theology, Christian ethics, and Jewish ethics, the study of moral and ethical questions was determinedly secular.

Today we have examples of books, still too few in number, that are not theology but take some of their inspiration and content from religion past and present. Responsibility may seem to be a thoroughly secular term, but if one digs into its history and implications the religious dimension becomes evident. The reader for whom I write is someone who considers religion to be important or at least not out of the question as an area of interest. The argument, nonetheless, is about data that are available to everyone, and it does not presume theological premises.

Although I express suspicions of the way "responsibility" is being pushed today, I do think a discussion of the term is a possible meeting point for all segments of the population. But any effective use of the term requires some careful distinctions that would open a different kind of conversation than those which usually swirl around the term today.

This book, like every book I have previously written, is a work on education. I subscribe to John Dewey's principle that "education is the workshop of philosophy." Education here means the reshaping of ordinary life through the conversations of men and women, adults and children, humans and nonhumans. The last of those three pairs may seem out of place; granted, conversation between humans and nonhumans is not easily accomplished. But the human relation to its nonhuman environment is the center of ethical, religious, and educational reform today. The humans should never forget that they share the earth with other creatures and that in relation to their closest animal kin humans have to listen as well as give orders.

The world of living beings is always the context of the intrahuman conversations that educate. There must always be a gentle reshaping of life's forms in any process that deserves the name education. The assumption that education consists of big people telling little people what to think is a cruel travesty. Conversation between mature men and women should gradually include children who can speak as well as listen, children who begin becoming responsible for themselves the day they are born.

The process of listening and then answering that I describe in this book is at the heart of all education. In the family, on the worksite, within the classroom, and through leisure activities education goes on every day, its effectiveness dependent on how deeply we listen and respond to the life within our own bodies and to the living beings around us. An analysis of responsibility that can illuminate education has to engage the major issues of today while keeping itself rooted in the moral and religious discussions of past centuries.

CHAPTER 1

TALKING ABOUT RESPONSIBILITY

This book is a reflection on the term "responsibility" and its close relatives such as "respond" and "responsible." A book-length study of a single word may seem excessive, but much depends on what the word is and how an author pursues the quest for its meaning. In the second part of this chapter, I explore the method of developing a grammar of usage around the meaning of a term and what such a study might contribute to a larger project of moral inquiry. Here in the first part of the chapter, I provide initial evidence for why "responsibility" is the right term to choose for the developing of a grammar.

The first thing to be noted about responsible/responsibility is an explosion in the frequency of its appearance. Throughout the twentieth century its use has continuously grown, and in the last two decades the talk of responsibility is everywhere. If the reader is not willing to grant this point, I can only suggest an experiment of listening for the word and noticing it in print. Among the many sources I use in this book is the editorial page of *The New York Times*. There is seldom a day when the word responsibility does not figure prominently in the *Times*'s editorials. A contemporary discussion of politics, art, economics, culture, religion, or ethics seems to be impossible without reliance on "responsibility." I will presently give a sample of quotations from newspapers, journals, popular literature, and scholarly studies to indicate the widespread use of the term.

The big problem I confront is not to find examples of the term's use but to bring attention to a complicated word that has blended into ordinary speech. A word can become so common that it almost ceases to be visible. It is taken to be an obvious idea whose meaning is patent to any speaker of the English language. And yet "responsibility" is a quite complex philosophical term with a puzzling history. One might

7

expect that there would be careful attention to its subtleties and complexity whenever it is used. Instead, it seems to fall under a rule of thumb that the more a term is used the less it is analyzed. Surely if everyone *assumes* the word's meaning, that meaning must have been made clear a long time ago. With the word responsibility the arguments often concern what adjective to place in front of it. In this context, the question is how the idea is to be applied not what the idea is.

Before taking up some examples of current usage, I have to acknowledge one possible interpretation of the widespread use of responsible/responsibility. There is a Taoist saying that "for a virtue to be conceptualized means that it is already moribund."[1] We begin to talk about a desirable aspect of life at the moment when we sense its absence.

In his book *Modern Times*, Paul Johnson begins by describing the intellectual revolution of the early twentieth century, which he finds embodied in Einstein, Freud, Joyce, and Proust. Johnson describes the effect of this revolution as one of "destroying the nineteenth century," especially its moral basis: "The nineteenth century saw the climax of the philosophy of personal responsibility—the notion that each of us is individually accountable for our actions—which was the joint heritage of Judeo-Christianity and the classical world."[2] Is Johnson correct in saying that responsibility reached its climax in the nineteenth century and has ceased to be in the twentieth?

If this view were to be correct it might not be surprising to find "responsibility" used the several dozen times it is in Pope John Paul II's encyclical *The Gospel of Life*.[3] That is, to many of his critics, the pope is asking for a return to a world that no longer exists. But what about all the other people who talk about responsibility? Are they praising responsibility precisely because it is no longer alive and, therefore, no one expresses opposition to the idea? Would there be less talk about responsibility if it were a vital idea? In this case, the endless calls for responsibility would be worse than useless; they would be a coverup of problems we cannot or will not face.

I take seriously the possibility of a coverup and the danger of being trapped into adding another layer of covering. I am also aware of the inevitable paradox in Taoist sayings of the kind I have quoted. If responsibility is "moribund" because of talk, then silence can add further covering. One needs talk of a peculiar kind (along with careful attention to silence) to discover the condition of the patient. A moribund concept is not neutral or nonexistent. Either it has to be resuscitated or else the corpse has to be cleared away. Either responsibility belongs at the center of contemporary discussions or else it is an obstacle to thinking effectively about our many overlapping problems. We will be able to decide which of these alternatives to follow only after exploring how the term is now being used and what are the limits of its effective use. Can the term responsibility be an entry point to speaking about all the important issues of today or is the task to reveal a fraudulent hope?

We can begin illustrating the use of "responsibility" by noticing that in the nation's political speech the word is celebrated by both political parties. No politician can be heard questioning whether responsibility is a good thing. Democrats and Republicans do have a significant difference in how they have talked about responsibility, dating back to the beginning of this century. In the last two decades, however, the difference seems to have blurred. Whether this change is a permanent one is likely to be clear only after another decade or two. What is clear now is that politicians of every background and ideology will be outdone by no one in upholding responsibility.

President Bill Clinton was not the first president to preach responsibility. But he may have been the first to use the term as a kind of mantra, that is, a word repetitively chanted as a sacred symbol. Throughout his campaign for the presidency, responsibility was a central theme. And when he delivered his first State of the Union Address, it was structured around a repetition of the word responsible. "What has brought us here over two centuries," President Clinton said, is "a commitment to opportunity, to individual responsibility." But then "for too long we drifted without a strong sense of purpose or responsibility." "I come here tonight," said Clinton, "to accept responsibility and I want you to accept responsibility with me." "As government creates more opportunity in this new and different time, we must also demand more responsibility in turn." Of welfare, Mr. Clinton said: "It is time to demand that people take responsibility for the children they bring into the world." Of the military, he said: "We can responsibly reduce our defense budget" though "we still have responsibilities around the world." Of his proposed tax on energy, he said: "It is environmentally responsible."[4]

President Clinton ran into severe opposition in trying to carry through on these calls for responsibility. His opponents, of course, did not disagree about the need for responsibility. Indeed, one could say that the main premise in Newt Gingrich's *To Renew America* is the statement "Republicans envision a decentralized America in which responsibility is returned to the individual."[5] The much heralded "Contract with America" had ten items, one of which was a proposed bill called "The Personal Responsibility Act."[6] Someone unacquainted with political discussion in the United States during recent decades might not guess that the title was for a bill on welfare reform. Both parties repeatedly said that welfare policy in the United States is disgraceful, inefficient, and in need of total overhaul. But the discussion was less about the actual money involved than about responsibility, with the government on one side and individual recipients on the other.

When the new Republican majority tried to force changes in these laws, they were criticized for being callous. Speaker Newt Gingrich angrily replied to his critics: "Our point is, who is being callous? Is it the people responsible for the conditions that the poor live in today, or the people trying to fix that? We are the people trying to fix that. For those responsible for these problems to claim some moral high ground is repugnant."[7]

George Pataki, who was swept into the governorship of New York State in the 1994 election, made "personal responsibility" the theme of his inaugural address. And unmistakably, welfare was at the center of this theme. Governor Pataki painted the choice in clear lines: "When government accepts responsibility for people, then people no longer take responsibility for themselves. Individual responsibility and personal freedom are inevitably linked."[8]

At that moment there were few voices to be heard in opposition to this claim. Who is going to defend the proposition that people should *not* take responsibility for themselves? One group that did question the enthusiasm for "personal responsibility" was the United States Conference of Catholic Bishops. They happened to be meeting the week after the November 1994 elections. A spokesman, Bishop John Ricard of Baltimore, began his criticism by acknowledging that "there has to be personal responsibility." He then went on to say: "We also believe the society has a responsibility for those who cannot care for themselves."[9] The bishops continued to press their criticism in the following spring as these policies were discussed: "Society has a responsibility to help meet the needs of those who cannot care for themselves, especially young children."[10] Whether this kind of criticism is effective will have to be examined later in detail. Certainly, one has to look carefully at the opposing choices that are assumed to be the range of possibility.

When politicians speak of "personal responsibility," often with a primary reference to welfare recipients, they are exposing just one small part of a cultural upheaval. At the intersection of law and psychotherapy (twin pillars of United States culture) is a question of whether responsibility can be pinned down anymore. The courts, television talk shows, schools, business dealings, hospitals, social work are engulfed by confusion about who—if anyone—is responsible for what.

The extreme form of the problem is a phenomenon called "victimization." If the claim to be a victim is believed, the person cannot be held responsible. No one doubts that some people are the victims of human oppression or nonhuman disasters, and that the resulting physical or psychological damage interferes with their performance of ordinary human actions. They are "not responsible," at least in some aspects of life or to some degree. But what happens when millions of people lay claim to the status of "not responsible"? The question goes well beyond the welfare mother who is receiving $400 per month to support her family. In fact, the game is open to almost everyone who wishes to play.

A number of famous court cases in the 1980s and 1990s brought the "abuse excuse" to prominence. They were a manifestation of something already widespread; in turn they probably spread the idea further. Clever lawyers were able to convince juries (or individual jury members) that although the defendant clearly did the deed, he or she should not be held responsible. The juries in these cases refused to convict. In one of the best-known cases, which involved two brothers, Lyle and Erik Menendez, the prosecution failed to convict the defendants despite the fact that they killed their parents and went off on a spending spree with the money. The successful defense was based on a claim, now regularly used, of sexual abuse. In this case, the alleged abuse had happened many years previously, and the alleged victims were old enough to remove themselves from the situation. Similar defenses have become commonplace in the criminal justice system, the pleas of "not responsible" made by the rich and powerful as well as by the poor and helpless.

In the most famous case of all, the O. J. Simpson marathon, this element was present from the beginning. A few days after Simpson's arrest, District Attorney Gil Garcetti said: "I think that eventually he will admit that he did it but that he is not responsible."[11] Eyebrows were raised over the appropriateness of the district attorney making this statement. But no one, whether lawyer or casual observer of Court TV, had to ask what the statement meant. In his quasi-suicide note during that same week, Simpson had said that he felt like he was a victim. He did not explain the basis of the feeling, though undoubtedly he could have traced the feeling all the way back to childhood, and he could have recounted the heavy burden of high expectation, fame, and fortune.

We thus seem to have a deep fissure in the country between those who employ the language of victimization to evade responsibility and that part of the population which ever more fervently urges that people take responsibility for their lives. The people who consider themselves responsible citizens fear that they are losing the battle and that a rapid erosion of responsibility is in progress. Arlene Croce, a well-known dance critic, wrote a long, biting attack on the glorification of suffering and victimization in the arts. Her conclusion was "that victimhood is a kind of mass delusion that has taken hold of previously responsible sectors of our culture."[12]

In reaction to the seeming erosion of responsibility, there is likely to be applause when a public official declares that he or she "takes full responsibility" for a difficult decision. Certainly there is courage shown when someone candidly admits doing something foolish or criminal and is willing to accept the unpalatable consequences. "I acknowledge my responsibility in this sordid affair and must therefore submit my resignation and accept the punishment."

In recent decades, however, some public officials seem to have discovered that simply announcing that one "takes full responsibility" can turn attention from the foolishness or illegality of a policy to the courage and tenacity of the decision maker. The announcement becomes the last rather than one of the first steps to correcting the failure.

Public officials in such cases are simply doing what the public seems to want and what the press clamors for. There are few metaphors more frequently used in journalistic discussions of the government than Harry Truman's description of responsibility as "the buck stops here." I wish to argue later that this homey but inappropriate saying obscures any useful discussion of responsibility. It leads to presidents, governors, and mayors being routinely brought out to declare "I take full responsibility."

Consider the notorious case of the federal government's handling of the Branch Davidian compound in Waco, Texas. Within hours after the disastrous events were played out, Attorney General Janet Reno said in a press conference that she took full responsibility for what had happened: "I made the decision. I am accountable. The buck stops here." Then after twenty-four hours of being pressured to do so, President Clinton finally said that he was responsible. The press was not impressed. *Newsday* declared that "the president deliberately distanced himself from the decision to move in, laying responsibility squarely on the shoulders of Janet Reno."

Janet Reno garnered extremely favorable comments in the spring of 1993 not for actions taken by officials in the justice department but for knowing where the buck stopped. *Newsday*, after criticizing President Clinton, contrasted him with Janet Reno: "Her unstinting honesty in accepting complete responsibility for the decision was a rare display of integrity."[13] One did not have to be a cynic to guess that Reno's blanket assumption of responsibility would function as an obstacle to discovering who was responsible for what. After a year's reports on the Waco disaster and after House investigations two years later, one thing was clear: responsibility for all the mistakes in this fiasco would never be discovered.

The Oklahoma City bombing in 1995 revealed the continuing undercurrent of bitter feelings about the unresolved question of responsibility. At that time, Janet Reno sounded a rather different note in reacting to critics: "It is unfair, it is unreasonable, it is a lie, to spread the poison that the Government was responsible at Waco for the murder of innocents."[14] Her statement is undoubtedly correct but not adequate. Particular people in the government who advised Reno were partly responsible for many innocent people getting killed; and yet government reports on the event were unable to assign fault to anyone in particular.

It is not necessary to impugn Janet Reno's motives. But in this case as in numerous similar cases, a public official taking full responsibility subverts any serious inquiry into where the responsibility lies. I wish to argue that in any complex action, the official cannot take full responsibility; it simply is not there for the taking. And when the

rhetoric outdistances the reality, the result is obscurantism that undermines appropriately responsible action.

When whole nations are involved, questions of responsibility get
especially complicated along with being emotionally charged. The
passage of time does not of itself settle these issues. In fact, the relation
of the present generation to the past only complicates things further.
Unless a clear idea of responsibility is brought to bear upon the best
historical data, past events keep coming back to haunt us. Various fifti-
eth-year remembrances of the World War II era rekindled bitter memories. How does the idea of responsibility apply to Auschwitz, Pearl
Harbor, Hiroshima, the Iron Curtain, and other ungraspable events for
which we assign proper names? Perhaps it makes no sense to ask the
question of responsibility, but it does not seem to go away.

In 1991 the mayor of Honolulu asked President Bush to invite
Japanese participation in commemorating Pearl Harbor, only on the
condition that they apologize for the war. Deputy Chief Cabinet Secretary Ishihara Nobuo replied that "the entire world is responsible for
the war" and that the United States should apologize too. "It will take
tens or hundreds of years before the correct judgment is delivered on
who is responsible for the war."[15]

The era of World War II is especially rich in examples to be discussed, but international incidents continue to occur that spark heated
discussions of responsibility. When two nations or two factions within
a nation start fighting, most people outside the situation realize that
responsibility is extremely difficult to pin down. But the combatants
themselves usually see things in dramatically simple terms: the other
side started it; the enemy bears full responsibility for all the killing.
However difficult it is to analyze responsibility in situations of this
kind, thousands and even millions of lives can depend on responsible
parties understanding the past and the present of conflicts.

There is another area where responsibility is as complex as it is in
international affairs. The relation between the human race and its total
environment forms the backdrop of all questions of responsibility.
Over recent centuries, and especially in this century, the power of
human beings has greatly expanded. As the mastery of the physical
world has proceeded, the sense of human responsibility has also
expanded. Similar to the way a corporate structure multiplies the
effect of personal decisions, so technology has made human agents

capable of altering life on earth. What happens to the meaning of responsibility in a high-tech world?

From the late Middle Ages until recently in this century, the governing assumption was that science was liberating "man" and that science's by-product in the form of technology was subduing nature. Whether or not "man" was going to be able to bear the responsibility for this power over nature, the question itself seemed clear. Daniel Callahan, in a book on aging and death, writes: "Where once we human beings, as moral agents, stood helpless in the face of nature, whose workings were outside the range of our responsibility, now everything is in some sense thought to be our responsibility."[16]

If indeed it is thought that everything is *in some sense* our responsibility, we are still left with figuring out in what sense. In the last several decades there has been a questioning of the terms that the seventeenth, eighteenth, and nineteenth centuries gave us to work with. The abstractions of "man" and "nature" hide the currents of exchange between concrete existents: men and men, women and men, men and women and trees, men and women and fish. The nature supposedly being subdued was not a separate reality from human life.

Not surprisingly, technology has its most paradoxical effect in the marvels of modern medicine. Medical technology can extend an individual life, an accomplishment that can be a blessing. But simply extending the length of individual lives is raising new questions about human responsibility. Studies indicate that the majority of deaths in United States hospitals are "negotiated."[17] At the center of the negotiation are the patient, the physician (or medical team), and technology.

To turn on a machine and to turn off a machine are acts that involve responsibility. But so does not turning off a machine that has already been turned on, a choice to let the machine's logic dictate results. We are only four decades into the contemporary era of medicine, probably still at the threshold of this new sense of responsibility for relating life and death. At present, there seems to be confusion and frustration. Daniel Callahan captures some of the new-found disappointment at the moment of our triumph: "We have done nothing less than to make mortality itself our fault, our responsibility. By making humans responsible for everything, and making it irrelevant whether they act by commission or omission, we have created an impossibly heavy and unbearable burden."[18]

In trying to cope with the complex decisions of the modern world, we have created a class of people called "professionals." Whatever their specialty, these people are supposedly trustworthy because they are guided by a professional code of ethics. The central term in most of these codes is "responsibility." A professional is above all else a responsible person. What exactly is entailed by this professing of responsibility? Sol Linowitz, in a book lamenting the state of the legal profession, writes: "By the acceptance of his license to practice law, he has also accepted a responsibility to act as more than an advocate."[19] Linowitz is saying that the lawyer is not simply responsible for doing good for his client. The lawyer's responsibility is in relation to something greater. The court? The legal profession? Justice?

As another example that may be less exalted but is by no means trivial, there are professional athletes. A strike by professional players is shocking. A professional does not do that, should not have to do that. Beyond the million-dollar endorsements, there is a responsibility to the game, to the fans, to history. On the day that Michael Jordan returned to basketball, the reason he gave for returning was "Young guys are not taking their part of the responsibilities as far as love for the game. This certainly has affected the integrity of the game."[20] It was not clear which players or which practices Jordan was referring to. However, no sportswriter had to ask the meaning of being responsible to and for the game.

As a final example in this introductory survey, there is a paradoxical use of the term that would be almost amusing if it were not so often deadly. "Responsibility" seems to be the term of choice for terrorists. Perhaps "terrorists" is a term open to challenge; one group's terrorists are another group's patriotic leaders or front for justice. In either case, there are people who plant bombs, hijack airliners, and assassinate presidents. The actors in these dramas are fond of "taking responsibility." When the group has less chance of being believed, they are said to "claim responsibility."

The bombing of the World Trade Center in February, 1993, offers a typical case. In slightly shaky English, the group had its say in *The New York Times*: "We are, the fifth battalion in the Liberation Army, declare our responsibility for the explosion of the mentioned building." An unusual twist in this document is a subsequent use of "responsible" to explain the reason for the bombing: "The American people are responsible for the actions of their government and they must question all of the crimes that their government is committing against other people."[21] A nice symmetry is established here: the responsibility for crimes by U.S. government/people is met with responsibility for the bombing of U.S. building/people.

Why are terrorists so attached to the word responsibility? The terrorists probably do not know; they are following a script used hundreds of previous times. Everyone knows how the telephone call from the secret bomber goes: "We the ____ liberation group take responsibility for this strike against the ____ oppressive regime." But no one is certain why the message got formulated this way in the first place. I would guess that "responsibility" was originally chosen for its part in the message because the term is so often used by proper, conservative guardians of society. To apply the term to secret and violently disruptive acts is a deliberate taunting of all those people who call themselves the responsible members of society. "You keep urging that people take responsibility for their actions," say the terrorists; "we are taking it."

A sufficient number of examples of "responsibility" have now been provided to indicate the spectrum of use and the intriguing complexity of the term. Subsequent chapters will indicate several hundred other examples grouped in a way to penetrate the coverup when the term is used as a blunt instrument rather than with fine distinctions that take us somewhere. We need now to spell out what a grammar of use entails.

A Moral Grammar

This essay is a work of popular philosophy in two senses. First, it is addressed to a popular audience who are concerned with the moral climate of the country and moral questions of daily life. Second, the approach to the material is popular, although in a way that may not be immediately obvious. At the center of this book is the way ordinary people speak in their ordinary lives.

This second point requires some explaining. I begin with the premise that everyone (with some possible few exceptions) has a knowledge of morality. That knowledge is expressed in dinner table conversation, business reports, newspaper editorials, television talk shows, political speeches, classroom instruction, and every other place that people express judgments about the good or bad state of things.

This presumption is not a naive optimism that people are "naturally good" or that they usually do the right thing. All I presume is that there is present in people's thinking and speaking a sense of what good and bad, right and wrong, mean. What better place to begin a study of morality than with what is implied in everyday life and activity?

Plato may have been the first to maintain that you cannot teach something to someone unless he or she in some sense already knows it. Plato developed a metaphysical apparatus around this experience: eternal ideas, transmigration of the soul, a spiritual world beyond this one. One need not accept Plato's whole philosophy to accept his insight that people know more than they are immediately aware of knowing. Plato believed that statements of daily life need probing if they are to deliver any profound truth.[22]

This belief was developed by Aristotle and medieval philosophy, finding further resonance in contemporary thought. Our deepest intuitions and sensibilities get expressed in language that is never as adequate and accurate as we would like. When people pronounce "Of course he is guilty," or "Suicide is wrong," or "Animals have rights," they are likely to have some hold on the truth. At the same time, the truth is likely to be expressed in distorted or incomplete fashion. Words such as "guilty," "suicide," and "rights" cry out for clarification. Dictionaries cannot settle the matter; writers of dictionaries can only clear away general confusions and gross misstatements. Other writers have the task of questioning the basis of these ideas and how, if at all, these ideas refer to this individual or this group at this time.

Most of us are not inclined to pursue these matters as far as possible. When challenged ("How do you know that homosexuality is immoral?" "What good does capital punishment accomplish?" "Why does raising the minimum wage hurt the poor?") each of us has a store of information and reasoning more or less well founded. That is usually enough to back up what we have said. Occasionally, our storehouse of data and reasons is persuasive enough to convince the challenger; occasionally the reverse happens and we get convinced by the challenger. However, it seems safe to say that most such arguments end in a standoff. The experts on *Crossfire* or *The News Hour* do not seem to have a higher success rate with their arguments than do randomly selected disputants at a local bar.

This seeming ineffectiveness of moral arguing can be taken as evidence of the futility of efforts such as the present one. But the fact that most disagreements end in a draw, yet continue to occur, can suggest the need to dig further. If nine out of ten (or ninety-nine out of one hundred) arguments seem to go nowhere, what happens in the one case where progress, if not total agreement, is evident? When two people disagree strongly on an important matter, either both parties are wrong, or one party is right and the other is wrong, or both parties are right in what they are asserting but have not found the terms to express what they agree upon. The first two of these possibilities will eventually work out to a conclusion. The third possibility, more common than might at first be supposed, is what needs careful and patient concern.

Take what has been one of the most extreme cases of disagreement in the United States: abortion. One is not likely to surmise from news accounts that most people in the country agree on most of the important things about abortion. That is, most people are, at the least, uneasy about the widespread practice of abortion, and they question the motivation behind many abortions. But most people are also in favor of abortion being legally available.[23]

There is a minority at both ends of the argument who take a stronger stand, admitting little or no doubt that their formulation of the problem is the right one. Even these two groups, when questioned in depth, reveal some similarities, for example, a respect for the development of life in the womb and a concern for the welfare of children.[24]

In the case of abortion, the issue has been so emotionally charged and politically intractable that any serious inquiry and search for agreement have been overwhelmed by political lobbying. I do not fancy that I have the key to solve the problem. However, I do claim to be addressing an indispensable piece of the problem if there is to be any progress. What is analyzed here offers one of the possibilities for enlarging the area of agreement. For example, Carol Gilligan has a well-known study of women considering abortion.[25] The women in the study repeatedly refer to "responsibility" in interesting ways that invite examination.

This book, *A Grammar of Responsibility*, is intended to be practical. My intention is not just to offer interesting ideas, though I hope the ideas are in fact interesting. Even less so is this book advice on how to lead a moral life. I seek to be practical in the sense of looking closely at human practices and the way we describe them. I am more interested in words than in ideas; I resist leaving behind the words for the sake of a system of ideas.

Nearly all of the arguments here are linguistic, not in the sense of defining words but rather in asking how we use our words. In such an approach, the conclusions remain debatable, or put otherwise, there can be no final conclusions. The reader can only be invited to try out a position and see if it makes sense. A tryout requires running the proposed use of language through one's whole linguistic system, a process of months and years rather than a momentary consideration. With a little help and some concentrated effort, everyone can take part in this game; and everyone can succeed. Anyone can change the way he or she speaks even if it takes a long time.

In one sense, therefore, the book is clearly practical, concerned with the practice of speaking. Whether it is practical in the sense of effecting changes in people's lives remains to be seen. All I ask at the start is that examining the way we speak be allowed to compete with the "solutions" offered daily in the press, television, books, and churches. Someone says we first have to change attitudes; someone else says we need to change society; some others say parenting, job opportunities, the legal system, or violence on television is the problem. Who is right? No one is positive, but one possibility is that everyone is right.

Many things need improvement, and one does not have to be an expert to recognize most of these things. The question remains of *how* to get at a hundred different problems with effectiveness and with some assurance that we are not just attacking symptoms. I am not proposing to step above issues, problems, and failures to survey the fray from a higher viewpoint. I propose instead to explore the ground beneath the battles so as to find the way to connect disparate moral problems.

Perhaps many other eras have also believed that they were in a time of moral crisis, that the old ways did not work anymore. Certainly in the United States, where memory has always been short, we are susceptible to a mistaken belief that our age is completely novel, that in the past all parents loved their children, children did not experiment with sex, people cared for their neighbors, drugs were nonexistent, and so forth. Whether we are better or worse than our ancestors is debatable. But something has changed: our awareness, or at least our ability to be aware, of conflicts among people everywhere in the world. Every moral framework threatens to be overwhelmed by an avalanche of data that never stops.

We do not lack expert opinion on any subject imaginable; we also have a widespread skepticism about all advice. People may seem to lack information about what they are doing to their bodies, to their spouses and children, to their neighborhood, to the ozone layer. Occasionally that is the case; a youngster may be ignorant of the danger of AIDS, the effects of tobacco, the killing effect of crack. Far more often, young and old are surfeited by the excess of information available. Further advice, sermons, and lectures on the topic only increase resistance to accepting knowledge as something to be acted upon.

In this situation, one of the most interesting analyses of contemporary morality is Alasdair MacIntyre's *Three Rival Versions of Moral Enquiry*, the Gifford Lectures of 1989.[26] Each year since its inception in 1889 some famous person has delivered these lectures on morality. MacIntyre, it seems, was the first lecturer to raise the question of whether *lectures* on morality still make sense.

When Adam Gifford established this lecture series, few would have questioned the value of lecturing. The educated gentlemen of Edinburgh in the 1880s were confident that they possessed the essential principles of morality from which lecturing could proceed. MacIntyre quotes Henry Sidgwick, a leading moralist of the time: "Principles will soon be everything, and tradition nothing. . . ."[27] Thus, the main task was to add detail to the principles and show their applicability to the mass of people who are not so well versed in the principles. The lecture was the most appropriate format for moral exposition: clear, calm, rational, certain. MacIntyre takes as emblematic of this attitude the ninth edition of the *Encyclopedia Britannica*, which began publication in 1875. The enlightened wisdom of the world's experts was available to everyone in the stately prose of the *Encyclopedia*.

MacIntyre identifies two minority views at that time: one exemplified by Friedrich Nietzsche's *Genealogy of Morals* in 1887; the other by Pope Leo XIII's *Aeterni Patris* in 1879. Nietzsche's book traces morality back to its roots in an attempt to go "beyond good and evil." The papal encyclical began a restoration of the medieval form of inquiry, best realized in the work of Thomas Aquinas. In most respects, Nietzsche and Leo XIII are at the opposite ends of the universe. But MacIntyre finds a link between them in their opposition to the lecture format.

In MacIntyre's portrait of the three versions we are farthest removed from the gentlemen of Edinburgh in 1889, that is, from the lecture that tells us what the world of proper morality is and that expects us to assent to the advice of experts. There are still many people waiting to be told from the pulpit, the advice column, or the science book what is right and what is wrong. But the widespread erosion of a trusting attitude reveals the limits of that form of communication. Except under special conditions, lectures do not constitute the main basis for moral thinking and moral choice today.

If MacIntyre's analysis is correct, then our options are very limited: we can go back to ancient and medieval traditions represented by Leo XIII's appeal to a Thomistic synthesis; or we can go bravely forward with what MacIntyre describes as Nietzsche's guerrilla theater, unmasking the fraudulent basis of morality. Another possibility would be a strange combination of these two. As twentieth-century studies have shown, recovering Thomas Aquinas does not mean repeating what he said so much as rediscovering the dialogic or dialectical framework of his thought. Except in dialogue with the skepticism of today, Aquinas's majestic synthesis is not likely to get a wide hearing.

On the other side, Nietzsche's savagely critical epigrams may find easy assent among people who have no historical context. People in the twentieth century, with or without reading Nietzsche, have discovered the effectiveness of a guerrilla-theater approach to morality, especially if a television camera is in the vicinity. A group such as ACT UP, drawing attention to AIDS, demonstrates what a few individuals can do and will do after despairing of rational argument.

The more widespread sign of this despair is apathy rather than activism. Many young people in school will write down whatever their teachers wish them to say, but the least provocation will surface skeptical and cynical attitudes toward moral authority. A scene in Jean-Luc Godard's *Weekend* caught not just the spirit of the 1960s but a strand of twentieth-century irrationality. A professor and a student are conversing on a train. The student says: "First, we must blow up the Sorbonne." The professor asks: "And then what will you do?" The student replies: "I don't know, but first we must blow up the Sorbonne."

Nietzsche was not a bomb thrower but a philologist. His skepticism about moral systems arose from his studies of language and the evolution of moral concepts. On the central theme of this book, responsibility, Nietzsche plays a pivotal role, which I explore in the next chapter.

More generally, Nietzsche and his twentieth-century heirs (such as Michel Foucault) tried to point the way to a different kind of moral inquiry, based on historical research and expressed in a variety of literary forms.

The enemy in this kind of critical searching is the nineteenth-century lecture and the desiccated version of Christianity from which it issued. In medieval inquiry there was a place for the lecture (*lectio*) but only as a preliminary to further questioning. In rebelling against smug certainty and complacent experts it would be quixotic not to listen to the voices of the past and thoughtful reflection in the present. What Plato and Aristotle, Augustine and Aquinas, Plotinus and Eckhart tried to do in their writings could have new relevance today—how they proceeded as much as what they wrote. Each in his own way tracked the history of concepts and terms; each engaged in serious dialogue with contemporary opponents and problems of the past; each was aware that human life is not infinitely malleable, but its limits are unclear. We are unlikely ever again to have the system of rules for which the nineteenth century used the word "morality." Our task is in one sense broader (life and its context rather than a morality); in another sense it is narrower (instead of a logical system of rules a few terms that have a chance of opening a conversation without preestablished limits).

What I offer in this work is a grammar of moral inquiry, or rather one element of such a grammar. We do not lack moral vocabulary. Nearly everyone knows more than enough words to speak the language of morality: rights, duties, values, conscience, virtue, fairness, freedom, decision, good. The trouble is that language does not consist only of words. How the words are put together determines whether a language exists and whether it functions well. The grammar of a language consists of the written and unwritten rules whereby the words interact with one another. Our problem in the late twentieth century is that we seem to lack agreement on any rules for our moral language. The moral guidebooks act only as a thesaurus: this word means the same as that word.

Educational proposals in the moral area hide the problem by listing good qualities we seem to agree upon. Most often these qualities are called "values," although there has been a recent resurgence of the older term, "virtues." Don't we all agree that children should be honest, truthful, fair, responsible, compassionate. . . ?[28] Then let us put aside all the distracting talk of moral confusion and start inculcating the agreed-upon values or virtues. But as we try to move from a list of desirable qualities to the people who are to assimilate these qualities, the method becomes crucial. Unless that question is wrestled with, the method usually practiced is to tell people what they should think and order them to behave in a certain way. And if they do not behave properly some external coercion should be available.

A more enlightened pedagogy does not simply tell people to be honest or truthful; it also provides helpful examples in good literature. William Bennett's *The Book of Virtues*, with its selection of literature, has been an amazing success story.[29] The approach is certainly an improvement over heavy-handed sermons or abstruse lectures on these virtues. The book does presume a fairly stable world of reasonable people ready to work on acquiring one virtue after another.

This method has a long history that never died out among part of the population. Two centuries ago, Benjamin Franklin kept a book in which he checked off the number of times he practiced selected virtues each day. Franklin's book was itself an adaptation of a book of virtues that could be found in each monk's cell two centuries before Franklin. Daily confession of failure followed the hour of spiritual reading. Christianity had absorbed into itself the system of moral virtues developed by the Greeks and Romans. William Bennett would perhaps not feel out of place among the Edinburgh gentlemen of the nineteenth century, the Philadelphia gentlemen of the eighteenth century, or the Roman gentlemen of the first century. I would not underestimate the value of such tradition. We cannot survive without honesty, truthfulness, courage, and so forth, nor can we survive without exemplars and stories to inspire activities that bear those names.

I would contend, nonetheless, that today for some people nearly all the time and for all people some of the time another kind of question flickers across the mind. The question takes various forms: Who says so? Why should I? What's behind this? What's the point of anything? Under the impact of this questioning, the acquisition of values or virtues gets blocked in some lives, and in other lives apparent virtues get upended. There may seem nothing new in this report. Human beings have always failed morally. Those who fail badly enough have to be restrained; the others have to try to improve. But while this regular shoring up continues, we also need to ask how we are using the language of morality, including the question of who is the "we" asking the questions.

I have chosen as the entry point to a moral grammar the term "responsible/responsibility." Of course, there is no grammar that has only one word; grammar implies the totality of interacting words in the language. Many other terms will find their way into a discussion of responsibility. A conversation on this topic has no preestablished limit as to what other important terms come into play.

The conversation also has no predetermined limit on who speaks. When the topic is language, the past obviously has a crucial part to play. How a term is used today cannot make much sense without some knowledge of past use. But who speaks for the past has no simple answer. The old saying that "history is written by the winners" presents an enormous obstacle to hearing the voices of the past. Nevertheless, historians today are very sensitive to this problem and dig at sources with new tools and new questions. Etymology and the historical evolution of language are indispensable to hearing the conflicts and seeing who came out on top. If one follows the word (not the idea), there are some nonarbitrary boundaries for exploring the past: certain people used this word in this way. Whatever sense one can make of this data, a definite body of material exists as the backdrop for present discussions.

In the present as in the past, how language is used depends in part on who is doing the using. A complete grammar would involve a study of everyone's usage. Because such a survey is unrealistic, representative samples have to be used. But one has to be careful about who steps forward as representative. If the question is responsibility, there is a strong tendency to seek the answer from those who have been designated "responsible people." Those people have already designated another group as "irresponsible," that is, as a group whose voices should not be heard on the topic.

It is precisely those groups that have been excluded from the common wisdom of what constitutes responsibility who might have a fresh and revealing outlook. No doubt there are uses of a term that are simply incorrect; they are too far from any historical continuity of meaning that the term has had. As Ludwig Wittgenstein notes, we rightly correct a child's misuse of a term. The purpose of such correction, Wittgenstein adds, should not be to give the child the right meaning but to get the child into the human conversation.[30] Judging between a simple error of understanding on the child's part and a creative insight by a child (or adult) is not always easy. Etymology is usually more help than an assumed definition of the term, definitions being what those in control of language have decided is the accepted meaning.

Young children, for example, may not be able to articulate their own moral grammar, but they are often sensitive to adult misuse of grammar. Children ask embarrassingly difficult questions such as why so and who says. Parents usually win a test of wills with "because I say so," although that answer does not solve the problem of the larger context for the child's questions. Rebellion during the teenage years often recycles the same questions, or it aims similar questions at other figures besides parents.

Consider this example of the recorded exchange between a man and his two-year-old daughter. The father says: "Behave yourself." The girl replies: "But daddy, I am being haved."[31] The adult may think that the child has misunderstood the word "behave." However, the child not only has heard the root meaning of the term but is acutely aware of the grammar of its usage. Two-year-olds know that adults assume you can either have yourself (under control) or else you can be had by others. This is a remarkably narrow assumption that arose only in modern times. Two-year-olds are among the world's experts in the experience of being had by others. The child protests at the premature narrowing of choice in the term behavior: to be had by yourself or to be had by others.

When scientists study behavior they have already locked themselves into a narrow world. Unlike two-year-olds, they are probably deaf to the origin of the term, whose meaning they casually assume. If there is danger in this assumption, what might be done as a correction? Can one expand the meaning of behavior? Or should one accept that there are inherent limits to behavior and therefore one has to complement studies of behavior with studies using another term (for example, interaction)? Is the best person to ask this question a behavioral scientist? Or should one listen to children in nurseries, old people in nursing homes, unemployed black men, mothers of three, and—if one could get an opinion—dogs on leashes?

A cynic may scoff at the possibility that such groups care about grammar; they may have trouble with the most elementary rules of English grammar, the rules taught in school. But in the grammar of power relations and the use of the language of control, their resistance to current usage and their assertion of alternatives are what saves their humanity.

People who suffer from poverty or political oppression may be experts at recognizing the misuse of moral grammar. Poverty and oppression do not create virtue; but they do force a kind of questioning from which the rich and the comfortable are protected. Every repressive government has learned to speak a language of freedom, democracy, respect, dignity, loyalty, hard work. Because the oppressor has stolen all the good words, the oppressed can only get a foothold by challenging how words such as freedom or loyalty or respect are used.

In summary, there are voices on all sides proclaiming a moral crisis. The crisis may not be worse than in the past, but it is a crisis undeniably made obvious by worldwide communication media. How is one to address concerns that threaten to overwhelm our sense of control? The immediate impulse is for "good people" to tell "bad people" to improve their behavior or else get punished. The telling can vary from "stop that" and "just say no" to uplifting literature and courses on ethics. Such efforts are needed and to an extent are successful. Most people do become law-abiding citizens.

There is, nonetheless, another set of concerns that the twentieth century cannot avoid. These concerns are not entirely novel, but throughout this century they have become widespread and urgent. The concerns are expressed in such questions as: Is there a valid morality? If so, where did it come from? How does an individual or group come to pronounce some things good, others bad. In short, how does one get started talking about a moral crisis without already having prejudiced the outcome by using words already prejudiced? The questions I am asking are so simple a child can ask them. They are also so difficult that the human race may still be at the beginning of getting adequate answers.

From a number of possible entry points, I choose "responsibility" as a promising term to pursue issues both big and small. My interest is not in convincing people that they ought to be responsible. That is, I am not giving a lecture on the value of responsibility. Instead, I am asking the reader to notice how the term responsibility has been used in the past, how it is used in the present, and how it might be used in the future. That is what I mean by a grammar of its usage. The value of such an exercise can only be demonstrated by the exercise itself. However, in the next and final section of this chapter I sketch the main lines along which the grammar is to be built in the following chapters.

Developing the Grammar

The first step in the process of developing a grammar, and in some ways the most important, is to trace the origin and history of "responsibility." Chapter 2 provides an overall outline of that history, highlighting the twentieth-century flowering of the term at the center of ethical discussion. The governing metaphor behind such a term often contains unexplored possibilities. The meaning that the term has had establishes both the strengths and the limitations of its use today.

After setting out this survey of source material, the book is organized in response to the seemingly insuperable divisions that stymie contemporary ethics. Chapters 3 through 8 recount five major divisions and show how responsibility is the needed bridge to overcome each of these splits. Some introductory comments on these five problems can be presented as a conclusion to this chapter. Addressing these problems and explaining why and how responsibility is the answer require the discussion in chapters 3 to 8.

First, much of modern ethics from the eighteenth century, and especially in the twentieth century, is built around a split between what is and what ought to be. There is not much discussion of this split; it usually shows up in the form of a slogan: "everybody knows you cannot derive an ought from an is." While I do accept that there is a difference between saying that something is so and saying something ought to be so, I do not accept the image of an unbridgeable gulf between two worlds of is and ought.

Responsibility is a term that can function as a bridge between what is and what ought to be. The term has those resources built into its etymology and history. Furthermore, the term responsible (and various cognates) still functions in ordinary speech as sometimes an assertion of what is and sometimes an assertion of what ought to be. If this is so, there is no need to try to derive ought from is; the task is to draw appropriate distinctions in the use of responsible/responsibility.

Second, twentieth-century literature generally accepts a split between individual and collective, or as it is often expressed, individual versus society. Public policy and political debates throughout this century have revolved around whether something belongs to the individual or to society. Is poverty the problem of the individual or is it a social problem? Is crime the failure of individuals or is society to blame? The political right throughout most of the century has talked about "individual responsibility." The political left, while seldom inclined to speak against individual responsibility, has usually insisted on an addition. Besides individual responsibility there is social responsibility. But given the root meaning of responsible, does it make any sense to talk of "social responsibility"? Is the language of any collective responsibility a primitive myth or is it an idea that is especially needed today in a world of nationalism and global corporations?

The endless debates on this point do not seem to accomplish much. Responsibility is most frequently employed in this debate not as a bridge but as what is to be divided. I will argue that a better grammar of responsibility can unite distinct though inseparable elements. But the discussion has to be reconstituted with other terms than individual versus society. Of course, it is impossible to eliminate that particular contrast, but in being assumed to be *the* controlling contrast it has mired the discussion in two opaque ideas.

This problem thus presents a double task: to examine the split or splits *within* the individual human being; and on the other side of the divide to examine the variety of groupings and organizations that are part of (a collective) human life. The term responsibility is capable of serving this complex set of relations, if it is used with precise distinctions that are in accord with its meaning. For proposing a bridge over this division, two chapters are needed in the text that follows.

Third, perhaps the greatest gap for human beings, but one strangely hidden by our language, is the one between humans and nonhumans. At the beginning of modern times a line was drawn between "man" and "nature." This division had the effect of obscuring the relation of men and women, as well as rendering invisible most nonhumans. The relation between "man" and "nature" was conceived as one of conquest and dominance, a prejudice that had to rebound to our own undoing.

A correction is now underway, but the language has not adequately changed. We are in a particularly dangerous period of trying to develop an "environmental ethic," one driven by the language of rights and equality. Individual problems, such as animal rights, wetlands protection, or garbage disposal are intensely debated, but often without much context. "Environmental ethics" still suggests a specialized branch of applied ethics rather than a central concern for the development of ethics itself.

I will argue that the environmental movement has to do much more with "responsibility." The grammar of the term suggests gradations, especially a distinctive character for human beings. I do not argue for "man" returning to dominance at the pinnacle of "nature" but for an end to the language of "man and nature." Men and women have to exercise responsibility in relation to the variety of living creatures with whom they share the earth.

Fourth, human beings have always had some division between past and present. The events of the present obviously have some dependence on what has happened in the past. The individual human being daily accumulates a personal history that influences each of his or her decisions. There are also family, ethnic, national, racial, and religious histories that situate the individual person. Are individuals or groups responsible in the present for what occurred in the past? Do individuals sometimes cease to be responsible because of what other people have done in the past?

The modern emphasis on the future adds a new dimension of complications. In what sense can the present take responsibility for the future? Does awareness of the future alter some of the determinations of the past? Included in the future dimension of the temporal issue is the relation of adult and child. Can we design an educational process that links present and past in a responsible manner and gives future generations the best chance possible?

Fifth, the final contrast is the difference between "us" and "them." It could be called a division between societies, though it is usually described as a difference of "cultures." What is at stake behind the issue of cultural variations on morality is a concern that at least some of our moral judgments hold up through changing conditions. Some people may profess a blasé indifference to the problem of cultural relativism: let everyone practice one's own moral code; no one should criticize another culture from the outside.

From at least the time of the Greeks, and probably long before that, there has been awareness of this problem. Groups have usually assumed that they were superior to foreigners. The Greeks called foreigners "barbarians" (to the Greek ear the foreign tongue sound like "bar . . . bar . . . bar"). The names for foreigners usually cast doubt on whether they are fully human. The problem of relativism was solved by making one's own group the standard of measure. In the twentieth century we have moved away from this assumption of superiority by one group; consistency within a culture has seemed to be the alternative. But as the twentieth century comes to a close, these disparate cultures are interacting with each other, and the need for a transcultural ethic becomes apparent.

Many people today would like to find a "global ethic" that would guide all people.[32] But who could possibly write it? Any attempt to assert ethical statements that are true for all times and all places comes across as naive and arrogant. The task of "responsibility" in this area is mostly to be a holding action. In the split between a parochial ethic and a universal ethic, we need a term that provides grounding in the particular and daily affairs of life. At the same time, the term has to be open without predetermined limits to accepting variations within a universal ethic. Especially during the next few decades, as cultures enter strange new mixtures, responsibility has to be the center for an ethic yet to be written.

If I am correct that responsibility is at the middle of all five of these splits, then a grammar of its use would be a service not only in ethics but across numerous disciplines. Along the way I will deal with other troublesome contrasts (for example, the relation of men and women, the relation of professional and nonprofessional work) where responsibility is a term continually being called upon. A grammar of responsibility is not a magic wand that dispels all dilemmas and heals all wounds. Responsibility draws its meaning and its strengths from all the terms around it. The meanings of numerous other terms have to be assumed or implied in laying out the rules for using responsibility. But if the use of responsibility is at least tentatively assented to, it will in turn throw light on many of these other terms, such as person, right, duty, freedom, choice, and guilt.

If this venture is successful, we should be able to sort out three kinds of issues. We could discover that on questions where we thought there was intractable moral difference, there may be more agreement than is assumed possible. We could then proceed to achieve further agreements. On other questions, we could discover that there are indeed insuperable differences. On those, we might get respectful disagreement so that one group would not persecute or harangue another group over differences that may be unresolvable. Finally, we could discover that some questions are not worth debating. The adjective "moral" has been misplaced, and the appropriate policy would be simply to stop trying to get agreement where none is needed.

I am tempted to offer examples of each of these three kinds of issues. But that would be to presume that I know how all of these debated issues would turn out if we had a better framework for discussion. I do not approach the topics in the following chapters as a neutral observer. But neither am I simply stating what I take to be the right view or correct opinion. My main interest is devising a framework for conversation and contributing to that conversation. Jane Flax provides an admirable summary of this attitude: "To pursue promising ways of understanding our experience is not necessarily to seek 'truth' or power in an Enlightenment sense. Rather it entails a commitment to responsibility and a hope that there are others 'out there' with whom conversation is possible."[33]

CHAPTER 2

HISTORICAL GLEANINGS

William Bennett's *The Book of Virtues* is a collection of literary pieces that illustrate and encourage the practice of traditional virtues. Included in the book is a section entitled "Responsibility." One can easily understand the inclusion of a section on this topic. In any list of virtues today, responsibility surely ranks near the top. Some people would rank it first among the virtues.

What is more than a curious fact, however, is that until this century responsibility was not likely to be listed as a virtue at all. There are two issues to be investigated in this connection, one about the reemergence of virtue itself, the other about the fact that responsibility was not considered a virtue. But if responsibility was not a virtue, what was it? A few words about the meaning of virtue are needed before a longer reflection is undertaken on where responsibility came into the historical picture.

William Bennett has been one of a small but growing number of writers who have tried to recover the language of virtue. The popularity of *The Book of Virtues* is evidence of considerable success in this movement. A few decades ago, "virtue" seemed to many people a simplistic and archaic term. For some it was too genteel in reference to women; for others it was too heroic sounding in reference to men. For many people it was too closely connected to religion. But any announcement of virtue's demise has proved to be premature.[1]

Whatever the contemporary status of "virtue," the term has a clear history stretching back to the Greek philosophers. Plato and Aristotle laid out a catalogue of "excellences" or virtues that should govern human life. In the *Republic*, Plato shows how both the individual and the state need to be regulated by prudence, temperance, fortitude, and—the proper joining of all the virtues—justice.[2] Aristotle devel-

oped descriptions of many other virtues, such as liberality, magnificence, magnanimity, patience, modesty, and friendliness. Each of the
virtues was a mean between excess and deficiency in a human sphere
of activity.[3] Roman philosophers, such as Cicero and Seneca, translated and adapted the Greek excellences into qualities of life that the
Romans saw as typifying the good, strong "man." Our English word
"virtue" is tied to these Latin connotations.

The Christian church, from its earliest centuries, absorbed the
Greek-Roman catalogue of qualities. Whether or not this absorption
was a healthy one for Christianity, there is no denying the influence. In
sophisticated versions, such as in Thomas Aquinas's *Summa Theologica*, as well as in popular confessional manuals, lists of virtues domi-
nate medieval Christian treatises. Christian theologians gave special
place to "the theological virtues" of faith, hope, and charity. But most
of the favorites of Greek philosophy, including the "cardinal virtues"
of prudence, justice, temperance, and fortitude retained a central place
in Christian life. The good Christian was the virtuous Christian. The
church was perhaps too successful in making virtue its own. Virtue
became associated in popular speech with the practice of (Christian)
religion rather than with excellences or strengths of human life.

The contemporary revival of interest in virtue draws some of its
energies from conservative Christian circles, but it also taps into the
search for a sustainable human ethic with or without religion. The idea
of virtue has a chance of being a bridge builder, linking disparate
groups who are concerned with the decline of Western civilization.
The inculcation of virtue at home and in school is a conservative
answer to the drift, confusion, and malaise that surround many young
people.

While a list of virtues that need inculcation may be of value I would
still question the presence of responsibility on the list. The inclusion of
responsibility is not supported by the history of virtues. If one is going
back to traditional virtues, responsibility is out of place. The other
virtues on Bennett's list (courage, perseverance, faith, loyalty) go back
centuries, some as far back as the Greeks. But there are no ancient or
medieval treatises on the virtue of responsibility. The question I
address in this chapter is why. Why was responsibility not a medieval
virtue, and why is it one of the most prominent virtues of the twentieth
century?

An initial explanation is provided on the first page of Hans Jonas's

The Imperative of Responsibility. In the past, says Jonas, "the range of human action and therefore responsibility was narrowly circumscribed." But now, he says, "the nature of human action has changed." The future has acquired a new importance. "The qualitatively novel nature of certain of our actions has opened up a whole new dimension of ethical relevance for which there is no precedent in standards and canons of traditional ethics."[4]

Jonas's image here is one of human power that continuously increases in its effect upon the future. People in the twentieth century—say, the designers of the Chernobyl nuclear plant—carry a heavier burden than anyone could have imagined in the seventeenth century or earlier. While this explanation of the change in responsibility undoubtedly has some validity, I do not think it gets at the central issue. Responsibility did not go from a lesser virtue to a more important virtue. Instead, it went from not being a virtue at all to the all-important virtue.

Jonas, like most writers on responsibility, gives practically no attention to the root meaning of the term and to the history of the term. Jonas and most writers on responsibility begin with the question of what we are responsible for. But to start from that point is already to have cut off most of the interesting story about responsibility; the starting point aborts the useful possibilities of the term. Before one can be responsible *for* something, one has to be responsible *to* someone or something.

In the third chapter this distinction between responsible to/responsible for is a major part of the basis for a grammar of use. In this chapter, I only wish to show that this distinction is not a strange, new idea that I am trying to impose. Rather, this distinction is evident in the etymology and history of response/responsible/responsibility. To be responsible is first to listen and then to answer. The first moment is being responsible to; the second moment is being responsible for.

The history of responsibility has two very unequal parts, the first extending into the late nineteenth century. During that time the emphasis is on being responsible to; responsibility for something is implied but is mostly unspoken.

Since the end of the nineteenth century, responsible for is explicit and insisted upon. At the same time, the basis of the term's intelligibility—the to what or to whom—is increasingly obscured.

In *The Book of Virtues* William Bennett introduces the section on responsibility with a reference to the Federalist Papers written at the time of the country's founding.[5] That use by Alexander Hamilton is in fact the earliest reference for the term in the *Oxford English Dictionary*: "Responsibility in order to be reasonable must be limited to objects within the power of the responsible party." A more interesting and revealing use of the term is found in the paragraph that precedes the one cited by Bennett and the *OED*: "I add, as a *sixth* defect, the want, in some important cases, of a due responsibility in the government to the people." With the term responsibility, and the more frequently used "responsible," the issue is nearly always *to whom* one is responsible.[6]

Many of the early uses of "responsibility" are within a somewhat esoteric legal context. But a revealing use of the term is by an author named Sayce in 1874: "It is only when the concept of the individual has been reached that the idea of responsibility begins."[7] The author has caught a glimpse of something occurring as he wrote, namely, the rise of the individual. That is not the whole story, but it is an indispensable part of the modern shift of emphasis.

Until the nineteenth century, responsibility was not a virtue but a precondition of virtue. Because the human being is the responding/responsible animal, then moral virtue is possible and necessary. In the late nineteenth century, responsibility came to the fore. But as the sense of being responsible for things became explicit, the sense of responsibility to something waned. Responsibility becomes the burden, perhaps the main burden, that the individual carries.

Some writers trace the beginning of responsibility to the age of Plato and Aristotle. In contrast to the Homeric age, which had preceded him, Plato ushered in the world of a rational morality. Aristotle worked out in finer empirical detail the elements of human action and a catalogue of human virtues. Some of what is now discussed under responsibility overlaps Aristotle's discussion of voluntary action and what should be credited to or blamed on the individual man. Nonetheless, Arthur Adkins, in his study *Merit and Responsibility: A Study in Greek Values,* is particularly struck by the difference between Aristotle's position on these topics and our own. The author raises the issue at the beginning of the book "why the concept of moral responsibility is so unimportant to the Greeks."[8]

J. R. Lucas may be right in saying that "responsible" often seems to be the best English translation available for Aristotle's term *phronimos*. But that happens because today the specific meaning of responsible has been obscured. It can now be taken to mean "all-around reason-ableness and reliability, not confined to any particular topic and enter-ing into most other desirable qualities of character."[9] That is, responsible has come to mean "a reasonable sort of guy."

The root of responsibility is an aural/oral metaphor: first one lis-tens, then one answers. Greek philosophy, especially after Plato, was not strong on aural/oral metaphors. As the poets and storytellers were replaced by "thinkers," metaphors of sight and visual form over-whelmed other possibilities. Plato's philosophy shows some of the tension between oral and written cultures. The nonwriting Socrates of the dialogues gives way to Plato musing—in writing—on the dangers of writing to memory. Plato's powerful "ideas" that have influenced all of Western philosophy were visual forms. Beyond the idea was a light purer than the sun; the good is found in the contemplation of eternal beauty.[10] To this day we demand that our leaders have "vision," and we think of knowledge as "taking a look."[11]

Responsibility, in its root meaning, begins with a word of address having been spoken. The responsible person is someone who listens, recognizes the word as a personal address, and is impelled to answer. The aural/oral element in Western thought is clearly traceable to Hebrew/Jewish origin. The pattern of address/response is evident from the earliest strand of the Bible. An old saying has it that "Wisdom alighted on three things: the brain of the Frank, the hands of the Chi-nese, and the tongue of the Arab."[12] Jewish, Christian, and Muslim religions stem from that spoken word.

The covenant, which structures the relation between Israel and God, is a pattern of direct address and a way of life in response. The word is addressed to a particular people in the present, but the covenant unfolds in a centuries-long conversation. What is required at any moment depends on what has been done previously. The command-ments are spoken demands that are part of a struck bargain. The people are to "obey," that is, to listen. The most important of the ten commandments is the first, which says: Listen to me above all else; don't try any visual, tactile gods as substitutes. The Jews would later be called godless because they could not show their gods.

The case might therefore be made that the basis of responsibility comes from the earliest biblical tradition. God questions Eve about the forbidden fruit; the murderous Cain is queried about his brother. Moses' discussion with God, the prophets' call for justice, and the Pharisees' discovery of an oral source of divine revelation are developments on the way to responsibility. The full emergence of the idea awaited the flowering of a more individualized morality, one that the Pharisees helped to initiate in the centuries just before the Common Era.

Besides this strong sense of the individual, what was needed for responsibility was a sense of divine judgment. At the time of the reform movements in Israel, an apocalyptic attitude embraced much of the religious world. A divine judgment hovered over human life as a whole and over each human being. Not only the people but each individual, in the innermost region of the heart, is to answer that call.

W. Cantwell Smith locates the origin of the concept of responsibility in the first century B.C.E.[13] This is the period of Jewish reform that led to both the Christian movement and to the rabbinic form of modern Judaism. Responsibility is the correlate of a divine day of judgment. Smith notes that belief in a day of judgment is a subset of religious belief in heaven and hell. That is, many religions might affirm eternal rewards and punishments consequent upon human activity, but responsibility required the specific image of human life moving toward a day when accounts are totaled up. Jewish religion has retained a strong sense of a personal God deeply involved in details of history; a personal judgment at the end of each life has also been retained but without much imaginative embellishment.

Christianity, in contrast, painted a dramatic day of judgment, pointing all of life toward a final personal encounter and the stripping away of all secrets. Each funeral service reminded the faithful that they too must prepare for that *dies irae* when they must answer to God's harsh judgment.[14] They needed a compassionate Jesus as well as the Virgin Mary and the saints to plead their case. Christianity, like Judaism and Islam, is a religion of command and response. Even when the impersonal elements of "natural law" were incorporated into Christian theology, the whole system was still personalized under commandment, a point insisted on in twentieth-century reform by the Catholic moralist Bernard Haring.[15]

Smith argues that in Christianity "irresponsibility is hopelessly bad; but responsibility is, at best, inadequately good."[16] He believes that the Christian has to be more than responsible. He seems to associate responsibility with the "works" that the Christian performs, whereas it is faith that saves. I think that there is some disparagement here of responsibility, which follows from how "responsibility" came to be used in twentieth-century theology. I come back to this point below in discussing the effect of Max Weber's use of responsibility.

I am not persuaded that the root meaning of responsibility relegates it to a secondary position in Christian thinking. Separating it out from faith is not warranted. In Christianity, as in Judaism and Islam, faith comes by hearing, by listening to a divine call. Faith is a response from the heart, a saying yes to a personal invitation. One could say that faith means being responsible *to* God. If responsible is taken to assert only what I am responsible *for*, then it may imply a claim for human works over against divine favor.

It is true, of course, that while in Christianity responsibility is the basis of Christian life, it needs expression in particular action. Human beings have a vocation or calling; their lives are a response to an act of the creator. Being responsible is not so much a virtue as the given human condition; responsibility is a metaphysical idea before it is an ethical concept. A person is responsible and is called to act responsibly. *How* the human being responds determines the direction on a path that moves inexorably toward a final judgment scene.

The pattern of divine creation/human response continued to underlie moral thinking into the beginning of modern times. The Protestant Reformation of the sixteenth century did not overthrow this way of thinking. Even without the imagery of purgatory and the intercession of Mary and the saints, the sense of divine judgment remained and, if anything, was heightened. No term is more central in the writings of both Luther and Calvin than "calling." They were intent on recovering the universality of the term over against the restriction of "vocation" to monks and nuns. Every Christian is called by God, and the response of each person is demanded. "My life has become addressed by the unconditional affirmation that not my self but my relationship to him constitutes the reason for living," wrote Luther.[17] There were no shortcuts to heaven or free rides on the merits of the corporate church structure. All depended on a merciful God who in justice could drop the sinner into hell fire. The sinner must accept Jesus as Lord and Savior so as to be saved by God's grace.

The Modern Pattern

In the centuries following the Reformation, Christianity was challenged by the rise of modern science and technology. A compromise of sorts was worked out, mediated by the concept of nature. Science took all of nature as its domain; religion could still lay claim to nature's God. The place of conflict in this arrangement was the extent to which the human being is an exception to the laws of nature. The humans were different in having the choice whether or not to obey God's laws.

The God who was needed by Descartes and his successors was a missing piece of an intellectual puzzle. Someone or something had to get the world moving, create the human soul, establish a system of rewards and punishments. The eighteenth-century French thinkers viewed the Christian church as a failure at handling the religious affairs of the universe. A modern religion was needed, stripped of ancient myth and doctrine, a religion for "reasonable men." Thus was born the religion of theism or deism, these two words interchangeable at the time of their origin. In Voltaire's *Dictionary*, the alternative to Christianity is theism, the belief in a "supreme being" whose existence and nature are evident to any logical-minded person.[18]

This religion of deism/theism is important background for the founding of the United States of America. The Declaration of Independence was addressed to all the nations of the earth in light of what "nature and nature's God" require. Thomas Jefferson, author of the Declaration, was influenced by French, British, and Scottish Enlightenment thinkers. Jefferson himself spent several years editing a version of the New Testament sayings of Jesus. This document supported the theism/deism which Jefferson assumed would be the religion of the new nation. Jefferson, Franklin, Washington, Madison, and Hamilton could not have imagined how powerful and lasting would be another religious strain in United States history, namely, enthusiastic, revivalistic, apocalyptic religious experience.

The nineteenth century in both the United States and Europe had a Christian church establishment that was fairly comfortable and socially acceptable. It had survived the challenge of eighteenth-century theism/deism largely by shaping itself to the image of the attacker. Christianity was able to describe itself as a form of theism, with a supreme being and a rational code of conduct. In the lives of many Christians this "natural revelation" was the main story. A "supernatural revelation" was an added source of knowledge so long as it did not conflict with science.[19]

Always at the edge of this respectable Christianity were visionaries and prophets. Their response was not to a mechanical system of rewards and punishments but to an impending day of judgment. Logically, these people were "a-theists" because they rejected the compromise of eighteenth-century theism, but many were intensely religious. A choice between theism and atheism was the parochial presumption of nineteenth-century European thinkers. In this contrast, faith as personal response to creator/sustainer/judge tended to be squeezed out. And responsibility as listening and answering lost the context of its intelligibility.

Friedrich Nietzsche stands out as the prophetic voice that ushers in the twentieth century. He died in 1900 after a dozen tortured years in a mental asylum. His reputation since then has had a torturous history. That reputation, along with his final work, was put into the hands of his sister Elisabeth, who had her own peculiar ideas about her brother's intellectual legacy. The association of Nietzsche's name with twentieth-century tyrants, especially Hitler, is largely the doing of Elisabeth. The claim of anti-Semitism is an unfair charge against a writer who usually expresses admiration for the Jews in contrast to his view of Christianity.[20]

Nietzsche leaves little doubt that in his view the enemy is Christianity, which "gave Eros poison to drink"[21] Nietzsche's task was to diagnose the illness of our love life and prescribe a cure. He saw more clearly than others of his era that theism versus atheism obscured the real religious question: the existence and nature of responsibility.

Underlying both Jewish and Christian movements had been the notion of a personal creator and responding creature. Both the theism and atheism of modern Europe silently put aside the loving but frightening figure of biblical history, the *creating* force in daily life. At the same time, "man" was supposed to go on with business as usual and pretend that nothing much had happened. Nietzsche would have none of it. He agreed with the question, though not the answer, that troubled Dostoyevsky: "Who is man going to love then? To whom will he be thankful? To whom will he sing his hymn? Rakitin laughs. Rakitin says one can love humanity instead of God. Well, only an idiot can maintain that."[22]

For Nietzsche, as for Dostoyevsky, "man" as responsible could not continue if there was no God to be responsible to. Nietzsche was as contemptuous of the easy atheism of the intellectual class as he was of the slack theism of many Christians. What had first been explicit in atheism and then had seeped into Christianity was the belief that "man" is no longer responsible to God; man is responsible for himself. Nietzsche challenged the sleight of hand in responsibility's shift of meaning. For Nietzsche, the earth had been unchained from the sun. If there is no longer a god, there is no longer man. Man—the responsible man that Christianity had invented—now had to be transcended.

Nietzsche set out to recount "the long story of the origin or genesis of responsibility (the task of breeding an animal entitled to make promises)."[23] According to Nietzsche, the Greeks had used the gods to keep a bad conscience at a distance; Zeus says that the humans "claim we are responsible for all their evils."[24] The Christian could not make that claim; God being both all good and omnipotent, man is responsible for his own failures. As a result, the good man is driven by a bad conscience. "What if the 'good' man represents not merely a retrogression but even a danger, a temptation, a narcotic drug enabling the present to live at the expense of the future. . . ? Morality itself would be responsible for man, as a species, failing to reach the peak of magnificence of which he is capable?"[25]

In Nietzsche's genealogy, Christianity was progress of a sort in providing a meaning for suffering, but its solution was vulnerable to the manipulation of ascetic priests. The will requires an aim and a meaning, which were supplied by Christianity. The suffering person says "somebody must be responsible for my discomfort. . . . But his shepherd, the ascetic priest, says to him: 'You are quite right, my sheep, somebody must be at fault here, but that somebody is yourself. You alone are to blame for yourself.'"[26]

Christianity, in Nietzsche's view, had brought forth the monstrous situation of a creature who instead of responding to a creative force is burdened with carrying his own guilt. Nietzsche sought to clear away the corpse of the Christian God. The problem was, in Nietzsche's paradoxical phrase, the *death* of God. Nietzsche proclaimed himself not an atheist, but the anti-christ. Only with the removal of the corpse could there be a rebirth of the gods of blood and life. The responsible animal was here to stay, but he needed something or someone to be responsible to.

"Man" was now called by the force of life and the vision of the future to bring forth a greater than man. Only an "over-man" or superman could step into the role to be played. Nietzsche was doubtful, however, that his contemporaries were up to the challenge: "Is there really enough pride, courage, self-assurance, intellectual energy, responsibility, freedom of the will, to make philosophy possible in our world today?"[27] Perhaps like the madman who announces the death of God, Nietzsche believed of himself: "I have come too early; my time is not yet."[28] But if the problem could not be solved at the end of the nineteenth century, it was possible that it would still be there at the end of the twentieth.

Nietzsche has had a profound effect in the arts, where terms previously used of God's activity are now routinely used of the artist. In the twentieth century the human being is the creator of art, technology, decisions, and knowledge. The eighteenth-century "man" who had hankered after some divine prerogatives has been installed as the creator of the universe. It is not exactly what Nietzsche had called for, fearing that man was not ready to step into the empty spot in the heavens. In a combination of great insight and deteriorating sanity, Nietzsche wrote from the mental asylum: "I would much rather be a Basel professor than God, but I will not push my egotism so far as to desist from the creation of the universe."

Nietzsche had brought the nineteenth-century sense of "will" to its greatest height, and at the very moment of this exaltation collapsed the sense of a human will into an eternal return. Hannah Arendt, in her history of the will, found that it was in early Christianity that will begins to emerge as a separate faculty, subordinate to reason; it was tainted at birth by sin and remained that way until modern times. Jean-Jacques Rousseau fought against the doctrine of original sin and gave to the nineteenth century a will ready to be the highest faculty.[29] What that meant for human beings, writes Arendt, "was absolute power over their own destinies"—a power, she adds, that would "burden them with a formidable responsibility for things whose very existence would depend exclusively on themselves."[30]

Barely had an autonomous will come on stage when it was subverted by the burden of sustaining the universe and escaping irrational guilt. Nietzsche was a precursor of Freud in exploring the dark underside of consciousness.[31] Just when it seemed the moment to proclaim that "man is responsible for himself," the seed of doubt was planted as to whether he is capable of being responsible for the slightest action. Two paths lead from Nietzsche. One begins by exalting the power of the individual's will but collapses into questioning a capacity to will at all. The other path retains individual willing, but the will is carefully circumscribed by society.

One step along the first path was called "existentialism." The only thing clear about the term is an emphasis on (human) existence. Implied in the term is a focus on will and human choice. The term was broad enough to encompass much of the mood of the twentieth century. Most specifically, it referred to certain European philosophers after World War II who struggled with guilt, despair, courage, and an uncertain future. The lonely individual could rely only on himself and what he made of himself.

The writer who most prized the title of "existentialist" was Jean-Paul Sartre. Sartre coolly proclaimed the death of God as a fact; there was no longer need for Nietzsche's horror before this unspeakable crime. Sartre bravely proclaimed that "man being condemned to be free carries the weight of the whole world on his shoulders, he is responsible for the world and for himself as a way of being."[32]

Responsibility plays a central role in Sartre's philosophy. However, he seals off the question of to whom or to what "man" is responsible. What takes over completely is being responsible for. A man is responsible not only for his actions but for his life. Sartre goes so far as to say "in a certain sense I *choose* being born."[33] It is difficult to understand this claim as literally true, but the direction of Sartre's thought is clear. The horizon being empty of gods, "man invents himself." His choices determine the meaning of his life, including his birth.

The existentialist mood has largely disappeared in the last decades of the twentieth century. One forceful influence has been concern for the environment. Sartre's celebration of "man outside nature, beyond nature" did not stand up well.[34] In some quarters the description is cause for mourning rather than celebration. "Man," it is now said, must return to nature, must give up arrogant pretensions. The rebellion against God obscured the fact that the world's forces dwarf all human efforts at control. The human claim to be responsible for everything can at moments of earthquake, flood, or volcanic eruption sound childishly naive.

Albert Schweitzer's *Ethics and Civilization* in the 1920s foreshadowed the ecological movement of a half century later. Responsibility plays a key role in the book. Schweitzer advocates a reverence for all life, both human and nonhuman. His emphasis is not on the active, controlling will but a letting be, and for an appreciation of all creation. "Resignation is the vestibule through which we pass in entering the palace of ethics."[35]

The ecological movement is only one of the currents undermining the sense of "man's autonomy" and control. If he cannot control the universe, is he even certain he can control himself? Since Freud, the dark side of human motivation has more and more clouded the certainty of reason's control, even when that reason seems brightest. "The most important thing about human actions," Nietzsche wrote, "is what is not intended."[36] What in the late nineteenth century was a seed of doubt about intention and choice is now a widespread mood.

The term "postmodern" is probably even vaguer and more ambiguous than was "existentialist." The word can shift meaning dramatically from one context to another; many authors who get classified as postmodernist repudiate the term. The term does at the least point to some crisis in the meaning of "modern." What is under threat is "autonomous man," the priceless gem of earlier philosophical quests. At the most radical level of questioning, the issue is not whether "man" is in control of himself but whether there is a self to control.[37]

What has played out in the twentieth century is the possibility that with the removal of God, "man" would also disappear. Everything had been staked upon the human will; but with no one left to answer to, the will is submerged. "With the elimination of intent and purpose, of somebody who can 'be held responsible,' causality itself is eliminated; nothing can be traced back to a cause once the *causa prima* is eliminated."[38]

Martin Heidegger was profoundly influenced by Nietzsche in this aspect of his thought.[39] For Heidegger, the Christian God had failed, and there was no replacement in sight. "Man" remains listener and answerer, but there is no call. What can we do about that? "We can do nothing but wait."[40] The final and necessary destruction of the will is the will not to will.

Listening for a word not spoken exposes one to political passivity or to getting swept up into causes of doubtful value. Heidegger's reputation has suffered in recent years as biographies have revealed a deeper involvement in Nazism than Heidegger ever acknowledged.[41] His abstruse philosophy did not lead to Nazism, but neither did it offer sufficient resistance to such involvement. The failure here is more than a question of an individual character flaw. The stream of twentieth-century thought within which Heidegger remains a key figure has undermined the pretenses of "modern man," but to what end?

In much of contemporary literature, what is being attacked is easier to grasp than what is affirmed. "In the postmodern view, humans are best understood not as unities but as processes of influence."[42] Can a process of influence be responsible for anything? If "autonomous man" as the unique exception in nature dissolves, does the distinctly human disappear? The alternative would be a new relation of human and nonhuman natures to replace the language of "man and nature." What is uniquely human emerges from the relation of men and women within an environment of nonhuman natures.

The other path of twentieth-century writing on responsibility prescinds from metaphysical speculation and locates the term within the context of "man and society." Man (the individual) is responsible to man (the society). This closed circle stops any probing into the ultimate basis of responsibility. The only practical question becomes what is a "man" responsible for? Here once again, replacing "man" with "human" or "man or woman" would not result in a different set of relations. What we need is a concrete description of men and women in a variety of communal and organizational structures, as will be described in chapter 5.

Max Weber is the dominant figure of influence for this meaning of responsibility. Weber did recognize that there are people who live their lives as a response to a calling they take to be divine. However skeptical Weber may have been in theological matters, he was as keen as Luther or Calvin on the importance of calling or vocation. In an influential essay, "Politics as a Vocation," Weber distinguished two ethics: "We must be clear about the fact that all earthly oriented conduct may be guided by one of two fundamentally differing and irreconcilably opposed maxims: conduct can be oriented to an 'ethic of ultimate ends' (Gesinnungsethik) or to an ethic of responsibility (Verantwortungsethik)."[43]

An ethic of ultimate ends or good intention means a disregard of immediate effects. That contrasts with an ethic of responsibility in which "one has to give an account of the foreseeable results of one's actions."[44] The ethic of ultimate ends/intention is identified with Jesus' Sermon on the Mount, in which he refuses to compromise with the coercive activities of the state. The historical Christian church, in contrast, by adopting an ethic of responsibility is contaminated by violence, and it falls short of the pure gospel.

After Weber's radical separation of the two ethics, the end of the essay is surprising: "An ethic of ultimate ends and an ethic of responsibility are not absolute contrasts but rather supplements, which only in unison constitute a genuine man—a man who can have the calling for politics."[45] This union does not occur when ultimate ends are seen to need responsibility. The people who talk about ultimate ends, writes Weber, are 90 percent "windbags" who do not understand what they are attempting. But coming from the opposite side, the mature man, who has been acting responsibly, may find his life leading to something ultimate. "Somewhere he reaches the point where he says 'Here I stand, I can do no other.' "[46]

Max Weber, writing at the end of the nineteenth century, identified pure, "otherworldly" religion with the preaching of Jesus. Any significant effect of Jesus' Sermon on the Mount is undercut when his teachings are praised as a beautiful, idealistic—and completely impractical—way of looking at things. However, this assignment of Jesus' teachings to the "otherworld" is disputed today. Christian commentators in the late twentieth century, with help from Jewish scholars, read the Sermon on the Mount as a call to take realistic steps to resist violence and "do love to one's enemies."[47] Gandhi, King, and other radical reformers discovered a practical-minded Jew in the Gospels. If one listens to situations of oppression at a profound-enough level, one's response will be politically powerful, even though politically unconventional.

It is an unfortunate choice of terms to say that the person seeking radical reforms through "ultimate ends" is not acting in a way that is responsible. Weber's man of ultimate ends is not interested in "this worldly" ends. "The Christian does rightly and leaves the results with the Lord."[48] Does Christianity encourage its members to disregard the results of their activity? I think that Christian spiritual tradition has always encouraged its practitioners not to be *attached* to the results of their actions. Christians are not to be overly concerned with being judged successful; ultimate judgments of worth need standards more ultimate than today's fashions. That is far from saying that "the responsibility for consequence is not on me."[49]

Undeniably, Jesus and the Christian movement did emphasize motivation, intention, and control of desire. Nearly all religious reforms do that. Read out of context, without reference to what they were attempting to reform, they sound removed from the political give and take of ordinary life. By setting up a contrast between the pure religion of Jesus and an ethic of responsibility, religious teaching is preserved for "otherworldly" types who like that sort of thing. Conversely, responsibility is severely limited to the practical realm of individuals in society; all questions of ultimacy or even a theoretical basis for responsibility are bracketed from discussion.

Weber was quite successful in teaching the distinction of ultimate ends versus responsibility to twentieth-century writers. The distinction was absorbed into "Christian ethics" (itself a new phrase) and secular ethics. On the Christian side, responsibility had to compete with what claimed to be the more specifically Christian attitude. That is, responsibility was suspected of not being entirely Christian. In secular ethics, responsibility for all practical purposes had the stage to itself. The other ethic, one concerned with ultimate ends, was left to the religious minded and had to be excluded from discussions of public policy. The debate now was *within* the ethic of responsibility, especially about the role of government. The contrast between individual responsibility and social responsibility arose as the language in which to carry on this debate.

Responsibility thus became a household name, a favorite of politicians, economists, psychiatrists, and practical-minded people who wish to shape up the world. Differences remain about how to achieve a responsible society, but no one doubts that criminals should become responsible citizens, that welfare mothers would be more responsible if they were working, that people should take responsibility for their decisions. If we are going to strive for consensus, stability, and unity, where better to begin than with the agreement that everyone should be responsible?

Those who have felt that there is something too slick about this consensus on responsibility have been forced into indirect sniping instead of direct attack. At the end of *The Autobiography of Malcolm X*, Ossie Davis describes Malcolm X as "standing in relation as he does, to the 'responsible' civil rights leaders, just about where John Brown stood in relation to the 'responsible' abolitionists in the fight against slavery."[50] This passage is a typical twisting against what "responsible" is assumed to connote. The "responsible" leaders take cautious steps, very concerned with upsetting monied or political interests. Davis, of course, does not want to say that Malcolm X was "irresponsible," so the quotation marks around "responsible" are to suggest that the people being designated as responsible do not own the term; that Malcolm X was every bit as responsible as they were. But when such sniping is made at "responsible leaders" there is no discussion of how our language got this way and what would be an alternative.

Christian ethics has had a worse dilemma. It could not simply be silent on the question of a basis for responsibility. Assuming a split between ultimate ends and responsibility, Christian writers had the choice of embracing ultimacy at the expense of responsibility or else joining in the discussions of the secular world's responsibility while seeming to slight the New Testament. As one might guess, the conservative end of Protestant Christianity emphasized the Bible and salvation from evil, while being suspicious of political remedies. The liberal forces of Protestantism emphasized church cooperation with the positive features of modern reform movements.

The liberal impulse perhaps reached its peak at the World Council of Churches' meeting in Amsterdam in 1948. The council promulgated a "responsible society model." With cooperation having been achieved among Protestant groups, and the first hints of Roman Catholic support, the World Council of Churches was ready to lead in the post World War II era. "Against conservativism and inertia, ecumenical thought emphasizes the changeability of human structures; as a result it issues a call to responsibility for active participation in social change."[51]

The "responsible society model" had a rather brief ascendancy in Protestant circles. In recent decades, the phrase has been used with some disdain to describe the complacent church attitude of the 1950s.[52] By the time of the Geneva Conference in 1966 and the Uppsala Assembly in 1968, there was severe criticism of a model too embedded in the middle-class values of Western Europe and North America. The criticism was more from the left than the right. Like other liberal groups in the 1960s, liberal church leaders were surprised to be outflanked by people claiming to be not conservative but more radically liberal. The strongest force for change came from the so-called Third World. "While the 'responsible society' was predicated on the basis of a stable society which, through democratic procedures, endeavored to realize a fair degree of social justice, the new forces were struggling for a new and just society. They called for a radical shift in power, a mobilizing vision, a total commitment and a concrete historical focus."[53]

Political radicalism could thus join forces with a conservatism rooted in the radical message of the gospel and the protests of Reformation history. A suspicion of established power and a defense of vulnerable people underlay the realignment of Christian ethicists. On the biblical foundation of Christian criticism, Protestant and Catholic Christians now worked together. The growing importance of the churches of Asia, Africa, and Latin America has been gradually changing the face of Christianity. In the United States, the Roman Catholic church shifted from a church of immigrants intent on proving their patriotism to a church often at odds with their government on issues such as economic justice, peace, capital punishment, and abortion.

One of the most interesting examples of radical Christian writing is *The Politics of Jesus* by John Howard Yoder. Drawing on a conservative Mennonite tradition, Yoder articulates a dramatic and challenging ethic based on the Gospel of Luke. Like other advocates of nonviolence, he shows the relevance of Jesus' preaching and the Jewish tradition from which it emerged. What is of immediate interest for my purpose is Yoder's use of "responsibility."

The Politics of Jesus reflects the fact that it was written at the time when the "responsible society model" was being criticized. Yoder chides his Christian brethren who get their ethics "from a 'responsible' calculation of our chances and our duty to make events come out as well as possible." He comes back repeatedly to the word: Jesus' revolution was based on the "rejection of both quietism and establishment responsibility"; other Christian writers are criticized for doing ethics by "trying to apply individual categories ('personalization,' 'responsibility') to social structures." And the suffering of the poor is in conflict with an "ethic of 'responsibility' or of power that can no longer at the same time claim to be Christian and bypass the judgment of the Suffering Servant's exemplarity."[54]

Like the passage quoted earlier from Malcolm X's autobiography, Yoder often puts quotation marks around "responsibility," suggesting that the term is being misused by its advocates; but he never raises the question directly. It seems to me that, precisely to carry out his project of relating the New Testament to the present scene, a richer grammar of responsibility would be of great service. In one passage Yoder intimates that possibility where he says there are times when "the most effective way to *take* responsibility is to refuse to collaborate, and by that refusal to take sides in favor of men whom that power is oppressing."[55] Here the term responsibility is almost turned upside down from his other uses, which are resigned to the meaning found in the 1948 World Council of Churches and the standard secular meaning.

Contemporary Retrievals

There have been a number of Christian and Jewish thinkers in the twentieth century who have tried to recover a deeper meaning of response/responsible/responsibility. Refusing to accept a contrast of ultimate ends and responsibility, they have been attracted by what is implied in being responsible: call/answer. Instead of moving between individual and society, they have started with larger patterns of dependence and interdependence. Human life is interpreted as a process of answering.

The most famous Jewish writer in this vein was Martin Buber. His provocative essay *I and Thou* was too Jewish for some secular readers, too secular for some Jewish readers. The work is clearly inspired by biblical ideas of creation, salvation, justice, judgment. Its premise is that all reality is relational: "In the beginning is relation." The two fundamental words are "I-Thou" and "I-It." While human life involves both kinds of relations, the humans express life at its best in the encounter of I-Thou. "All true life is a meeting."[56]

Martin Buber's great insight was taken up by other Jewish thinkers (Emmanuel Levinas, Franz Rosenzweig) and Catholic philosophers (Emmanuel Mounier, Gabriel Marcel).[57] More widely, Buber influenced many schools of philosophy and psychology. Under his impact on religious writing, human life was described as a divine call, and interpersonal exchange was taken to be the highest manifestation of the divine. In the secular world of psychology, the ultimate basis for human vocation was left blank, but Buber's emphasis on encounter filtered into practice. The presence and invitation of another person were viewed as the center of healing. Especially in the United States, where the impersonality of the Freudian analyst never fully took hold, psychology emphasized interpersonal exchange (Carl Rogers, Abraham Maslow, Rollo May).

As happens with many great insights that get turned into slogans, Buber's I-Thou easily lends itself to trivialization and sentimentality. Finding one's thou could be taken to be the only task in life. And talking things out could be taken as the solution to all problems. Still, this resituating of the personal at the center of philosophy and ethics has been of incalculable significance and is one of the keys to a grammar of responsibility.

Roman Catholic theology recovered a sense of responsibility along a different route. Karl Rahner, the greatest Catholic theologian of the century, wrote a philosophical dissertation, *Hearers of the Word*.[58] He reread Thomas Aquinas through the lens of Kant and Heidegger. The work was rejected by the conservative Catholic faculty as subversive of theology. It was criticized from the opposite direction as too easy an answer to the question asked by Heidegger. Rahner's work eventually triumphed within the church, although he did not concentrate on the implications for ethics or moral theology.

Catholic theology was transformed after mid-century by its confrontation with modern categories while it was also recovering its Jewish roots. Genuine Christian writing cannot leave out the flow of history, particular words that have been spoken, heard, and answered. The Christian story begins with words having already been spoken. The metaphysical premise is a being able to respond; the ethical question is *how* the human being responds. The transformation of the understanding of church, sacraments, and moral theology was underpinned by an understanding of divine revelation as human response to divine call; that is, there can be no revelation of God without human response-ability.[59] Insofar as this idea is grounded in the Bible, Catholic, Protestant, and Jewish writings have moved together more closely.

Some of the most profound twentieth-century writing on responsibility is by Dietrich Bonhoeffer.[60] His life, as much as his writings, exemplified the meaning of responsibility. He returned to Germany from the United States in the 1930s to fight the Nazi regime. Eventually, he was executed for involvement in a plot to kill Hitler. Bonhoeffer was much discussed in the 1960s for his prison notes that speak of a "religionless Christianity" and the experience of the death of God. His earlier writings unfortunately were not as widely read. Those works show a deep religious and ethical sensitivity that prepared him for his last days in prison. He was especially concerned with responsibility as a response to a divine call that each person must answer in his or her own life. But responsibility, Bonhoeffer insists, is always limited by the responsibility that fellow human beings have for themselves.[61]

One Protestant thinker in the United States deserves special note. H. Richard Niebuhr taught Christian Ethics at Yale Divinity School for many years. His book *The Responsible Self* was pieced together after his death.[62] Although fragmentary, the book is filled with brilliant insights. Like Rahner's *Hearers of the Word*, it is not a book of theology; Niebuhr calls it a work of moral philosophy that is profoundly affected by the author's encounter with the founder of Christianity. Niebuhr composed the ideas of the book while the "responsible society model" was in vogue, but he recognized that "society" is not the right word after "responsible." His interest is the nature of the self as the basis of all ethics.

Niebuhr proposed that there are three ways to conceive of the moral life: as a *maker* of one's life; as an *obeyer* of law; or as a *respondent* within a continuing process of interaction and interpretation. "Responsibility" may be employed in the first two cases: as a thing to be reached or as an obligation on us. However, in the third case, responsible is what we are: beings whose nature is to listen and to answer. Thus, the major question of ethics for Niebuhr is: "To whom or what am I responsible and in what community of interaction am I myself?"[63] The question is a powerfully practical one that calls for more of a theoretical basis than Niebuhr developed in *The Responsible Self*, though he did develop some of those ideas in earlier writings.[64]

Niebuhr did elaborate the process of responsibility with respect to time. Every action involves an interpretation of past events and some anticipation of the future. "Our actions answer to actions upon us in accord with our interpretation of that action."[65] Responsibility is temporal not just in the sense of being situated in time. More profoundly, we discover ourselves as present, having past and future as dimensions of the present, in the experience of ourselves as responsible beings.

Niebuhr also attempted to develop a "social" dimension to responsibility. Here he was less successful, both because of the fragmentary character of his work but also because of the inadequacy of the language at hand. Like Buber, he insisted on an interpersonal or intersubjective character to human existence.[66] But that does not of itself address communal, organizational, and environmental issues of responsibility.

Some of the great political figures of the twentieth century may offer examples of responsibility in action. They listened to what history and the concrete situations of their people said to them, and then they did the deeds that seemed called for. Franklin Roosevelt and Winston Churchill seem to have secured their places in history. As one gets close to the present, judgments are less certain. Contemporary Russia is not very kind in its judgment of Mikhail Gorbachev, though in much of the rest of the world he is honored as a man of courage and responsibility. Nelson Mandela survived years in prison; when the South African government called, he was ready to respond.

Most contemporary leaders do not have the time and the inclination to articulate a theory of responsibility. One remarkable exception is Vaclav Havel. Starting in the 1970s, Havel spoke eloquently of responsibility. With his art and his political essays he tried to live out his understanding of what responsibility demanded. Havel's writings include many of the distinctions I make in a grammar of responsibility. He is acutely aware of being responsible to a reality greater than the present regime. He is also aware of being responsible for the next concrete step, which for much of his life was a refusal to submit. Universality for Havel means being responsible to and for the whole. "A reaffirmed human responsibility is the most natural barrier to all irresponsibility. If, for instance, the spiritual and technological potential of the advanced world is spread truly responsibly, not solely under the pressure of a selfish interest in profits, we can prevent its irresponsible transformation into weapons of destruction."[67]

A final author might be noted here to indicate a possible opening in the discussion of responsibility. Carol Gilligan has had considerable influence on discussions of moral development. She refers in one essay to Niebuhr's *Responsible Self*, although I do not think Niebuhr was a formative influence. She also refers to Max Weber's two ethics, but she does not remain dependent on his use of responsibility.[68] I think that responsibility is prominent in her writing because she heard it from the women she interviewed. Furthermore, the women's usage reflected the meaning implied in Niebuhr's question: To whom and to what am I responsible?

I concentrate here on Gilligan's study of women who were considering an abortion, the study that led to her book *In a Different Voice*.[69] Almost always for the women interviewed, whatever their ambivalence about abortion, the question of who is responsible for deciding is clear. The woman herself is the responsible party; she has to decide either to have or not to have the abortion. Nonetheless, the women ponder responsibility at great length. They frequently talk of "responsibility to myself." They also talk of responsibility to the child—a future, hypothetical child. This concern is distinguishable from a responsibility for the developing organism within her own body.

Because the term responsibility arose frequently in the women's description of their moral action, it has come to play an important part not only in Gilligan's writing but in much of feminist literature.[70] As this happens, the danger is that the term is invoked as something which "we" agree upon and sets "us" against "them." If responsibility has the potential to bridge many opposites by going deeper than the divisions, it would be unfortunate to identify the term with one group, whether it be professionals, Republicans, Christians, or women.

Carol Gilligan developed a formula in which responsibility is central. The trouble is that her pairings set responsibility over against ethical terms that should not be opposites. She writes that "justice gives rise to an ethics of rights and care engenders an ethic of responsibility."[71] She does not entirely identify justice with men and responsibility with women. She does assume a meaning of justice that has dominated Western thought from John Locke to John Rawls, a meaning controlled by ideas of equality, objectivity, and rational calculation.

Gilligan is aware that such a meaning of justice can be used oppressively. She points out the ineffectiveness, even obscenity, of preaching justice at people when all the choices before them are patently unjust.[72] Responsibility in such circumstances often means listening painfully to all aspects of the situation and then choosing the least evil option. But what cries out for change here is, among other things, our idea of justice. Responsibility should not be an alternative to justice. It can be a revelation of injustice and a step toward transforming ethical systems that complacently claim to be built on justice.

One could write a grammar of justice similar to what I am trying to do with responsibility. Certainly, justice can lay claim to being the most important, most comprehensive, ethical term. Its roots go deep into both religious tradition and philosophical speculation. The biblical meaning of justice—what one author summarizes as "to sort out what belongs to whom, and to return it to them"—stands in considerable tension with Plato, Aristotle, and the image of a blind balancing of weights.[73] The history of justice throughout Western history is extraordinarily rich. Political and legal systems of the last three centuries create a dense thicket of conversation about the meaning of justice.

My choice to track the use of "responsibility" is not a choice against justice. It is rather a hope of being modestly successful at controlling the material. For every book on responsibility there are dozens or hundreds on justice. Until this century, "justice" had been used hundreds or thousands of times more frequently than "responsibility." Today, however, "responsibility" competes with "justice" in popular discourse, even if most of the scholarly literature on responsibility is restricted to specialized uses.

As indicated earlier, responsibility has been chosen as an entry point for discussing contemporary morality. It is a term implied as the basis for much of Western history. But it is a term whose explicit use is mostly in the twentieth century. The question that remains open toward the end of this century is whether its repetitive use is evidence of its effectiveness to get at contemporary issues or whether it is being wielded as an opaque instrument to avoid doing much about those issues. The following chapters articulate a use of responsibility that is based on history, etymology, logic, contemporary discussion, and practical need. Only when the grammar of responsibility is laid out can we judge if it is a theoretically consistent and practically effective category.

CHAPTER 3

FUNDAMENTAL DISTINCTIONS

The historical outline of the previous chapter situates responsibility in the paradoxical position that it occupies today. Its rise to the top was at the expense of a severing from its roots. On one side, responsibility can be a catch-all term for describing a generally good person; on the other side, most writing on responsibility quickly gets to technical and very specific issues. Nothing seems more widely agreed upon than the necessity of having responsibility; almost as wide an agreement exists that we are currently lacking it. Those who are confident that they are responsible people look for ways to get the other people to take responsibility.

If I am correct that our present grammar of responsibility is inadequate, is there any hope of changing the situation? Were it a matter of inventing a meaning that does not now exist or of reestablishing conditions of several centuries ago, the project would be doomed. Fortunately, the meaning of a term does not simply disappear; its etymology, as J. L. Austin says, nearly always trails behind it.[1] One can realistically argue for a retrieval of latent meaning, for highlighting one meaning over another. The richest meaning of responsibility is not necessarily the one that brings the heaviest burden. It is rather one that is based on defensible distinctions from a historical point of view and one that illuminates in new ways our moral language.

There is often a groping after the distinctions that are introduced in this chapter. Many people sense that the terms that are now used in moral discussion cannot break us out of our dilemmas. Responsibility is one of the most frequently invoked terms in such dilemmas. But usually the question of responsibility gets reduced to computerlike logic: x or y is responsible for a; x is or is not responsible for b; if x is responsible for c, x goes to jail.

Many people get frustrated at this absorption of responsibility into a legal calculus. They sense that some deeper meaning is hidden in the word. However, writing on responsibility that goes further quickly gets into the technical language of philosophical or professional specialties. For example, discussions about the responsibility of the physician are heavy on medical talk and not very probing about the nature of responsibility. These necessary inquiries into specialized areas are not ultimately fruitful unless they are connected at the base to a rich meaning of responsibility itself.

Most books that announce their intention to explore responsibility quickly make clear, often on the first page, that their interest is "moral responsibility." This distinction is understandable, even indispensable. However, one would think that the line between moral and nonmoral responsibility would draw attention. Can we understand moral responsibility without its relation to responsibility as a whole? But moral responsibility is most often isolated as a topic on its own so that the other element or elements in the set are unclear.

For example, in the introduction to *Perspectives on Moral Responsibility*, the editors immediately distinguish moral and *causal* responsibility. But lest the reader assume that causal is logically equivalent to nonmoral, a footnote adds: "It should be noted that the term 'responsibility' admits of a variety of uses in addition to causal and moral responsibility. For example, it is used to refer to legal responsibility, corporate responsibility, role responsibility. . . . In this Introduction we restrict our attention to the issues surrounding moral responsibility."[2] I find this clarification bewildering. Moral responsibility is assumed to be a special case of responsibility in a grab bag of things called "responsibilities."

The furthest extreme in this fragmenting of responsibility is a book with the startling title *Freedom without Responsibility*. One must credit the author Bruce Waller with a novel thesis; he wishes to get rid of responsibility without damaging freedom. But he is not, it turns out, opposed to all responsibility. Indeed, "there are 'responsible' persons who have substantial 'responsibilities' and who have been placed in such positions of 'responsibility' because they are self-controlled, deliberate, trustworthy. But all of that is a matter of *role* responsibility and must not be confused with moral responsibility."[3]

It is apparent that Waller is quite fond of the word responsibility; he accepts "role responsibility" but not moral responsibility. Even there, he accepts one "sort" of moral responsibility. A person is "moral-act responsible" but not "moral-judgment responsible."[4] What starts out in the title as a rejection of responsibility is really a book about the unfair blaming of people and the uselessness of punishment.[5] I tend to agree with much of what he says on these practical matters. But he has created a thicket of definitions that do nothing but obscure the intelligibility of the term responsible. Even for the purpose of rejecting moral responsibility, one has to have a fairly simple and logically coherent meaning for responsibility.

For exploring the fundamental meaning of "responsible" that funds a variety of uses, this chapter has four interrelated sections: (1) the continuity of meaning between human and nonhuman; (2) the continuity between is and ought; (3) the distinction between responsible to and responsible for; (4) the distinction within responsibility of right and duty. Each point builds on the previous ones without ever moving far from the root of "responsible": to listen and to answer. The English word goes back through the French *repondre* to the Latin *respondeo*. The German *Verantwortlich* parallels the etymology of the English word "answer." In European languages generally the image is the same: an address having been made, there is a return or answer.

Humans and Nonhumans

Are others than humans responsible? The natural inclination is to say "obviously not," assuming that the question means "moral responsibility." And, of course, by the usual definitions, only human actions can be morally responsible. However, the fact that not *all* human actions are morally responsible suggests that there might be something worth exploring here. Do humans share some nonmoral responsibility with the nonhuman world? The relation between moral and nonmoral responsibility *within* human life might be illuminated by asking about responsibility in the nonhuman world.

A responsible being is one that responds, or more precisely, is capable of response. How far does that characteristic extend? There is no obvious line beyond which response is totally out of the question. According to modern physics, the smallest particles of the universe cannot be exactly located because they respond to our pressing the search. Where to draw a useful line depends on how far we wish to extend a metaphor taken from human life. The full meaning we have of responding to a call addressed to a self comes from human experience. To what other beings can we attribute *something like that* without creating anthropomorphic fantasies that prevent us seeing what is before our eyes?

The question, I would insist, is not whether to extend the experience of "capable of response" beyond the human, but how far. All of human speech has some anthropomorphic bias; it is after all *human*. We compare nonhuman and human, and decide that some particular words appropriately apply to some beings and not to others. Some experiences cannot be attributed to things because those things are too far removed from the experience; no consistent grammar of use is possible. Wittgenstein uses the example of a machine having a toothache.[6] We know before examining any claims that a machine does not have toothaches; we simply do not talk that way. But can we talk about a piece of wood responding to the expert touch of a carpenter or a violinist? The wood is capable of responding in different ways; the expert draws forth a better response than someone who has no feel for wood.

Some people will not be persuaded that responsible should be extended that far. But even with a highly restrictive use of the term, does anyone doubt that a dog or a dolphin is "capable of response"? True, we do not hold dogs morally accountable for their actions, though that has been done in the past and we come rather close at times.[7] We do assume that they can, and should, respond to training. We work with patterns of behavior and see the animal's behavior in a larger context of interpretation. Should responsible be limited to mammals, to sentient animals, to organisms?

Mary Midgley in *Beast and Man* is one of the few authors who notices the breadth in the use of the word response.[8] She does so in the form of a complaint that "response" is a misleading term. She notes that response can be used for the highly sensitive answering of a conscious being and also for activities that are entirely mechanical. Her point in voicing this complaint is that the ambiguity can lead people to take the animal's responsive behavior as mechanical. Her theme is that "beasts" are more like humans than machines, and they deserve our respect. Mary Midgley's book was in fact one of the major contributors to the gaining of respect for animals. But is it possible that this respect (with appropriate gradations) should extend beyond the "beast."

Should not respect be extended to all living creatures, and could not the term response be appropriately used beyond both "man and beast"?

I would agree with Midgley's objection to the use of response and response-able as qualities of the mechanical world. When human beings build something, their responsibility may be carried out through the machine's activity. When we say, as we occasionally do, that the bridge is responsible for carrying thirty tons, it is usually clear that we are talking about how the bridge has been humanly designed. But sometimes this kind of use is the basis of confusion and argument. A report on suicide in 1995 carries the statement that "guns are largely, if not entirely, responsible for the dramatic increase in suicide rates for the nation's youths."[9] The authors had a point to make, but they misstate their case. The cliché that "guns don't kill, people do" needs a more precise rejoinder than saying guns are responsible for the increase of suicide. Responsibility needs assigning to the gun makers, gun sellers, politicians, NRA officials, and others.

More difficult to decide is whether respond/response should be used of mountains, oceans, deserts, trees, wind, rivers, and other powerful elements of nature. They are not living beings, though they are integral to the cycle of life. Much of literature, not to mention spiritual traditions, would be tongue-tied unless these elements were allowed some response.

With living beings, a consistent logic and grammar of responsibility clearly becomes feasible. Response is not a peripheral note to the notion of living. There is a within to the living being that interacts with an environment. Even minute living beings are respondents and contribute to the pattern of living beings. Speaking of the indispensable place of insects, the director of the Xerces society has said: "The world is going to go without golden lemurs and without any of a number of orchids, but invertebrates are responsible for all the ecosystem processes."[10]

Is it a legitimate use of the term to say that insects are responsible for the ecosystem? Clearly insects are lacking in some of the elements that are present in human responsibility. Just as clearly, there is something more at issue than in the case of the bridge being responsible for carrying a certain weight. However one explains the design of the ecosystem, insects do carry a heavy burden of responsibility for the functioning of human as well as nonhuman life. They respond according to the ways they are acted upon; when conditions change, they are capable of response in new patterns.

One reason why humans may resist attributing responsibleness to insects is that they go about their business without necessarily responding *to us*. If insects are threatened by human intervention, they will indeed respond in whatever self-protecting ways they can. But in the main, the insect world goes its own way, apparently oblivious of human hopes and fears, human plans for shaping up the world. It is not just that we feel our dignity has been slighted; rather we are unsure of how to interpret response/responsible if we are not part of it.

Moving in this direction toward the fullest meaning of responsibility, we can ask whether there are living beings that speak and listen in ways closely analogous to human speaking and listening. Do trees talk to people? Do people's plants do better when spoken to? These questions can be dismissed as silly if no play is allowed for the meanings of speak and listen. In 1974, the United States Supreme Court ruled that "trees have standing"; that is, a suit could be brought before the court in which trees are the claimant.[11] Of course, the trees (not unlike most of us) need a lawyer to be their spokesperson. Nonetheless, the court is willing to listen to trees, as well as cases of endangered species.

When Victor Frankl interviewed a survivor of the death camps, he asked her what had kept her going. She replied that it was a tree that she could see from her cell and she spoke with the tree. Frankl asked what the tree said. She answered: "It said to me, 'I am here—I am here—I am life, eternal life.'"[12] Did the tree really speak? The fact that one has not heard a tree speak is not proof that trees do not do so. One has to listen, to be attuned in ways that we may not be accustomed. Sometimes dire experiences, such as those of the woman in the death camp, change our attentiveness. Or at the other extreme, the exhilarating and majestic experience of being among trees a thousand years in age can resituate the meaning of listening and speaking. Those who respect the forest and are challenged by the wilderness discover that trees are responsive beings.[13]

One aspect of Martin Buber's *I and Thou* that has often been misunderstood is that his I-Thou word is not exclusively a human to human relation. He explicitly refers to a human relation to trees in which the pattern of address and response is present. A tree, in Buber's vocabulary, can be turned into an "it" when the human I sees the tree as nothing but lumber or wood pulp. A living tree deserves appreciative attention as one capable of revealing the mysteries of life and death.[14]

One of the most intriguing passages in *I and Thou* is Buber's description of his cat. He seems to credit the cat with some of the deepest revelations of life: "No other event has made me so deeply aware of the evanescent actuality in all relationships to other beings."[15] When we get to the sphere of domestic animals, we are unmistakably dealing with beings who are capable of response to our human speech, even while connecting us to primal forces we can only glimpse. Buber's choice of the cat is an appropriate one for exemplifying this link. Cats are the most popular domestic animal in this country. Children learn about responsibility in interaction with cats and dogs, as much as by any experience.

One also learns differences in animal responses. As T. S. Eliot's now-famous poem about cats dramatized, "you should address a cat, but always keep in mind that he resents familiarity."[16] As one saying has it, "when you call a dog, the dog comes; when you call a cat, the cat says leave a message and I'll get back to you." Some people do not much like this independence of the cat. Should not these cared-for animals respond with more alacrity to our wishes? Cats do not follow easily, whether behind human or cat. In *The Tribe of Tiger*, Elizabeth Marshall Thomas writes that "kittens follow their mothers, to be sure, but cats make their own plans and decisions, each individual taking full responsibility for himself or herself with no one else to show the way."[17] Such passages in Thomas's books on cats and dogs are criticized for excessive anthropomorphism, but she always accords respect to the animal's autonomous existence. Thus, to her question of what do dogs really want, her answer is: each other.[18]

There is something else worth noticing about the human interaction with dogs, cats, horses, chimps, and other animals that people come to have affection for. The person expresses care for a particular animal by providing food, shelter, and even conversation. The animal responds with signals of appreciation, such as purring or a wagging tail. That in turn evokes further caring by the human partner. Why does a human "owner" come to feel responsible for *this* dog or *that* bird? In large part because the particular animal has exhibited its own responsibility, that is, its ability to respond to the care of *this* human being. By most standards of logic, this process seems either unfair or utterly haphazard. A stray animal shows up at the door, and the human being comes to feel responsible for this animal but not for a million other strays.

This process of growing into responsibility, or at least feeling responsible, is not confined to human treatment of a nonhuman animal. The person–dog or person–horse relation prefigures some of what goes on between humans. With human to animal relations one can see the beginnings of reciprocity pertaining to response. The animal's ability to respond does not reach equality with the human. But the interaction, reciprocal action to whatever degree, generates the experience of being responsible. We become responsible over a period of time by finding a response in another being that in turn evokes a response in us. Given the time required and the complexity of the movement, those to whom we can *feel* responsible are few in number. And without some feelings being involved, responsibility will not survive on the basis of rational calculation.

In human relations we would like to have some guarantee that those few whom we feel intimately related to are worth our time and effort. Choosing a marriage partner or a close friend ought to have more direction and logic than adopting a stray cat. Nonetheless, in human affairs we are confronted with people, starting with family members and extending to chance encounters, who are part of a narrow circle to whom we feel responsible. We may sometimes try to shake off the feeling and convince ourselves that responsibility toward a drug-addicted brother or a cheating business partner is not different from responsibility toward five billion other people. But if a bond of reciprocal response has developed over the years then, though I may not have chosen these people, nonetheless fate, luck, randomness, or divine providence keeps the meaning of my responsibility rooted in these people.

The movement from insect to human world seems to involve both a more generalized capacity to respond and a narrower focus of response. As humans come to conceive of moral responsibility, it is important they do not forget the simple, bodily feeling out of which this moral stance emerges. We are morally responsible because we can first feel our bodily response to a world of particulars outside of our own bodies. We become morally responsible as we guide our physical and emotional responses to things we need, animals we care for, humans we love. At some point along a continuum, we draw a line to distinguish the realm called "moral" responsibility. That realm is understandably what most interests us, but it will not be intelligible if it is severed from its nonmoral roots.

Is and Ought

This second point, the continuity between what is and what ought to be, has been prepared for by the first point. To be responsible is a term that can both describe the way the world is and also indicate how we should act. This range of meaning is not based on confusion, let alone equivocation. "Responsible" is simply one of those words that we need, and in fact do use, to indicate continuity between our statements of what is and what ought to be. There is a line drawn through responsibility to distinguish (not separate) is and ought. That line is never entirely clear-cut and is not stationary in an individual's life.

A human being is the responsible being, or the most responsible of all the animals. A one-day-old baby is, in this sense, responsible. We are now acutely aware of the importance of the infant (even the fetus) as a response-able being. An environment of people and things evokes responses in infants and young children. This environment has relevance to the individual's later sense of (moral) responsibility. We do not attribute moral responsibility to the child until he or she has developed powers of deliberation and choice. Before that age, the child is responsible but not morally responsible.

Responsible in the second or moral sense means being held accountable for good or bad behavior. When we say that people should act responsibly, we are demanding that they fulfill obligations, obey the law, and otherwise be good people. Of course, in the first sense, people are always acting responsibly, however ethical or unethical their behavior. The moral demand of responsibility, therefore, is not to acquire something that is missing but to somehow change the direction of what is already present. A person who fails to act in ways accepted as ethical is called "irresponsible." Thus, we have the paradox: Only a responsible being can be irresponsible.

It is important to note how clearly this distinction is built into the term. The difference between nonresponsible and irresponsible is neither haphazard nor a unique case. A similar clear distinction is made with other important terms. For example, we carefully distinguish between nonrational and irrational, the second word connoting psychological if not moral failure. An irrational person has lost control of his or her life; irrational acts are prone to violence and self-destruction. There are innumerable nonrational beings that do not have the power to reason. Only a rational being can be irrational.

Similarly, "professional" is a term applied to people, work, or behavior. What does not fit the category is called nonprofessional. The laborer, the amateur, the layperson are terms indicating nonprofessional status. When the term "unprofessional" is used in reference to work or behavior, it always signals a lapse, a breach of ethical conduct. Once again the paradox: Only a professional can act unprofessionally.

When "responsible" is a description of what is, its opposite is "nonresponsible." When "responsible" is a demand to act in an ethically proper way, its opposite is "irresponsible." It is incorrect to say of a small child that it is irresponsible; but it is proper and necessary to say that the small child is (morally) nonresponsible.

By examining the whole range of responsibility, I have extended the term beyond the human adult to include the child, and beyond the human world to (at least) our next of animal kin. That context should act as a reminder that even when a human adult is called responsible, the term can still mean "capable of response" as well as meaning a requirement to act in an ethically proper way. A human adult *is* responsible; and a human adult *should be* responsible.

The advantage in having this term is that ethical advice to others or ethical striving by ourselves can be undertaken with the modest aim of improving what is there. Indeed, so long as people are not acting irresponsibly, they are probably more responsible than is recognized. The disadvantage is that responsibility is exposed to being a banal term that comes in for routine praise. Urging that we act responsibly is neither helpful nor courageous if that is what everybody does every day. Unless both the continuity of is and ought and also the distinction between them is recognized, then calls for responsibility take us nowhere.

My claim that "responsibility" can cover what is and what ought to be is in conflict with a cherished maxim of modern ethics, namely, that one cannot derive an ought from an is. That maxim may be true, but it assumes that there is a realm of statements that describe the world in morally neutral terms.[19] When ethical issues are subsequently raised, it is assumed that they have to be stated as prescriptions of how the world ought to be instead of how it in fact is. Thus, the dilemma of "is versus ought" is also stated as "fact versus value," and "description versus prescription."

Instead of trying to "derive" the second element from the first in these pairs, I have begun with a term that can and is used to unite (while distinguishing) statements of what is and what ought to be. If the "is versus ought" dilemma of modern ethics is to be coped with, other terms have to complement "responsible" in tracing the continuity of is and ought. Nevertheless, even the existence of one term can show that an absolute division between a world of fact and a wish list called "values" is a recent invention that has been assumed without proof.

For overcoming this division, the language of "fact and value" will never work. The two terms have been defined in modern times to be opposites with no bridge between them. A fact is simply there, a neutral datum that confronts the mind. A value is something to be willed or chosen; it is what persons cherish or stand for. As modern science turned the world into a collection of facts, one form of resistance in the eighteenth and nineteenth centuries was to posit a realm of *values* untouchable by impersonal science. These days it is common to see "responsibility" designated as a value. That is a disastrous tendency. Of course, responsibility is not a fact, either. It simply has no place in a world divided between fact and value.

A more interesting, even if ultimately unsatisfactory, language to explore is "description versus prescription." There is at least a little give in this language. Presumably the prescription, if not *derived* from description, is expected to flow from what has been described. Speakers and writers, nevertheless, assume that these two are separate worlds. Authors repeatedly write: My job is to describe, not to prescribe.

The defense seldom works. Although an author may clearly state that the book is intended as description not prescription, readers and reviewers regularly take something else from the book. One place this inevitably happens is in writing on "human development." Authors are rightfully wary of claiming to have universal theories of human development after interviewing a few dozen or a few hundred people.

Gail Sheehy's popular book *Passages* is intended to be description not prescription.[20] Neither enthusiastic readers nor skeptical reviewers took the book's contents that way. Starting with the word "development," the language is not descriptive—at least in the sense of objective fact reported by neutral observer. "Development" for at least two centuries has accumulated a meaning of how things *should* go. Each time a developmental stage is given a catchy title the author's feelings are revealed. Even if one were to do nothing but report the raw data of interviews, the choice of material and the arrangement of the data would involve the author's evaluative judgment.[21]

As another example, take what is in one way the ultimate theory of human development: Elisabeth Kübler-Ross's stages of dying. The author wishes to describe not prescribe.[22] However, millions of readers became convinced on reading the book that the five stages are the way people should die. And there is ample evidence in the text itself that the author thinks that, with sufficient time and a good counselor, the dying person should reach acceptance.[23]

Kübler-Ross was trying to find out how people were dying and how better they might be served at this stage of life. She did not wish to say how people must die, but she also did not study dying patients as scientific objects. She talked to the patients, listened at length, wrote down and shaped what they had to say, and discerned a pattern that she named with emotion-laden words (denial, anger, bargain, depression, acceptance). *Neither* the language of description *nor* that of prescription is adequate for her study.

Consider the most obvious case, if not the origin, of the language of description versus prescription: medical practice. If I have an ailment, I go to a physician. With the tools of modern medicine, the physician establishes the facts of my case. He or she writes a prescription which the pharmacist fills. If all goes well, the medicine cures the problem. The pre-scription is what is written before, that is, what supplies the solution. If the de-scription can be done with objective, even numerical, standards the description is all the better.

I realize that the above is something of a caricature, but it is not too far from the way the medical profession was at its most arrogant. The "doctor" became the expert who knew what was wrong and knew what to prescribe for a cure. These days physicians are more likely to listen to their patients, try to explain things so that the patient will work along with the physician on whatever therapy is used in the attempt to heal. That is, description/prescription does not even hold well today in medicine.

Consider an alternative metaphor from another profession: the law.

If I am accused of a crime, I will hire a lawyer. We subsequently talk at length. He or she becomes my advocate in court. What is said and how it is said are crucial to convincing the jury. If one route does not work, another can be tried. If the advocacy is successful, the result is not a cure for all my problems, but I am allowed to get on with my life. In this metaphor, each statement has to be factually not false, but it is always someone's rendering of reality in emotionally freighted words. The process is one of advocating that one way of naming reality is closer to the truth than any other available way.[24]

In my examples above of developmental theories, Gail Sheehy or Elisabeth Kübler-Ross would have been in a stronger position by saying: I have listened to people; I have shaped an argument from their words to advocate a position I believe in. I am sure my theory of stages is not false. My way of naming stages is pointing in the right direction, although each key term has some connotations I do not subscribe to. Kübler-Ross could have said of her most important term "acceptance": I use this term both to describe what people do throughout life (they accept it every day); I also use the term to indicate where people should end life, with a fullness of accepting that can embrace denial or anger or other emotions that I have not named.

In writing on human development or in other areas where an ethical dimension is unavoidable, every choice of language involves advocacy. A "factual description" can exist in numbers; but once language is used, someone has to decide which words are best to get close to the truth. When language is carefully advocated, the speaker is aware of the range of connotations that could be playing in the listener's (juror's) mind. The speaker tries to exclude what may mislead, but not by trying to reduce words to algebraic definitions. The ambiguity of the old, rich words is precisely what the speaker plays upon to evoke deeper levels of human truth.[25]

In this book "responsible" is my choice. I make no claim that it is merely descriptive—in the sense of an objective fact obvious to any reasonable person. I advocate the term as theoretically revealing and practically useful. This choice involves my advocating that Martin Buber or H. Richard Niebuhr is closer to the truth of the matter than is Descartes, Locke, or Kant. Whether the reader will agree with the choice is likely to depend on whether "responsible" can be presented as both comprehensive and consistent. A grammar of its use is intended to show just that. By being able to include statements of what is and what ought to be, "responsible" opens out on a rich conversation about the moral life.

Responsible To and Responsible For

The previous two points establish the basis for the most important distinction within responsible: to and for. As I recounted in the previous chapter on the history of the term, "responsible to" was the usual way of using the term until the latter part of the nineteenth century. Then, "responsible for," which had played a secondary role, took over to the near exclusion of "responsible to." I do not argue that we should go back a century or more, but the question of "responsible to" never went away and cannot go away. The failure to notice that "responsible to" is a question at all vitiates much of the writing on responsibility.

Hans Jonas's *The Imperative of Responsibility* is one of the most detailed studies of the use of "responsibility." Jonas says that there are "two widely differing senses of responsibility": (1) accountability for one's deeds and (2) responsibility for particular objects. Although this is a distinction within the use of "responsible for," Jonas is oblivious of the far more basic distinction of responsible to and responsible for; this distinction, among other things, would explain the link between his two senses of responsible.[26] Only in a few spots where he is referring to the future does Jonas use, without comment, "responsible to."

In pursuing the meaning of this distinction of to and for, one should note a quirk of the English language that blurs this point. "Responsible" is often followed by "to" but in cases where that word is part of an infinitive. The meaning is still responsible for. If someone says "it is his responsibility to act," that is equivalent to "he is responsible *for* acting." When an infinitive is used after "responsible," the question of to whom and to what is not being addressed. However, I suspect that at some level of consciousness the issue is present, and the use of infinitives after "responsible" has the effect of seeming to deal with this unresolved question.

The one place today where a conscious use of this distinction is regularly employed is in bureaucratic organizations. For many people the question "to whom are you responsible?" has a clear answer: my supervisor in the next office up the pyramid. In ordinary circumstances, this reply is sufficient to justify the actions of secretaries, soldiers, and street sweepers. But when a crisis hits, an investigator wants to know "who is responsible for this?" The movement up the pyramid is assumed to stop somewhere. In this way arises the metaphor of "the buck stops here." But this picture needs examination in light of Hannah Arendt's brilliant analysis of bureaucracy. The most frightening thing about bureaucracies, Arendt claims, is that when you get to the top you find that nobody is in charge.[27]

For now, I wish to explore the meaning of responsible to, within which the bureaucratic use of the phrase is a residue of a much fuller meaning. Later in this chapter it will be important to narrow the focus of "responsible for," but that narrowing process can occur only as we widen the lens of "responsible to." The simplest answer to the question "to what and to whom am I responsible?" is: everything and everyone. That answer may not seem to be of any help; it would not be unless we explore with some concrete detail the process of trying to be responsible to everything and everyone. In practice we all come to trust some sources more than others, but the principle remains of not closing out anything or anyone as a possible source. I can only take up responsibility for my actions as a consequence of what I am responsible to.

While reformers badger us about our failure to be responsible (for), they are usually oblivious that the main failure lies in what we are responsible to. In practice, there is not a sequence of only two steps but instead a constant cycle. Reform has to break the pattern whereby "to" limits "for," which in turn can distort the ensuing "to." Some of these intricacies of the individual's inner life will be dealt with in the next chapter.

We can begin tracing "responsible to" by saying that the individual has to be responsible to himself or herself. I noted previously that the women in Gilligan's study of abortion frequently refer to being "responsible to myself." In another context that could signal a self-centered person cut off from others. But in this case, "responsible to" means listening to what is going on in one's bodily life as the touchstone for contact with reality. Trying to be responsible *for* my life when I have not first listened to that life is sure to be disastrous, either by excess in overmortgaging my resources or by deficiency in not knowing what use to make of my talents.

A main theme of Thomas Moore's popular book *Care of the Soul* is stated at the beginning: "If I see my responsibility to myself, to a friend, or to a patient in therapy as observing and respecting what the soul presents, I won't try to take things away, in the name of health."[28] Moore's use of "responsible to" here is deliberate; "responsible for" would violate his meaning. Respecting what one discovers in being responsible to oneself is the basis for respecting others—both people and things. "Responsibility to" is without preordained limits; situated at the center of the human heart, it is open to the grandeur of the universe. The result of this openness is what Moore calls a "soul ecology: a responsibility to things of the world based on appreciation and relatedness rather than on abstract principle."

Other human beings do play a special role in the calling to be responsible. Being responsible to oneself is possible only within the presence of responsive people who provide the calm security required for quiet listening. Kenneth Eble in *A Perfect Education* writes that "good teachers are almost infinitely responsive. Boys and girls become good students for teachers who provide for the first time, a response to what they feel most deeply."[29]

Responsibility to everything is, therefore, embodied in response to ourselves in a context of intersubjective exchange. From here a discriminating intelligence has to decide which incoming information is worth attending to. We can listen or we can shut our ears; we can listen with more or with less of ourselves.

Perhaps to allay some suspicion here, the question should be explicitly raised: Does the very existence of the question I am asking, "to whom and to what am I responsible," imply a religious answer? Undeniably, the idea of responsibility arose in the religious context of a divine day of judgment. The modern world has struggled to sever the term from this religious origin while not only retaining but heightening the sense of responsibility. Can that be done? Does the project self-destruct without a religious answer for "to whom am I responsible"? I would say that a religious attitude of some kind is implied, though the imagery and the institutions that grew up around divine judgment are not necessarily implied.

The nineteenth century went about the business of methodically trying to replace religion, asking who or what, instead of God, we could be responsible to. The twentieth century tried to eliminate the question of responsible to, but ironically we are now awash in new religious movements. I am trying to make the question explicit in a context that gives us more choice of answer than deciding either that

"God is back in charge" or else that "we are in charge, responsible to no one."

In John Stuart Mill's *On Liberty*, the author's first use of "responsible" refers to the European liberalism of his time, which believed that it had solved the problem of to whom the rulers of the nation are responsible. Since the rulers, the people, and the nation are now seen as one, "the nation did not need to be protected against its own will. There was no fear of its tyrannizing over itself. Let the rulers be effectually responsible to it, promptly removable by it, and it could afford to trust with power of which it could itself dictate the use to be made."[30] Mill was suspicious of (the rulers of) the nation being responsible to (the people of) the nation, of "it" being responsible only to itself. There was too neat a symmetry in the arrangement that hid the clash of competing interests. Taking his cue in part from the United States, Mill insisted on the need for guarantees of liberty so that people would be free to pursue happiness. Neither the nation, nor society, nor humanity was ready to be the recipient of religious devotion and unconditional trust. Implied in that skepticism is an appeal to something greater than nation, society, or humanity, whether the "it" is named.

There will probably always be disagreement over how to characterize the object of religious devotion, but it is perhaps possible to characterize a religious attitude as one responsible to everyone and everything. One of the classic attempts to describe this attitude was written by William James at the end of the nineteenth century. He is commenting on an exchange between two writers, Margaret Fuller and Thomas Carlyle. Fuller had said "I accept the universe"; Carlyle had sarcastically replied "Gad, she'd better." James gets underneath this exchange with his reflection: "At bottom the whole concern of both morality and religion is with the manner of our acceptance of the universe. Do we accept it only in part and grudgingly or heartily and altogether? . . . If we accept the whole, shall we do so as if stunned into submission—as Carlyle would have us—'Gad we'd better'—or shall we do so with enthusiastic assent?"[31]

When we turn from "responsible to" to "responsible for," we find the phrase everywhere. In what follows, I wish to situate its meaning in relation to "responsible to." When this context is missing, as it usually is, then there is a strong impetus to expand the area for which one is responsible. That is, if someone says "I am responsible only for myself," the statement almost inevitably draws rebuke as too narrow a view of responsible. Indeed, the statement by itself is too narrow, but the remedy is not to expand what we are responsible for. The proper route is to complement what one is responsible for with what one is responsible to.

As the context of "responsible to" comes into play, then "responsible for" can be focused more narrowly. The statement "I am responsible only for myself," instead of accepting too little for which one is responsible, actually claims too much. At any particular time, I am responsible for specific actions of my life. Through the course of a lifetime of development I become more responsible for the character of that life. However, no one can say without qualification: I am responsible for myself.

Consider this exchange in the much-praised book *Habits of the Heart*. The interviewer is Steven Tipton; the woman interviewed is a psychotherapist.

Q. So what are you responsible for?
A. I am responsible for my own acts and what I do.
Q. Does that mean you're not responsible for others, too?
A. No.
Q. Are you your sister's keeper?
A. No.
Q. Your brother's keeper?
A. No.
Q. Are you responsible for your husband?
A. I'm not. He makes his own decisions. He is his own person. He acts his own acts. I can agree with them or disagree with them. If I ever find them nauseous enough, I have the responsibility to leave and not deal with it anymore.
Q. What about your children?
A. I—I would say that I have a legal responsibility for them, but in a sense I think they are responsible for their own acts.[32]

The hectoring tone of this interview indicates that the interviewer cannot believe what he is hearing. Elsewhere in the book he says of this woman that she "is caught in some of the contradictions her belief implies. She is responsible for herself but she has no reliable way to connect her own fulfillment to that of other people."[33] However, nothing in the book's description of this woman indicates that she "has no reliable way to connect her own fulfillment to that of other people."

She is a hard-working wife and mother, involved in community affairs. Perhaps it is the interviewer who is confused about how to formulate the question of responsibility. The woman may be answering a different question—the question actually being asked—than the question the interviewer is trying to ask but does not know how.

The woman gets it about right: she is responsible for her acts (not as Tipton paraphrases her answer "responsible for herself"). She does not substitute her responsibility for other adults, each of whom is responsible for himself or herself. She makes an appropriate exception for her children; the parent has a legal and moral responsibility for some of the child's acts. (The issue of children will be explored in chapter 7.) The repetition of the interviewer's term "keeper" is an appeal to the Bible, the assumption being that the Bible says I should be my brother's keeper. But in the Bible, God does not deign to answer the murderer Cain, who asks "Am I my brother's keeper?" If God had, he might have said: I did not ask you to be his keeper but to be his brother. Brothers are neither for keeping nor for killing.

If the interviewer had asked the question "Are you responsible *to* your husband, brother, sister, children," I am certain the woman's answers would have been yes. And an interesting conversation might have ensued. The woman is a psychotherapist and presumably knows about listening to people. She lives a life not of isolated privacy but of responsiveness which sweeps wide. It is the breadth of that "responsible to" which allows her to say with precision and clarity: I am responsible for my acts. As a psychotherapist she could probably have gone on to say more precisely what acts she is responsible for and some acts over which she may not have control.

Far from being typical of a selfish-sounding generation, this woman is unusual for resisting the grandiose rhetoric that so often accompanies talk of responsibility. As a figure of speech in a literary work, the expansion of "responsible for" may be understandable. When Dimitri in *Brothers Kamarazov* says "we are all responsible for all. . . . I go for all because someone must go for all," the reader is exhilarated by the grand gesture.[34] But when a philosopher is reflecting on the scope of "responsible for," the proper restriction needs to be stated. As Bonhoeffer notes: "There can, therefore, never be an absolute responsibility, a responsibility which is not essentially limited by the responsibility of the other man."[35]

When Eugene Levinas says we are "responsible for all who are not

Hitler," one is likely to think his provocative exclusion of Hitler is the problem, whereas it is his saying that I am "at every moment responsible for the others, the hostage of others. I can be responsible for that which I did not do and take upon myself a distress which is not mine."[36] Levinas's blanket responsibility for everyone would exhaust the individual trying to accomplish it, and it is disrespectful of the freedom of others.

Two relevant points are raised by this quotation from Levinas. He rightly says "I can be responsible for that which I did not do." I am responsible for what I do; however, that includes *acts of omission*. If there is clearly a reason why I should do something and I fail to act, I am responsible for the act of not acting. If I am leaving a party with a friend who is drunk and I make no effort to stop him from driving his car, I become partly responsible for the accident that follows. The culpable action is an omission of action.

As a political example, take the case of the 1982 slaughter at El Mozote in El Salvador, a disgraceful episode in recent United States history. Especially disgraceful is the fact that there were eyewitness accounts and newspaper reports, but it took eleven years for the United States government to acknowledge its complicity in the massacre carried out by the army. Even then, Thomas Enders, who had been Assistant Secretary of State for Latin American Affairs, defended himself by saying: "I did not deny the killing. . . . I have responsibility for not having been able to confirm it."[37] His not confirming is indeed what he is responsible for, though he says disingenuously that he was not "able to confirm it." What he means is that he sent two men to find out but they never got there. After that, the main effort seems to have been to impugn the reputation of the *New York Times* reporter on the scene.[38]

The second relevant point about Levinas's philosophy is that it is profoundly affected by the Holocaust. Any ethical distinction should be tested against the Holocaust. The distinction between responsible to and responsible for does not detract from the reality of the Holocaust. I think it would be serviceable in trying to examine the Holocaust.

The point I wish to emphasize at present is that Levinas seems at times to be referring to other people who cannot be responsible for themselves. That happens, of course, in less extreme cases than the Holocaust. I can become responsible for an adult human being when that person cannot be responsible for his or her own actions. In most cases, that is a temporary condition but there are also permanent situations. An illness such as Alzheimer's disease may totally disable a person, although it is important to recognize any ability to respond for oneself that a disabled person retains. Responsibility for another becomes complete in cases of permanent and irreversible coma.

In both temporary and permanent incapacity, who should step in to be responsible is not always clear. Generally, we assume that a family member or a close friend becomes responsible. When that is not feasible, a professional person or a judge may have to be responsible for someone's well-being. It can also be the case that pure chance puts me in the position of being responsible for the safety or health of someone. If I find someone unconscious on the street, I am responsible for that person, or more exactly, I am responsible for my actions, which temporarily substitute for the actions of the unconscious person. A court will not usually hold me responsible if I walk by, and urban experience today can seem to make that acceptable. But ethically I am responsible for doing something, if only to dial 911.

Children are the other main exception to the principle of not being responsible for other human beings. I have reserved that discussion until chapter 7. Animals are somewhere between responsible adults and nonresponsible things. I can be responsible for an animal's welfare in specific ways, but animals ought to be allowed their own activity. The animal's desire to establish a rhythm of eating, sleeping, and going off on its own should at least get a respectful hearing. As for things, human beings are responsible for that which cannot speak for itself. Sometimes that means speaking for a particular mountain, river, or forest range. At other times it means acting for the general good of the environment.

In short, we are generally not responsible for other people; we are responsible for things. Very often in writing on responsibility the assumption is exactly the opposite, that we are responsible for people but not for things. In the Steven Tipton interview above, he asks about husband, sister, brother, and children. He never got to the things. If he had asked the woman whether she was responsible for the flowers in her front yard, he would have gotten the yes he was so intent on getting.

"Responsibility for a thing" is a shorthand phrase that needs the context of "responsible to." Hans Jonas writes that there are two different senses of responsible: for one's acts and for things. These two should be held together in the phrase "responsible for my acts in their relation to things." If I am responsible for things (and sometimes by exception, people), it is because, having listened to them, my actions respect their degree of autonomy. For things, my acts are a substitute for choices they cannot exercise. For people, my acts substitute for specific acts that another person is not in a position to do.

Jonas writes that "the captain is master of the ship and its passengers, and bears responsibility for them."[39] Not quite. The captain bears responsibility for his actions that guarantee the passengers' safety; that is not the same as saying the captain is responsible for the passengers (what they eat, who they sleep with, how they dress). I would not go on a boat that had a captain who thinks he is responsible for me. The distinction is important because Jonas uses this example to claim that the statesman is likewise responsible for the people over whom he has power. I certainly do not want a politician thinking he is responsible for me; I want a politician who, responsible to the best interests of the people, is responsible for his or her own actions.

Beyond saying that a president or a mayor is not responsible for me, I am saying that *I* am not responsible for me. I am responsible for some of my acts. This distinction makes a difference when I am urged to "take responsibility for your life." It is not there for the taking; much about my life is outside my control. Some people are so swamped by the idea of "being responsible for their life" that they never get as far as taking the first step in the right direction. Other people feel supremely confident they are responsible for their life, their future, their fate, their destiny. One sharp pain in the chest can prove them wrong.

Rights and Duties

The previous three sections in this chapter set the basis for effectively relating responsibility to right and duty. In recent decades, this question has been muddied by the development of a cliché: what is wrong with the country is that we need to have responsibilities as well as rights. We do indeed need both rights and responsibility, but they are not the same kind of thing. Responsibility is not really a "thing" at all; it is a process within which things called "rights" emerge. What needs pairing with rights are duties or obligations.

In December, 1994, when President Clinton looked for a program to counter the Republican landslide in November, he came up with a set of benefits grandly named "The Middle Class Bill of Rights." When the president returned to the theme in his January State of the Union Address, he noted parenthetically that it should be called "The Middle Class Bill of Rights—and Responsibilities." That addition would seem to signal a drastic change in the proposal, but no change was apparent. Nor did any commentator question the addition of the word "responsibilities." Politicians know that today when you say "rights," the proper form is to add "responsibilities." No one will object and nothing effectively changes beyond the more palatable rhetoric.

It is three decades since the American Bar Association established a section on "Individual Rights." While the section was still under proposal, its name was changed by adding the term "responsibilities." One person who has been a member of the section since its beginning complains that it has done little throughout its history except to deal with rights.[40] Perhaps the author of this complaint should consider whether the well-intentioned phrasing of the title was flawed from the beginning, that rights plus responsibilities always seems to equal rights.

A group of writers called "communitarians" has been especially vocal on the topic of responsibility. The group published a platform and continues to publish a stimulating journal, *The Responsive Community*. The platform that the group published is headed: The Responsive Communitarian Platform: Rights and Responsibilities.[41] Amatai Etzioni, the most prominent member of the group, explains: "We aim for a judicious mix of self-interest, self-expression, and commitment to the commons—of rights *and* responsibilities, of I and we."[42]

While I am in favor of responsibility, I think it is a losing battle to try to win by addition. Neither historically nor logically does responsibility fit there; worse still, that position prevents responsibility from playing the important role of being the ground of both rights and duties. The preamble to "The Declaration of the Rights of Man and the Citizen" in 1789 says its "purpose is to serve as a constant reminder to the members of the body social, not only of their rights but of their duties."[43] That is the straightforward language that is still most helpful when the concept of right is explored: one person's right can be another person's duty or obligation. A society that talks about rights without at the same time talking about duties is creating a logical and practical mess.

Why in much of contemporary discussion is the term "duty" replaced by "responsibility"? Is this just a twentieth-century translation of a nineteenth-century word? To an extent the answer is yes, but this substitution gives to the term responsibility a burden it cannot bear. "Responsibilities," as things we take, is not given any intelligible connection to the process of human life. However, "responsibility" seems to have a softer, more acceptable sound than "duty," with its prim and strict Victorian overtones. So, responsibility as a general idea is embraced instead; it is, after all, in part of its meaning, what we are.

The first moment of responsibility is being responsible to. It is not a thing I possess but a process within which the "I" is formed. Religious traditions moved from that gift of life to duties or obligations entailed by the gift. At the top of the list is thanksgiving. That and other duties (obeying one's parents, caring for the earth, telling the truth) are connoted by the term "religion." Mosaic law was said to have six-hundred and thirteen commandments, but they could be subsumed under three, two, or even just one commandment.[44] Religion consisted of duties in response to God.

No religious group produced a bill of rights. The assumption seems to have been that one must trust that God will do right by us. "Even if he slay me, I will trust him," says the beleaguered Job. Religious people were somewhat naive in this attitude of trust. God may be trustworthy, but organizations, which are unavoidable for any religious group, might very well need stipulations that limit the power of officials.

At the beginning of modern political theory, that is what a right meant; "rights," said Justice Holmes, "mark the limits of interference with individual freedom."[45] A person's rights are most clearly stated in negative terms: not to be killed, not to be tortured, not to be prevented from speaking. The United States Constitution would not have been ratified except for the addition of a Bill of Rights, a series of severe restrictions on the government's power.

During the last two centuries the idea of rights has tended to move from protections to "entitlements."[46] A person reading the Bill of Rights today might be disappointed; it does not state all the good things I am entitled to. The United Nations *Universal Declaration of Rights* is oriented more positively. It begins with the rights not to be

killed and not to be tortured, but it eventually gets to rights to education, to a good wage, to health care, and so forth.[47] For the last half century, no one has argued that these latter rights are not good things. The
nagging question has been how do such rights exist without someone
enforcing them; if those are rights, there must be obligations entailed
by somebody or some organizations.

As right has moved from "a very frail attempt to set at least some
limits to abuse and cruelty"[48] to being the series of good things everyone is entitled to, it has nearly banished any other ethical currency.
Especially in the United States of America, we have almost no other
way to formulate ethical issues except in the language of rights. Understandably, every group of people who have suffered in any way
demand their rights; unfortunately, one group's rights quickly conflict
with another group's rights. And, without any other language to medi-
ate the conflict, the result is either paralysis of government or violence.

The most obvious and painful example of this conflict is abortion, as
it has been argued in the United States. The controversy is so strident
because both sides use the same language of rights and cannot give
any ground. In her helpful book *Abortion and Divorce in Western Law*,
Mary Ann Glendon demonstrates that there are other ways to deal
with abortion. She writes that in the United States abortion is thought
of as a conflict of rights, the right to life of the fetus versus a woman's
right to privacy. "The two seemingly irrevocably opposed positions
are actually locked within the same intellectual framework, a framework that appears rigid and impoverished when viewed from a comparative perspective."[49]

Given the historical record of the United States as a place insistent
on rights, it may seem hopeless to think of changing things. I do not
expect there will be a fundamental change. The United States considers it a glorious tradition that it champions human rights. And indeed
there remain many places on earth where some powerful outside force
should demand an end to killing and torture. The United States will
probably continue to play the part of outside critic. But for its own survival, as well as for its role as preacher, some qualifications in the
meaning of rights and some appreciation of other approaches are
urgently needed. The formula "not just rights but responsibilities"
fails to accomplish either of these needs.

What has to be worked at is an integral linking of right and obligation within a larger ethical discourse. And the ethical itself needs to be

situated in a world where talk is about beauty, joy, pleasure, hopes, dreams, sorrow, mourning, rebirth. The United States is a very moralistic and litigious society. The threat of suing for one's rights is never far below the surface in disagreements. When these rights are brought up, duties should be too. However, we could also look for ways to speak in which neither rights nor duties govern the conversation.

We will continue to need the protection of rights, such as life, liberty, and—in Jefferson's phrase—the pursuit of happiness. The government can only promise to allow the pursuit, not guarantee the happiness. The government should not unduly interfere in how an individual pursues happiness, but the government has to protect that space by seeing that individuals or groups do not violate the basic rights. John Stuart Mill, the apostle of liberty, could still speak of "things which wherever it is obviously a man's duty to do he may rightfully be made responsible to society for not doing."[50] Those duties, Mill says, are "assignable obligations" on the part of another. Thus, for Mill both the rights and the duties are "responsible to society." I have expressed some doubt that society can be the ultimate reference for "responsible to." Nonetheless, both rights and duties depend on the experience of being responsible to someone or something.

I do not propose to take out the word "society" and replace it with another term. For the present, no single term will do. Responding to is at the heart of life; the range of its objects includes elements that are more particular than society, as well as realities greater than society. The ecological movement may eventually help us to recover our relation to a reality immeasurably greater than the human.

Instead of urging people to accept their responsibilities, we would do better to try to develop their capacity for response. People who are responsive—to beauty in nature, to care for family and friends, to the intellectual excitement of learning, to the satisfaction of artistic work—will generally accept that they have some duties or obligations. They are responsible for their actions as law-abiding citizens. Such people do not generally feel the constraint of law. Instead the law can function educationally by encouraging or discouraging behavior. The law guides "individual choices as to behavior by presenting them with reasons for exercising choice in the direction of obedience but leaving them to choose."[51] That would be a new legal framework for responsible people, for those who can listen to guidance, make up their own minds and act without coercion.

CHAPTER 4

SELF-DIVIDEDNESS
AND RESPONSIBILITY

This chapter addresses the question What is personal responsibility? The addition of the adjective "personal" is something of a puzzle; all responsibility would seem situated in the person. Nonetheless, when responsibility is being urged on people, they are usually told to take personal responsibility. Is that in contrast to "impersonal"? Or is the adjective redundant and simply added for emphasis?

One possibility is that personal responsibility is used in contrast to some kind of *collective* responsibility. The insistence on the personal is in contrast to the government or other organizations having the responsibility. This meaning often does seem to be the case. The adjective "personal" is often a code word in such things as a proposal to cut welfare benefits.

A term that is related to personal is "individual." But both in etymology and ordinary usage, individual has some different connotations. In the first chapter I said that responsibility is a bridge over five divisions, one of which is the opposition of individual versus collective. The contrast in that language is between one unit and many units. "Individual" means what is not divided, what is the ultimate unit in a measuring of people or things.

For addressing the rift between the individual and the collective, the discussion of this chapter has to be joined to the following chapter. There is a problem on both sides of the individual/collective divide; each half requires extensive surgery. Because one cannot say everything at once, the discussion of this chapter could be misread as affirming a private, individualistic (rather than personal) responsibility.

My first step in trying to avoid such a misreading is to use personal rather than individual as the basis of this chapter. I have admitted that "personal" is sometimes just a throwaway term, unthinkingly used to indicate the speaker is serious. Nevertheless, it is the right term to begin with in transcending a split between the individual and the collective.[1]

The term person has a somewhat strange etymology and origin. A person is someone who speaks through a mask. The term person comes late in philosophical history, not from the Greek philosophers but from controversies in early Christian history. It was coined as part of a pair with "nature." Whereas nature is the answer to the question "what," person is the answer to "who." The law courts and the psychologists have controlled the term's meaning in recent history, but the original meaning has not disappeared.

Two notes of "person" are relevant to the present discussion. The first is that persons are speakers; the oral/aural metaphor which is at the base of responsibility is embodied in persons. A person is related by address and response to other personal beings. The second note is that a person is not transparent; something is hidden behind the mask. At least two different questions (who, what) can be asked about personal beings. Within a person there is always some dividedness. There may even be more than two elements within the person, but in any case the personal is not a simple, indivisible unity.

The person is certainly not transparent to an onlooker and usually not easily explainable to himself or herself. Otherwise, the plays of Shakespeare and most of the world's literature would not exist; nor would lawyers, psychotherapists, priests, social workers, and most of the "helping professions."[2] And yet it is amazing how many theories of human action assume that human beings are rational agents who calculate the benefits of a course of action and proceed accordingly. Economists are often criticized for failing to incorporate any psychological complexity into their theories.[3] Even sophisticated theories such as John Rawls's *A Theory of Justice* are criticized for assuming a simplistic idea of the individual who calculates decisions on a rational basis.[4]

Mary Midgley notes that the powerful impact of Freud has been due largely to his injecting other motivation for human action than a calculus of self-preservation.[5] Freud highlighted the fact that people often do not know why they are doing what they are doing, that what may seem reasonable to a person is coming from nonconscious drives. The unmasking of our seemingly rational life had also been undertaken by Karl Marx. Ironically, but not inconsistent with either Freud or Marx, their followers have become entangled with their own ideological masks. So long as persons remain speakers of language, the mysteries of human motivation and the dangers of destructive action are not likely to dissolve into a clear liquid.

Given this incapacity of a person to master its own self, what can be said about taking personal responsibility for one's life? As a lifelong goal, that may be a realistic hope. But what one can hope to do today is to accept responsibility for those actions that are sufficiently under one's control. Such responsible actions are possible for nearly everyone. And some behavior in each person's life is not under the direct control of the person, but there may be steps that would eventually lead to a more direct control.

Which actions am I morally responsible for? The answer to that question pushes us to another level of questioning: I am responsible *for* what I am responsible *to*. This principle lies on the side of "is" rather than "ought"; it is not a moral principle stating what should be. Nevertheless, it is a necessary but neglected step in deciding moral responsibility. A person carries out morally responsible actions in relation to what is heard. Moral deficiency is mostly a hearing failure. "The general recipe for inexcusable acts is neither madness nor a bizarre morality but a steady refusal to attend both to the consequences of one's actions and to the principles involved."[6]

This formula may seem to be a complicated way of saying that vice is ignorance, a position often attributed to Socrates. That position is salvageable if *ignorance* is understood as complex. When *ignoring* and not just a lack of information is indeed the problem, moral failure can follow. Central to medieval moral theology was the category of "culpable ignorance"; people are indeed ignorant of their duty, but they are so because they have deceived themselves.[7]

"Responsible" is a useful term to get behind the self-deceptions and find out how progress could happen. Instead of assuming entities such as free will, reason, or "the affective domain," one can discuss a single dialectic of responsible to and responsible for. This simple line of inquiry does not deny the value of sometimes discussing will and reason, intelligence and emotion, instinct and drives, self-interest and benevolence. But it is also possible to summarize the moral problem by asking to whom and to what are we responsible. Moral improvement comes about by broadening and deepening the range of that response. That can sound simplistic if one neglects the fact that responsible to depends in part on what we have previously been responsible for. Trying to influence the play between to and for is the complex task of moral reform.

I said in the previous chapter that the first step in being responsible to is listening to one's own bodily self. I realize this proposal might be misconstrued as an endorsement of selfishness or narcissism. But those words describe individuals who do not realize that their self is split into speaker and listener. To know what the self really needs or wants, one must listen quietly and wait for deeper levels of the self to have their say. D. H. Lawrence wrote: "All that matters is that men and women should do what they really want to do. . . . The desires of the moment are easy to recognize but the others, the deeper ones, are different. It is the business of our chief thinkers to tell us of our deeper desires, not to keep shrilling our little desires into our ears."[8]

This listening to oneself is the first step not the whole process. I will speak later in this chapter and in the following chapter of the many voices to be heard if one is to be responsible to oneself. The premise, for the moment, is that the voices of others are heard when one can listen to one's self in its ambiguity and depth. William Doherty, in a severe criticism of psychotherapy's effect on today's moral climate, complains of "expressive individualism . . . in which responsibilities to others are reduced to responsibility to oneself."[9] I would agree that there is nothing inevitable about this process. Nonetheless, if one is truly responsible to oneself, the voices of others will be heard.

Self-Divided: The Record

The contention that the person is always self-divided is not just a theory of one school of philosophy or psychology. The difference between "I" and "me" is encoded in all of our conversations, including the silent ones in our own heads. The subject who uses the nominative pronoun is distinguished from the object who can be spoken about in the third person: him, her, it. The I and me are not necessarily at war with each other; they may very well be in agreement. Even to know that, however, the I has to listen to yearnings, impulses, and tendencies of me. The historical record shows that the elements that make up the self or person are not always in accord.

It would be difficult to find either a religion or a philosophy that did not recognize a division of elements within the human being. At least since the rise of reflective self-consciousness in history, the pattern has been one of postulating a certain kind of dividedness in life and then, especially in religious practice, providing a way out, a way toward healing or unity. The descriptions of a brokenness or multiplicity are endless, varying in the severity of the conflict perceived.

The crudest picture would have the two elements, A and B, as good and evil. The solution would be for A to escape from or destroy B. In this case, the "self" turns out to be not the tension of A and B, but instead A temporarily imprisoned in B. This philosophy or religion has always been attractive. The enemy being clear, there is no listening needed. At times of historical crisis, the attractiveness is increased. In the middle of famine, plague, or war, the idea that an evil power reigns in history and in human bodies seems plausible, and one's only recourse is to identify with the pure spirit that is on the side of good.

The world's major religions and philosophical schools usually have a more complex play of forces. Instead of A versus B, there may be a C that mediates or casts a swing vote. Or instead of A versus B, further analysis reveals A1A2 versus B1B2 with possible conversation between A1A2, B1B2, A1B1, A2B1, and almost a dozen other possible combinations. The aim of such inner conversation is not to do away with the elements but to keep them in proportion and maintain a unity of harmonies. The *yin/yang* distinction in Taoism is an example of a gentle, peaceful division in which passivity is revealed as a kind of action, and harmony thereby becomes possible. Less well known is the Jewish *yetzer hara/yetzer hatov*. The split between the passive *hatov* and the aggressive *hara* can lead to evil acts; the latter as the basis of greed or lust is the more suspect. But the remedy is not to banish either principle; it is to establish a fruitful tension in one's life.[10]

Greek philosophy, with the rise of a more reflective and speculative outlook, described sharper tensions and contrasts. In *Medea* appears the following line: "I know indeed what evil I intend to do; but stronger than my deliberations is my *thymos* which is the cause of the greatest evils among mortals."[11] Pitted against deliberation on good and evil is an inner force or drive, *thymos*. The term is sometimes translated as "spiritedness," a reality that challenges cold, sober, rational calculation. Plato uses this same term, *thymos*, as the swing vote or crossover element in the conflict of reason and emotion. If *thymos* can be induced to serve on the side of reason, then the three elements can live in a well-ordered life. In contrast, the man who gives in to superficial desires will lead a disordered and unhappy life. Of the tyrant, Plato concludes: "Just because he always does what he pleases, he never succeeds in doing what he really wishes."[12]

St. Paul in the Christian New Testament had and still has a profound impact on Western religion and philosophy. Paul's Epistle to the Romans poses the dilemma of the self divided against itself: "I do not understand my own actions. For I do not do what I want, but I do the very thing I hate."[13] Augustine and Luther became the interpreters of a Pauline doctrine of universal bondage in sin. The need was for a savior who could break out of the prison from the inside of human nature.

The Christian doctrine of an incapacitated will directly challenged the Greek explanation of vice as ignorance. Yet the two were able to be blended, at least by Augustine and the Middle Ages, if not by Luther. At times this cooperation provided subtle analysis as in the moral theology of Thomas Aquinas. The popular version of Christianity, however, has often been a simplified Platonism in which body is at war with soul. The sensual, especially sexual, drives of the body are thought to tend to evil; the beleaguered will, representative of the soul, tries to withstand the onslaught of the senses. When that image reigns there is not much room for being responsible to one's bodily self. Responsibility is to God and to the grace of God which frees the will.

The Christian doctrine did offer an explanation of the experience of self-dividedness. Paul, Augustine, and Luther struck a resonant chord in describing a free will that was not free; from their origin humans cannot quite master their own tendencies. The *Times Literary Supplement* once said "The doctrine of original sin is the only empirically verifiable doctrine of the Christian faith."[14] This is a slight exaggeration since a doctrine of "original sin" is only one way to interpret the experience; nonetheless, the doctrine did ground Christianity in the most powerful of human experiences. As Austin Farrer says: "The person doing evil never says to himself: 'I want this,' but something like 'this is what I do, must do.'"[15] The will freely succumbs to some larger force operating within the person.

Modern philosophy from the beginning was intent on banishing the interlocking doctrines of original sin, redemption, bondage of the will, liberation by grace. But after several centuries of explaining evil in strictly rational terms, thinkers in the twentieth century have had to confront stark images of evil and human destructiveness at an unprecedented level.[16] In the twentieth century, philosophy, science, and the arts have produced other descriptions of the inner conflicts that give rise to self-destructive behavior and outward violence.

What seems most strange in surveying modern thought, from the sixteenth and seventeenth centuries onward, is that Christian doctrines were not so much banished as dressed up in more presentable appearance. The splits of body and soul, reason and will, man and beast, not only survived but were sharpened further. But now the means for dealing with the splits had been dismissed without being replaced. René Descartes is usually credited with being the first of modern philosophers. His search for an indubitable first principle led him to a thought, the thought of "I exist." He could then only establish a connection to the external world by trusting that God would not deceive him. As Etienne Gilson said of Descartes, when he searched his own mind for an answer, what he found was the catechism answers he had learned as a child.[17]

The catechism may have been a voice in Descartes's mind, but he was looking rather than listening. What he discovered by looking for the truth was a thinking mind with no firm relation to a living organism. One of the most perceptive comments on Descartes's experiment is by Timothy Cooney in *Telling Right from Wrong*. Concerning Descartes sitting in his room and systematically doubting until he reached his one certain idea, Cooney says it is unfortunate he did not stay at his task for another five or six hours. He then would have cried: "I'm hungry." And his second certainty would have been: "I know how to satisfy my hunger." Instead of knowledge being equated with abstract conceptions, knowledge would have had an ethical dimension from the beginning. "Our ability to satisfy some of our desires is our most certain link between mind and world."[18] Or in the terms I have suggested, our ability to act, including the act of speculative judgment, starts with our being responsible to our own desires and interests. The moral life is not a separate sphere tacked onto a theoretical outlook and built on a shaky premise of free will.

Freud's work was shocking to people for several reasons, one of which was the undermining of free will. The human being was portrayed as a product of forces outside of conscious awareness. The self-dividedness was at first described by Freud with the contrast of conscious and unconscious. Later he elaborated his description as a split between "I" and "it," with another player, the "over it" holding some of the balance.[19] Freud was enough of a man of his time to equate the "I" with reason and to look to rational control as the answer. In the United States a popular Freudianism was propagated as an optimistic belief that by getting rid of repressions and external restraints we would all become "adjusted." Freud's own view remained darkly pessimistic; the search for pleasure always remains at odds with culture or civilization. The individual could only hope to progress from hysterical misery to common unhappiness.

Are we better off after the Freudian revolution? We certainly talk more about problems that had been hidden, especially sexual problems. Freud and his successors have given us ways to understand the dynamics of human personality. The result has been a dismantling of many external restraints on behavior. It is not clear that personal understanding and "self-control" have adequately developed as a substitute for outside control. John Stuart Mill writes of the world Freud was born into: "In our times, from the highest class of society down to the lowest, everyone lives as under the eye of a hostile and dreaded censorship."[20] Mill's pleas for liberty from restraints in that context now have to be read in a radically revised context.

Whether or not we are better off, we do seem challenged to be "responsible for" in ways no previous century has felt burdened. Some people are enthusiastic about this new responsibility; with our new insights into human personality, we will be able to take on more responsibility for it. Erich Neumann has been one of those enthusiasts of depth psychology. He has an essay comparing the "new ethic" and the "old ethic." His interesting choice to represent the old ethic is St. Augustine. The difference between the two ethics, says Neumann, is captured in a text where Augustine "thanks God that he is not responsible to Him for his dreams."[21] While in Neumann's new ethic we are responsible *for* our dreams, Augustine was concerned about the One *to* whom he is responsible.

Augustine, in contrast to many modern rationalists, would have taken dreams seriously as revelatory of life. What he denies is that he is *responsible to* God for them. Neumann's ethic also denies that we are *responsible to* God. The real difference would seem to be that Augustine's denial relieved him of a burden, but the twentieth-century ethic throws the burden back on us.

Neumann surely does not wish to burden us with responsibility for all the contents of our dreams; that, say, dreaming of murder makes one responsible for murder. What he presumably wishes to affirm is that unconscious processes and conscious life are integrally related. Our conscious acts are influenced by forces outside of our direct awareness (as Augustine well knew), and dreams are a connective link. Our conscious acts do influence what we dream and vice versa. What we are responsible for shades off into areas beyond our immediate, direct, and conscious control, because we can indirectly influence that area.

William Butler Yeats, in the frontpiece of a collection of poems, *Responsibility*, quotes from what he calls an old play: "In dreams begin responsibility."[22] There is a positive as well as a negative possibility implied here. Dreams are not necessarily a museum of unspeakable horrors and sick longings. For the man such as Yeats who would write a poem, he has to respond to his dreams. For a man or woman to do anything, dreams are an important source to listen to because they both reflect and influence conscious life. The "daydream" more than the night dream is closer to conscious control, closer to what we are responsible for. But the determination to bring all dreaming under control would block the well of inspiration that Yeats is naming.

I would be wary of anyone taking "full responsibility" for what he or she does. The person who says that is often clamping a stiff rational control upon drives, desires, and dreams that refuse to be so ordered. It is similar to a person claiming to speak "the whole truth." That is an admirable aim, but it is not within the ability of persons to speak the whole truth. They can make a series of true statements (which is in fact all the court can demand). The whole truth is not within their purview, which is why confirming evidence is required in a court. And the person trying to take full responsibility for what he or she does is limited to responding to the partial truth available.

One could have almost guessed that the letter which O.J. Simpson wrote to his wife after beating her and which she kept in a safety deposit box begins: "I've taken full responsibility for this."[23] Like millions of others before him, Simpson was not lying. He simply had no grasp of what had impelled his violent action. Without a wider and deeper responsibility to self, taking full responsibility is a dangerous illusion.

The case is most tragic when the *victim* of abuse is the one who takes "full responsibility." Greg Louganis, in his autobiography, describes being beaten and raped by someone who at their next meeting acts as

if it had never happened. "I didn't expect him to apologize," writes
Louganis, "because I thought I was the one who was in the wrong. . . .
I took full responsibility for what had happened and told myself that
as long as I was good, it would never happen again."[24]

Guilt and Criminality

Responsibility is closely related to but should be distinguished from
guilt. The immediate occasion for talking about responsibility is usually the failure of responsibility. However, to understand failure one
has to keep in mind what success is.[25] The idea of "responsible to" is
positive in meaning. People are regularly responsive often in ways
that are expected and at times in ways highly praiseworthy. People are
also "responsible for" all the good human actions performed each day.

As human beings have increasingly taken on responsibility for
everything, they have also taken on the burden of every failure and
deficiency. And in this situation, responsibility and guilt are more
likely to blur together. An exploration of responsibility is too quickly
assumed to be asking "who is guilty?" And that locks the question into
a calculus of x is or is not guilty. The question takes the form of a court
trial that presumes at the end either a judgment of guilty or not guilty.

Guilt can be an appropriate feeling when one has clearly failed to do
one's duty. But responsible to/responsible for is about shades of difference, various degrees, and a constantly changing process. In that
process, if guilt comes in at all, it should be near the end. The court
must sometimes say that someone is guilty for having violated the law.
The individual person usually does not have to make such a judgment.
A person can judge another's behavior as wrong while leaving open
the question of moral guilt. Even when someone does something
wrong, guilt is at the extreme of a continuum that includes shame,
remorse, regret, feeling tainted, and so forth.[26]

In trying to get rid of feeling guilty before a heavenly tribunal, the
twentieth century sometimes seems to have pulled down the feeling of
guilt as a suffocating cover. Heidegger's idea of guilt is that "human
existence is guilty to the extent that it factually exists."[27] Karl Jaspers
distinguishes a metaphysical guilt from a moral guilt. Jaspers was
struggling with the problem of a collective responsibility on the part of
the German people for Nazi crimes. Jaspers's metaphysical guilt

"makes each co-responsible for every wrong and every injustice in the world"[28] As with Heidegger's metaphysical use of guilt, saying that all are guilty evacuates particular judgments of guilt. Guilt should be the result of someone doing something despicable, knowing that it is despicable, and knowing that alternative action is possible.

In contrast to guilt, responsibility is a never-ending process of listening and speaking that involves a person to varying degrees, directly and indirectly. The degree of responsibility for unethical behavior depends on excusing factors. Sometimes actions are done inadvertently, especially when the moral weight of the action is slight. J. L. Austin writes: "'I did it inadvertently' will do as an excuse for treading on a snail, but not for treading on the baby." That is, treading on a baby needs a better excuse than "I just wasn't paying attention to what I was doing." In that instance, I am responsible for inattentively being responsible to.[29] Aristotle believed that there were some offenses (for example, matricide) for which there was no excuse.[30] These days we can find an excuse for just about any action, which may mean that we understand human action better or else that we are lax in accepting responsibility.

I think that Bruce Waller goes too far in what he calls "non-fault naturalism." For Waller, since we are incapable of sorting out good people from bad people and passing judgment on who is at fault, we should stop altogether judgments of fault. "The non-fault naturalist will be drawn to the conclusion that fundamentally there is little difference between the vicious and the virtuous: 'There but for a few differences in fortuitous environmental contingencies go I.'"[31] It is possible, however, to have an alternative to his choice between harsh judgment of fault and judgment of non-fault. This other possibility is that we are each at fault on specific occasions; that we are fallible in judging our own faults, let alone those of others; that we ought to resist passing definitive judgments on the persons of others, but we can and sometimes should judge that certain actions are at fault.

Criminals are people who have committed grave faults and are judged to be adequately responsible for what they have done. The community sometimes has to restrain a person and deter future violations. "Swift and certain" response is the only kind that is likely to be effective if the purpose of punishment is both to improve the person as well as protect the community. Gregory Vlastos credits Protagoras as the first Greek to clearly distinguish revenge and punishment.[32] More than two millennia ago, Protagoras taught that "men do not punish others for natural or chance defects, but they punish them for failure to learn. In fact, in civilized societies, punishment is a sort of teaching."[33] Unfortunately, what Protagoras took as the mark of civilized societies has never entirely triumphed in the civilized world. It is obvious that if the state punishes by putting prisoners in brutalizing prisons, the purpose is not to improve the prisoner. Whatever may be the purpose, what is in fact taught is brutality.[34] The recidivism rate of a typical prison provides ample evidence of the success of the teaching.

The alternative to educating the criminal away from crime is a view of punishment as the restoration of a balance in the universe. Much of religious history seems influenced by a mystical sense of pain being expunged only by the exacting of equal pain. The executor of the pain usually has to be thought of as a representative of divine judgment. Where there is no God assumed, pain for pain seems only to be revenge, an attitude prized by nobody, and one all but certain to cause more violence.

Dostoyevsky seems to have believed that society had to balance suffering and that "psychologically the criminal needed his punishment to heal the laceration of the bonds that joined him to society. So in the end Raskolnikov the murderer thirsts for his punishment."[35] There may be some limited validity to this principle that punishment is good for the criminal and is even desired by the criminal. George W. Webber, who has spent decades educating prisoners, says: "The guys take responsibility for what they did. But they can say, 'Look, I messed up, I've done awful things, I've committed murder, I deserve punishment, yet at the same time I was victimized by a vicious, corrupt, awful society that never gave me a chance.'"[36]

Obviously, an educational principle does not extend to capital punishment, which is based on despair of ever healing the bond to community. Other than feeding a feeling of revenge, there are not even plausible arguments in support of capital punishment. It has been abolished almost everywhere in the civilized world, though it has made a strange and frightening reappearance in the United States.[37] In 1846, when capital punishment was in fact rare in the United States, a legislator said: "After every instance in which the law violates the sanctity of human life, that life is held less sacred by the community among whom the outrage is perpetrated."[38] That sentiment had seemed to penetrate the country a century hence but to have receded in the subsequent half century.

One aspect of capital punishment that is relevant here is the fact that condemned killers sometimes say they deserve it. "Many a murderer," writes David Dennett, "has no doubt of his own culpability." Of the condemned, brutal murderer Richard Harris, Dennett writes: "It is noteworthy that Harris seems to accept responsibility for his life."[39] I think that what is more noteworthy is that Harris is wrong in accepting responsibility for his life. If Harris had accepted responsibility for certain acts and had accepted that punishment was appropriate, then he might have been on the road to not being a criminal. Capital punishment renders the issue moot.

Killers have been taught that moral responsibility is the mark of the human. One way for them to affirm their dignity in the face of dehumanizing incarceration and execution is to "accept responsibility." As their last thread of dignity, accepting a degree of responsibility can be healthy. But an acceptance of capital punishment by the prisoner does nothing to exculpate the executioners. The prisoner has bought into a view of responsibility, expressed by John Spenkelink, the first person executed in Florida after the resumption of capital punishment: "Man is what he chooses to be. He chooses that for himself."[40] Perhaps this Sartrean posturing provided some manner of relief for the prisoner. Intelligent people in the criminal justice system have no excuse for thinking that the criminal accepting responsibility for his life in any way justifies taking that life.[41]

Freedom and Self-Governance

Behind the discussion of guilt, culpability, and crime is one of the ultimate philosophical issues: the nature of freedom. I do not propose to offer any solution to this much debated topic. However, the play between responsible to and responsible for throws light on a few aspects of human freedom. Popular speech tends to identify freedom with free will or choice or "making decisions." Philosophical discussions of freedom tend to subvert popular images and assumptions.

The Greek idea of freedom did not assume a free will. The basic freedom was that of movement: "I can" rather than "I will" was the criterion of freedom. Aristotle's term, *hekousion*, is usually translated "voluntary." Voluntary acts are subject to praise or blame. Such acts could sometimes include those of children or animals. A person who is physically coerced does not perform a voluntary act; the threat of violence, in contrast, would not make the action involuntary. The action remains voluntary if it is not haphazard and is performed with one's possession of physical and mental strength.[42]

Aristotle's severe view of the extent of blame has generally been dismissed. We are much more aware of factors that impair freedom and take away responsibility for actions. Still, he was at least trying to root human action in bodily integrity, extending voluntariness even beyond the human. What I noted in the previous chapter about responsibility being applicable to children and animals parallels his use of voluntary. It is at this level—where responsible for is dependent on responsible to—that reflection on freedom is most fruitful.

The later isolation of a faculty called "free will" had the effect of blocking out perception of this relation. Dwight Moody, one of the most famous Christian preachers in the late nineteenth century, used to proclaim: "It is 'I will' or 'I won't' for every man in this hall tonight. . . . The battle is in the will and only there."[43] Although Aristotle was blind to some excusing factors, the modern obsession with the will created a self-dividedness in which the will was asked to be the lone defender of the fortress of the self.

The popular view of free will has become embodied in the contemporary phrase "make a decision."[44] Self-help talk in books and on television relentlessly urges us to make decisions. If one cannot make a decision, then one is lacking in maturity, courage, or strength of will. The image is of an engineering project in which one's life is under construction and decisions are to be *made*. The harder the decision is, the more it will contribute to "personal growth." Unless one is making decisions, one is not taking responsibility for one's life.

It is an interesting fact that centuries ago people got along without making decisions. People did decide on a course of action that flowed from habitual ways of acting. In that framework, virtue, as a habit, sets the direction and then deciding becomes smooth and easy. Freedom is not based on *hard* decisions but on softly following the best tendencies of the whole organism. Drawing on the long history of Christian moral tradition, Stanley Hauerwas writes: "Morally the most important things about us are the matters about which we never have to make a decision. Thus nonviolent persons do not have to choose to use or not to use violence, but rather their being nonviolent means they must use their imaginations to form their whole way of life consistent with their convictions."[45]

The path to greater control of self has its own strict discipline, but it is not much concerned with will control. The choice to do good is easy—if the whole body is aligned on that side. Human beings do *decide*, a word that means "to cut." The will acts similar to a film director. The director sees various takes on a scene from the imagination and finally says "cut, that's a wrap." Freedom is exercised through a negation of other possibilities. Sometimes when everything works together exceptionally well the director has only one take on the scene. Freedom does not necessarily mean choosing between A and B; it can simply mean saying yes to A by saying no to all else.

Paradoxically, then, the responsible person might move in the direction of fewer choices. Freedom need not mean a "wide range of options." At the least, those options need not include self-destructive paths. A person responsible to his or her organism will come to exclude many possible choices as stupid or evil. David Dennett asks: "Doesn't a considerable part of being a responsible person consist in making oneself unable to do things one would be blamed for doing if one did them?"[46]

What would be the culmination of this process of exclusion? Can the paradox be sustained that freedom would mean acting as one *must*? In relation to the widespread assumption that freedom means always being able to do anything I choose, such a notion of freedom sounds self-contradictory. Indeed, we seem to have gone full circle to the earlier quotation of Austin Farrer that the person doing evil never says to himself "I want this," but "this is what I must do."

There are some characteristics that apply both to the unfree person, submerged by an impersonal force, and to Max Weber's "mature man" who finally decides: Here I stand I can do no other. Not only Martin Luther but numerous other great characters in history have fearlessly stood up before tyranny and declared: I cannot, I will not be moved. Everything has led up to that moment so that the "I" does not flinch, whatever the repercussions. The difference between the two ends of the spectrum of freedom is nicely captured by Michael Polanyi: "While compulsion by force or by neurotic obsession excludes responsibility, compulsion by universal intent establishes responsibility. . . .

The freedom of the subjective person to do as he pleases is overruled by the freedom of the responsible person to act as he must."[47]

Most of us most of the time play in the middle range, compelled in neither of the two ways Polanyi cites. We value our choices, and we rightly use choice as a test of freedom: I could do something different from what I am doing. The claim to be doing what I *must* is always a dangerous one. At best, it is often premature; at worst, it is the claim of charlatans and deluded cranks with a future likely to be disastrous. The tragic thing about human affairs is that we all work with fallible criteria in judging ourselves as well as others. Often it is only after a person's death that we recognize cases of heroic freedom. John Brown can be a hero of the twentieth century after being shot as a criminal lunatic in the nineteenth. Joan of Arc becomes heroine and saint centuries after being thought of as a foolish and headstrong hearer of voices.

The attempt to imitate the determined hero is dangerous. Each person has to find a path by listening to his or her own life in all the particularities of time and place. A rush to reach the place of a vocation where I do what I *must* do can lead to following a Jim Jones or David Koresh, or, less apocalyptically, to living in a desert retreat or an urban ghetto when one is not prepared to do so.

Even marriage vows, despite the commonality of the practice, are an extraordinary claim to know oneself well enough to say: I forsake all others and "plight my troth with thee." The divorce rate suggests a problem in being responsible to oneself and others before one can claim to be responsible for marriage vows. A complaint after the wedding that "I want my freedom" is evidence that the vow was not an act of freedom, even though there was no external coercion. "Playing the field" is desired by the person who has not reached the freedom of saying and knowing with the whole self what it means to say: This is the one.

David Dennett argues that freedom does not mean I could have done something different. After the fact, it is clear that all of the process that led up to the moment would have that outcome and only that outcome. Freedom is not an exception to natural causality nor is it the insertion of arbitrariness. Dennett cites a medieval moral doctrine that the most saintly and blessed are those unable to sin.[48] There is a danger here of overemphasizing the culmination of the movement at the expense of our day to day experience. For medieval theology, the blessed in heaven and the human nature of Jesus are incapable of sin. The rest of us are in a different position.

While it is true that what I did in the past—in those exact circumstances—I could not do otherwise, the future holds different possibilities. "It is not the capacity for choice but the evaluation and formation of wants that is central."[49] That is, I can learn from the past so that in *similar* circumstances (they will never be the same), I can do better than in the past. "The free man," writes Buber, "intervenes no more but at the same time he does not let things merely happen. He listens to what is emerging from himself, to the course of being in the world."[50]

When a faculty of will is thought to dictate orders to the body, the implied image has reason and will at the top of a pyramid. The body with its senses, emotions, and drives is imagined to lie underneath, always threatening to erupt. And when the reason cannot placate primal urges, the only defender against chaos is "will power." The will does not know what is far beneath it; trying to find out what is there would be a distraction from making hard choices, or might entice the will to drop its guard.

If freedom depends on being responsible to, a different image emerges. The place to listen is from the center rather than from the top. Instead of a bulwark or a dictator, freedom requires an emptiness, a space for listening. The governing is along democratic lines with voice and vote for every concentric circle out from the center. As in every democracy, there are competing interests whose cooperation can be gained only with patience and negotiation. Drawing upon Bishop Butler's eighteenth-century political metaphor for conscience, Mary Midgley writes: "What rules is our own center. It is indeed a 'governor,' but not an alien, colonial one. It is our own sense of how our nature works."[51]

The moral problem here is not usually violent eruptions of uncontrollable force but rather the fragmenting of forces that have to blend into a unified self. Midgley comments on two furious letters to the editor in a newspaper, one angry at cigarette advertising, the other angry that there is candy at the supermarket checkout counter. The angry letter writers are saying: How dare you set me against myself. "Perhaps it is a perfectly proper protest against fissiparous forces too strong for the center to cope with."[52]

What is wanted by our senses and drives is good, otherwise it would not be wanted. But because of competition among our desires, the center must try to find what is good in a stronger sense, what the organism as a whole wants. The votes must be lined up before cutting off debate as a decision. Reason supplies an evaluation of past successes and the likelihood of unified action now. Reason's chief tactic is often delay. "Waiting makes real wishing possible and real wishes make waiting possible."[53]

Beyond Our Control

Before describing further the self-governing process it is necessary to admit that there are human failures who cannot or do not succeed in this process. Some human beings have been so maimed at birth or have experienced such trauma during life that their freedom is completely impaired. Since the last century, these people are said to have a mental disorder. It took a long time to establish a clear demarcation between the insane ("unhealthy") and the criminal.[54] The criminal is held responsible for illegal acts; the mentally insane are to be treated as lacking responsibility for their actions. And, of course, it remains the case that we are sometimes unsure whether a particular person is in the one condition or the other.

The puzzling and confusing situation is people who are seemingly "normal," functioning as ordinary citizens. But at some moments or in some area of life, they claim to be and/or appear to be incapable of acting freely. In the past, this condition was assumed to be an unusual exception. Today an increasing number of people claim that their freedom has been so violated that in a specific area of life they should not be held responsible. A man's excuse for beating his child is that he was beaten as a child. Or a girl's excuse for shooting her father is that he has sexually molested her.

It would be dangerous if a society could no longer recognize immoral behavior or if it no longer had sanctions against it. To excuse a person for mitigating circumstances can be distinguished from condoning a person's bad behavior. As to whether a person should be "held responsible" for the bad behavior, we would do well to think in degrees. The jury may have only the choice of guilty or not guilty. But in asking the question of responsibility, both of others and ourselves, the question is usually how far we are responsible and how we might take the next step toward greater responsibility.

Instead of dividing the world into victims and nonvictims, we might better realize that each person has areas of life not completely under his or her control. Some people have suffered more than others, but an exemption from responsibility for their actions would not be a help to them. Whatever genetic and hereditary factors are combined with a person's upbringing and surroundings, response to the present and responsibility for present action is possible.

People entangled in bad behavior that has gone on for years cannot just suddenly do the right thing. What they *can* do is something better than the self-destructive behavior they have been engaging in. It may still be bad behavior, but relative to the past it is better behavior. Changing "behavior," that is, the external part of human activity, is to be combined with a change of attitude. The person has to "accept" (a more appropriate word than "take") some responsibility for some actions. No more and no less should be demanded.

Glenn Loury properly distinguishes between fault and responsibility, but his use of this distinction fails to clarify the problems of the black underclass he is describing. Loury writes that "whatever *fault* may be placed upon racism in America, *responsibility* for the behavior of black youngsters lies squarely on the shoulders of the black community itself." He attributes both too much and too little to the black community. Not the black community but the black youngster is responsible for his or her behavior. And the white community no less than the black has to be responsible to the problems of black youngsters. Members of the black community can be responsible for changing the conditions of these youngsters' lives, but the black community cannot do it alone. "Fault" can be assigned not only to racism but to particular actions of government, business, and educational leaders.[55]

The classic case to study for severe impairment of freedom is alcoholism. Aristotle thought that acting under the influence of liquor simply added a second level of blame.[56] We are more understanding, having decided to call alcoholism a "disease." Like other drugs to which the body can become addicted, alcohol consumption overwhelms the self. The center cannot hold. The person who for whatever genetic and environmental reasons cannot control the use of alcohol has to avoid it altogether. Alcoholics Anonymous is rightfully famous for having developed an effective program of treatment. It has at times been criticized for embracing too much Christian language, but its main strategy has proved remarkably successful. If anything, it suffers from too much success and the inevitable imitations that can trivialize the approach.[57]

Alcoholics Anonymous is a story of responsibility. It embodies many of the distinctions proposed in this book. First, the person who up to this moment was only a drunk has to say aloud: I am an alcoholic. Speaking the name is indispensable. Then one has to be responsible to oneself at a deeper level than heretofore. This is helped by being responsible to a community and one person in particular within the community. All of this is in relation to being responsible to a "Higher Power." Then one has to accept responsibility, not for the rest of one's life, but for one's actions one day at a time.

As for the past, one has to be responsible to it, gaining whatever understanding is possible while not drowning in guilt. The appeal to a greater power is a move that relieves a person of being the only cause of his or her situation. Accepting that experience and explanation allows one to be responsible to the community members who are a permanent auxiliary. Failure is not unexpected or terribly surprising, but it does not have to be total reversal. Some of the steps can be quickly retraced, and the issue can be brought back into focus: To whom and to what are you now responsible? Are you willing to accept responsibility for your next step?

The experience of Alcoholics Anonymous has valuable lessons to teach both to people with other severe addictions and also to the general population. Drug treatment programs have little chance of success unless they incorporate something similar to AA's understanding of responsibility. Thirty-day treatments of rich people that pronounce individuals cured or aggressive police action in urban ghettos are inadequate responses. Alcoholics Anonymous is a constant reminder of what a comprehensive struggle with addiction entails.

What AA can teach the wider population is exposed to being trivialized by innumerable programs that imitate the "Twelve Steps." In a country that thrives on therapy, the mechanics of these programs can be a temptation more than a cure. That is, many people are all too willing to say that whatever their failing, it is not their fault, it is a disease deserving of sympathy. And since it is a condition they are not responsible for, what they look for is therapy rather than moral improvement. The peculiar approach of AA is that while using the language of disease, the program is still moralistic in its demands. One starts with a permanent condition that is not one's fault; but every action *in relation to that condition* is one for which the person must accept responsibility. Many of the programs that imitate AA do not maintain this tension of responsible to and responsible for.

No doubt there are problems in peoples' lives that are out of their control. Some of these problems are bodily addictions; at least the body is so habituated to the practice that a change cannot be accomplished simply by making a firm resolution on December 31. One has to listen to the body and enlist others in support to stop smoking tobacco, eating sweets, or drinking Pepsi Cola. The body has its own logic that must be listened to.

Some apparent addictions do not seem to be based in the genetic code or in bodily conditioning. Gambling or shoplifting or sexual exhibitionism destroys many lives; those who suffer from one of these self-destructive behaviors feel captured by an alien force. The plight of such people deserves some combination of sympathy for the condition along with a demand for responsible action *within* that condition.

The issue of personal control can be brought home to everyone with the issue of diet. All of us have a diet that began developing at birth, if not a few months before. It is almost impossible to make fundamental changes in one's personal diet, although over a period of years a person can make some significant shifts. Letters regularly appear in the newspaper that begin "I have tried every diet there is. . . . " The inevitable conclusion is that nothing works for me and therefore you should feel sorry for me. The person who has tried every diet would first have to discover that he or she has always had a diet. One cannot go on and off diets. One has to discover what one's diet is and some of the reasons why it is what it is.[58]

The situation in the United States would be amusing if it did not include such economic fraud, personal frustration, and disastrous health problems. While starvation remains the common condition around the world, the United States agonizes over an obesity problem in a third of the population. And a large part of the other two-thirds seems obsessed with the latest diet fad or with feeling guilty over eating a piece of chocolate cake. Never has any country at any time been so awash in data about healthy eating. But the information does not seem to translate into people eating healthful and enjoyable food.

Tens of millions of people seem blinded to their own eating pattern and to their ability to improve it. They are at the mercy of a forty-billion-dollar diet industry that finds an endless stream of takers. The failure rate for these products is somewhere between 95 and 100 percent. The people buying the products know the failure rate; it is their own experience. You can hardly turn on a television program without hearing of a product that will take off ten pounds in two weeks or your money back. What is enticing is that the claim is correct. While a person tries to lose weight, the body cannibalizes itself, assured that after a short wait the pressure will be removed and the body can resume the pattern it has had for decades. For most people, it is not that difficult to lose ten pounds in two weeks or whatever the ad maker claims. What is nearly but not totally impossible is to change one's diet.

Genetics and heredity make control of weight more difficult for some people than for others. Each of us has to respond to our own makeup whatever it is. Similarly, some people were more fortunate than others in the developing of diet in childhood. That, too, must be responded to, whatever was the wisdom or ignorance of one's parents. Some people have more money to spend on better quality food; it is not easy maintaining a healthful diet for oneself and one's children in poverty. Ironically, however, poor people are not the ones on television saying they are not responsible for their poor eating habits.

Overeating (or undereating) is not a grave moral problem in itself. However, the moral life is buttressed by daily rhythms and routines. In most traditional religion, there is considerable attention to how people dress, what and when they eat, the times at which they go to sleep and arise, how they exercise, when they remain silent, and so forth. Today these daily manners are usually overlooked or dismissed as irrelevant when experts talk about "making good decisions." Traditional practice presumed that if you take care of the small things, you will not have to agonize over the big things.

The point of discussing diet here is not to point a guilty finger at overweight people. Many of them are drowning in guilt already. The reason for the discussion is that one's diet is almost a perfect experience to analyze for being responsible: to and for. Everyone has a daily experience of what the question is. Practically everyone has blind spots in understanding his or her diet and how to find one's ideal diet. To handle this issue in an appropriate way one has to be aware of and respond to the heredity and condition in which one was born; one has to be responsible to past eating habits that still affect the organism; one has to be responsible to easily available material on healthful diet; one has to be responsible to family and friends with whom one shares meals; one has to be responsible to people in the world who are undernourished. Instead of torturing myself with guilt because I have enough to eat, an appreciation of good food should compel me to help others who lack food. If one is responsible to one's diet, then responsibility for what one eats is done without difficulty and without destroying the simple, human pleasure of sharing food and drink.

The other area that affects everyone and requires responsibility is sexual feeling and expression. There are many parallels with what has been said of diet. We are each born with predispositions that condition all of our sexual experience. In the twentieth century, we have discovered how important is early childhood experience. There will probably never be a firm statistic on how many children are sexually abused, but even estimates on the low side are frightening. Especially during the last decade a culture of sexual victims has arisen. No one doubts that there are adults who were horribly abused as children, but a whole industry of memory recovery is generating intense debate and criticism.[59] Without having to go into the details of that debate, I can reassert the principle that all adults have to respond to the childhood that fate or providence has given them.

Nearly all adults have some difficulty in responding to sexual life because of distortions in childhood and because of the continued warping of vital information. As with information on nutrition, the country brims over with sexual talk. Yet people, especially in the teenage years, are often astoundingly ignorant of elementary information. By most indicators, progress over the last half century in understanding one's own sexuality and living at ease with one's sexual practice has been slight. Unfortunately, it took the AIDS epidemic to force into the open some frank discussion of sexual hygiene and the practices of birth control. AIDS has created new awareness and spread information; it has also increased anxiety and done little for sexual joy.

Sexual life, like diet, is important to a moral life and for similar reasons. It is a way to be responsible to oneself every day and through that responsibility find a bond with other people. Sadly, that is not usually the way guardians of morality think of sexual life. Sex is feared as the leading eruptive force under the will. Any time it spills out into the public arena, there are anxious cries to tamp it down, get it out of sight. At times in life people do need strong safeguards, but overall they eventually have to accept their sexual condition, whatever it is, and be responsible for their own sexual practices.

Present attitudes and policies have generated a multibillion dollar pornography industry which is in the open and an unimaginable underground industry. Pornography gets tied in with prostitution and drugs, destroying untold lives. Periodic raids on particular establishments do nothing except move the problem for a while. Perhaps the saddest fact is that pornography does not even do what it promises to do, which is to supply erotic stimulation to undernourished sexual lives and imaginations. When the legal restraints were removed several decades ago, there was a wild rush to say the forbidden word and to show the previously censored activity. Having done that, pornographers had nowhere to go; they seem not to know what eroticism is. The product became joyless and unimaginatively repetitious.

The personal dividedness that is the theme of this chapter has almost always been associated with the sexual division of the human race. Yin and yang are often referred to as masculine and feminine principles. Western thought traditionally identified the rational spirit with men; the body, with its uncontrollable drives, was attributed (by men) to women. One can hardly doubt that the division of the sexes and the experience of self-division are somehow related, but not in the simplistic way of saying that men are rational, women are nonrational.

No solution to self-dividedness can be effective without including attention to sexuality. That does not mean a direct attack on what are thought to be immoralities. Rather, the question of homosexuality, which has finally begun to be discussed in the last thirty years, is one key to everyone's sexuality. And changes in the relation of men and women promise to alter in drastic ways how to be responsible to oneself and to others.

Voices Within

As the previous section indicates, being responsible so as to achieve greater control of one's actions means attending to voices that speak to us. There are always competing voices in the different levels of our lives. Sometimes we cannot tell if the voice is our own from an earlier time or if the voice belongs to someone else. Nonetheless, there would be no voice at all unless there were beings beyond us, calling us to engage ourselves with a reality that goes beyond our self.

A popular notion of "conscience" as a voice that tells us right from wrong is an oversimplified version of how we judge the rightness or wrongness of an action. We have a conscience because we have a consciousness; the two terms have a common root. The basis of right and wrong is implicit in our first grasp of consciousness, and except for the mentally sick person, the voice of conscience is never entirely stilled. Vaclav Havel writes: "We must trust the voice of our conscience more than that of all abstract speculations and not invent other responsibilities than the one to which the voice calls us."[60]

Conscience nevertheless needs education, a practicing in the skill of sorting out which voices selectively to attend to.[61] Education in this context need not mean years in school or courses in ethics. A caring childhood probably does more than anything to develop a sensitive conscience, even though the buzz of ordinary life can obscure what moral sensitivity a person has. Hannah Arendt states the paradox of conscience by saying that only really bad people have clear consciences.[62] Those trying to do their best usually have some feelings of failure and guilt. Help can come from enlightening the conscience with information; most people's sexual lives are not that startlingly different, but they may feel guilty if they know little of statistics on sexual practices. Conscience is a power to know, not a magic storehouse of truth.

In the movie *Silkwood*, the heroine, Karen Silkwood, is not a very admirable person. However, she stumbles on knowledge of dangerous practices in the nuclear power plant. Taken to Washington, she is told by union leaders that she has a "moral imperative" to do something. Although she is barely aware of what the words mean, they strike a responsive chord. She goes home and starts doing courageous things to amass knowledge and organize the workers. To her confused and questioning boyfriend she says: I have a moral imperative. As Thomas More says in *A Man for All Seasons*, sometimes a person has no choice except to become a hero. A voice is heard demanding an answer, and the person, sometimes to his or her surprise, responds. Other voices had prepared the way, though which ones are often lost in the thicket of memory.

Pity the person who early in life shuts out the voice of parents or caretakers because survival seems at stake. The rap musician Tupac

Shakur, on the way to a prison cell, said: "My mother was a revolutionary Black Panther and all that. But I also saw my mother as a crack addict. So I answer to no one. I follow my heart." Journalist Murray Kempton responded in his elegant prose: "The child is well advised to distrust any heart that instructs him to answer to no one."[63] The choice, as Kempton indicates, is not between listening to one's heart or listening to another person. We listen with the heart to voices. How well we listen and to whom we listen depend on many factors, some beyond our control.

A person who was inundated with foolish, abusive, or criminal voices early in life is going to have difficulties later on, unless circumstances provide a wealth of countervailing voices. Nevertheless, each of us retains the ability to be responsible for responding to, for taking a step away from whatever bondage the past leaves us in. A man at age thirty-five or sixty-five can one day stop blaming his parents or an unfortunate accident for all the woes of his life. It is not the time to declare: "I am responsible for my life." But it may be the time to say: "Being responsible to my life, I accept responsibility for taking a step toward reform of this life."

I have restricted this discussion of voices mainly to other people, especially parents and friends. "Human beings," wrote John Stuart Mill, "owe to each other help to distinguish the better from the worse, and encouragement to choose the former and avoid the latter."[64] There are other voices and other connections than those I have adverted to, the description of which belongs in the next chapter. Especially in our day, there are groups and organizations and institutions that are inevitably part of being responsible to. Personal self-dividedness cannot be solved exclusively by interpersonal exchanges. Or put somewhat differently, the physical individual that is a human person is related to other large entities that have some of the characteristics of a person. It is to interaction with these constructed persons that we turn now.

CHAPTER 5

CORPORATELY RESPONSIBLE

This chapter extends the discussion of the previous chapter by extending the meaning of the term "personal." It deals with bodies (corporations) of more than one human being that have characteristics of the personal. This extension of "personal" stretches the term beyond common usage, but a basis for so using the word goes back in history for many centuries. Some corporations have long been recognized as *legal* persons. However, it is often assumed that such a use is a "convenient fiction." The issue of responsibility raises a question whether the personhood of corporations is morally real or just a figure of speech.

I wish to emphasize that there are two distinct questions at issue in this chapter which is entitled "corporately responsible." Consistent with the distinction used throughout this book, one has to ask about being *responsible to* corporations before asking whether and how corporations are *responsible for* actions. The first question is important on its own terms and would deserve attention even if the answer to the second question were that corporations are not morally responsible for anything. I think that corporations do have responsibility for some actions. But that question is best addressed only after exploring how corporations of many kinds are involved in every act of responsibility.

This chapter, therefore, not only follows chapter 4 but dovetails back into its meaning of personal. I have said that these two chapters are an attempt to overcome the split in modern ethics between individual and collective. Chapter 4 was mainly concerned to show the inadequacy of "individual"; this chapter does the same with "collective." Both are concerned with the "personal" as an alternative to the split itself of individual and collective. Persons are beings that can be responsible for actions; before that, persons are beings that listen and answer. The question of responsibility cannot be handled if the only choice is between individual and collective. It *can* be dealt with by distinguishing between different kinds of persons.

When the division is between individual and collective, responsibility inevitably gets assigned to the first. Individual responsibility plus collective responsibility equals individual responsibility. Peter French, who more than any other writer has sought to change this equation, writes: "Almost all Western moral philosophers have approached the subject of responsibility armed with the assumption that the only interesting and important things to be said on the topic must be about individual human beings."[1]

There is nothing particularly wrong about either of the words individual or collective. It is just that they do not provide any texture for exploring responsible to and responsible for. For that exploration, the description here is of a relation between the naturally existing person and various groupings that sometimes act with sufficient unity to be responsible for actions. Those groups that perform responsible acts are called *artificial persons*.[2] Their existence depends on artifice, on the deliberate designing of their ability to act as a unity.

Sometimes, of course, a collection of individuals is just manyness, individuals without a distinctive pattern of operation. But if interaction occurs over a period of time, there usually grows up an organizing pattern. There are no firm rules in our language for differentiating groups, communities, organizations, institutions, conglomerates. I use the word "corporation" as a comprehensive term; it has a sufficiently rich etymology and broad history to serve this purpose. The biggest problem with "corporation" is that in the twentieth century the business world exercises undue control. I deal with the *business* corporation toward the end of this chapter as one example, admittedly one very powerful example, of a corporation. But the premise of the discussion is that all personal responsibility is in some way corporate, and some corporate activity carries personal responsibility for actions.

Peter French, in explaining why the idea of responsibility became individualized and segregated from corporations, writes: "The grand individualistic tradition that characterizes much of our moral thought has its taproot in Western religion's conception of personal salvation. . . . Morally, organizations and collectives do not exist and, mutatis mutandis, the notions of corporate and collective responsibility are illusionary."[3] I do not think that this statement does justice to the medieval church, which had a strong sense of corporateness. It is true that the Christian (and Muslim) conception of "personal salvation" was in the background of later Western individualism. But to the extent that the salvation was *personal* and not just *individual*, there remained an integral connection to body, community, and organized power.

The Christian and Muslim doctrine of the resurrection of the body was an affirmation that to be a person requires bodiliness.[4] The bodily or corporate human being interacts with other corporate entities. In Christianity, one could be saved only with the corporate efforts of the church, the "body of Christ." The medieval Christian was responsible to God, but the keys of the kingdom had been given to church ministers. It was not enough to confess one's sins to God in private; one had to submit the sins to the church tribunal in the sacrament of penance. The forgiveness of God was expressed by the church's representative.

At the least, it seems highly paradoxical to say that medieval Christendom believed that "morally, organizations and collectives do not exist." It seems more likely that our individualistic notions of morality arose in rebellion against the communion of saints and the mystical body. Jean Piaget's criticism of Christianity comes more from this direction. He writes in his *Moral Judgment of the Child* that "only in theology, that is to say, in the most conservative of our institutions, does the idea of Original Sin keep alive the idea of collective responsibility."[5] For Piaget as for most writers in the late nineteenth and early twentieth centuries, "collective responsibility" was a primitive myth that Western Enlightenment was finally freeing us from. Responsibility, it now seemed clear, was an individual's task. However, in the past few decades the question has come back to haunt us. World War II, especially the horror of the Holocaust, revived the question, and it has not gone away. Peter French mentions that he got interested in the question because of the Vietnam War.[6]

By the seventeenth century the movement to an individualistic responsibility was becoming evident. As I traced in the previous chapter, the Cartesian revolution placed the burden of responding on the individual's reason and will; thus the individual was not the bodily organism but the mind in its solitariness. Descartes, Leibniz, and many others at the beginning of modern philosophy were brilliant young mathematicians. Corporateness could be left behind in their minds. But any philosophy with a more psychological or political bent could not so easily sunder the ties to bodiliness. Peter French invokes the names of Rousseau, Burke, Hegel, and Bradley in support of the thesis that the human being starts out a *potential* person. He or she has to cooperate with corporate reality in becoming a person. "To be a full-fledged human moral person is to find a place (or places) in the structure of corporate entities."[7]

There is a parallel or analogy here with the distinction in chapter 3 between the nonmoral and moral meanings of responsibility. A human infant is a responsible being; it responds to its own body and the people and things of its environment. The infant, however, is only potentially a morally responsible being. It becomes morally responsible for its actions as it acquires a wider and deeper sense of responsible to. That begins with the infant's relation to the parent or caregiver. But before the child becomes morally responsible, he or she has to run up against organized power and take a stand on competing interests.

On the whole, corporations enhance human freedom, making possible the full flowering of personhood. The individual-becoming-person tries out various masks or roles in the corporate world, discovering, adapting, and inventing the person he or she becomes. This description may sound too rosy. Inevitably there are "role conflicts" that require difficult, sometimes painful, resolution. The principle nonetheless stands: human freedom can only be exercised in institutions, organizations, and corporations.

In our day this principle may sound outlandish, given the connotations of institution or corporation. The institution is widely thought to be the great enemy of individual freedom. The bigger the institution, the bigger the threat that it seems to pose to individual freedom. The government runs the biggest institutions, and therefore it is from the government one needs the most protection. And, indeed, the Bill of Rights and the check-and-balance system of the government seem built on the premise that one cannot trust the government's institutions. Other institutions that gather power within their walls—universities, churches, big business—are also not to be trusted. Roman Catholics today, who are upset at what pope and bishops say, attack the "institutional church," presumably on the belief that a noninstitutional church exists.

I do not carry any strong brief for the term "institution." It is over-worked in the twentieth century and does not help much to locate exactly what kind of institution and what policies of that institution are blameworthy. Like people attacking "the system," the rejection of institutions is a cry of frustration that usually obscures who or what is the problem. To the extent that the term institution is used, it should simply be as an aspect of experience by which human beings are linked to one another through set structures. In general, "corporation" has more flexibility and better connotations than does "institution."

I have acknowledged the fact that most times when people say "corporation" they mean business corporation. Life in the corporate world suggests offices in skyscrapers rather than the pleasures of the body and the person's relation to the dozens of communities and organizations that make up personal life. It may seem quixotic to fight against the business world's takeover of the corporation. Yet, there is enough in the meaning of the word to stage a resistance. For example, there are plenty of not-for-profit corporations that are not mere anomalies. They stand in a tradition many centuries long of bodies that bear hardly any resemblance to AT&T, GM, or Exxon.

Before describing examples of corporations and their responsibility, it is necessary to make an extended comment on the term most often paired with individual: social. When people talk about individuals taking responsibility for their lives, the contrast is very often to *social* responsibility. Sometimes the term comes up in discussions of big business; more regularly it is associated with government programs where the individual has failed his or her responsibility. As an alternative to "collective," social is an advance in clarity and particularity. Unfortunately, it does not go far enough to get at the question of responsibility. Just as with collective, the addition of individual responsibility and social responsibility usually equals individual responsibility. Someone or some group may succeed in changing that equation but history does not give any firm backing for that hope.

Social/Society

When Margaret Thatcher was the British Prime Minister, she antagonized her liberal opponents by dismantling much of the country's social-welfare policy. The justification she gave in a line that became infamous is that "there is no society, only individuals and their families." The claim infuriated her critics in part because she was using liberal language against itself. To say that society does not exist is an exaggeration but not a preposterous claim. The term "society" on its own says very little beyond referring to a group of individuals. In the language that Thatcher—and many of her critics—assumed, if society does not exist then indeed only individuals do. (It would have been interesting if someone had thought to ask Thatcher whether the monarchy, the British government, or England exists.) The alternative to beginning with "individual" and "society" is to begin with persons in a variety of communal and organizational relations.

"Society" has become the twentieth century's word of choice to summarize the human situation. The social sciences took over the study of the human being, looking at men and women not in their individual biographies but in their congregating patterns. To say that "man is social" tells us only of a characteristic "he" shares with many animals. Society means living together and interacting.

The United States is rich in studies of social interaction. One influential school, called "symbolic interactionism," concentrates on symbols of communication. This viewpoint does bring out specifically human characteristics. Its strength but also its limitation is that "it implicates the individual with society and society with the individual."[8] Studying the interaction between individual human beings has produced fascinating data; Erving Goffman's studies of how people stand in elevators or pass each other on the street are illuminating.[9] The data are useful so long as social interaction is not made equivalent to the entire field of human relations.

When individual and society are assumed to be the ultimate markers, everything else gets spoken of as units small or large "in society." A main question then about any organization is how it helps individuals to get along in society. The concern of the schools in the twentieth century has been to *socialize* the child. Emile Durkheim's influential writing on education placed "socialization" as the aim of education: "Education, far from having as its unique or principal object the individual and his interests, is above all the means by which society perpetually recreates the conditions of its very existence."[10]

Similar to education, the government is thought of as something existing "in society," and its purpose is defined by and for society. There are constant debates about how the government should balance individual interests and social needs. "The dilemmas of the black underclass pose in stark terms the most pressing unresolved problem of the social and moral sciences: how to reconcile individual and social responsibility."[11]

"Society" did not start out as an abstract, comprehensive term. Greek philosophers did not really have a word for what we now mean by "society." Aristotle describes the human being as the political animal, one that lives in the city (*polis*) and engages in speech.[12] Society was a Roman invention, a recognition that human beings can form "associations" for a multitude of purposes. A *societas* was a grouping for a specific purpose, much like the word "association" still connotes in English today. When the Christian church first appeared in Rome it was confused with a funeral society.

The church, of course, had bigger ideas, offering itself as a nonpolitical and nonethnic association destined to encompass the earth. It sought to gather all the nations to itself, not on the basis of the Greek city-state or Jewish bloodlines but by call of God in Christ. Later in the Middle Ages, theologians reflected on the form of the church itself. The description then given of the church was a "perfect society," a description that was not a boast of human artifice but a praise of God.

Within Roman law, *societas* got tied down to its mundane meaning as one type of organization. The law distinguished between *societas* and *universitas*. The first was a contractual arrangement among individuals, the assets of the group remaining in possession of the contractors. The second was an entity distinct from individual human beings; it possessed rights and obligations as an organization. Thus was born the notion of legal personhood. Organizations that qualified received this recognition as a privilege bestowed by government. A society, in contrast, did not have rights or obligations. It could not be legally responsible for actions.[13]

A more developed form of legal and corporate actor began in the thirteenth century. The granting of town charters by the king in England created a sense of autonomy for towns, such as Cambridge, distinct from the natural person of the king. Something similar happened in continental Europe with individual churches having their existence as corporate actors. The business corporation got its start with trading companies (for example, the East India Company) and banking companies that began as family enterprises but became independent actors.[14]

These two strands of history—the worldwide gathering of the human race and the contracting of a small partnership—met at the beginning of modern times to give us the meaning of "society." By the eighteenth century, the perfect society of the church was badly fragmented, but the hope and need for a universal gathering of the race did not recede. Society became a kind of church without Christ to which one must belong, even if reluctantly, to receive one's credentials as part of humanity. What underwrites and sustains society is a "social contract."

A number of thinkers, including Locke and Rousseau, elaborated versions of the story whereby the human race contracts with itself to get things started. Rousseau acknowledged the mythical character of the story: "The man who speaks of the 'state of nature' speaks of a state which no longer exists, which may never have existed, and which probably never will exist." Still, it is necessary to have this myth of an original contract "in order to judge correctly our present condition."[15] Each human being accepts the protection of society while taking on contractual obligations as a social being.

Rousseau was not enamored of this overarching society. He hoped that there would be a time when the individual would be perfectly congruent with the "general will," but until then man (the individual and natural man) and society would be at odds. Rousseau was a forerunner of modern psychology in trying to explain how, starting with untainted individuals, society can produce deluded and vicious characters. He distinguishes between two kinds of love, one in touch with human nature within the self, the other mediated by society's other individuals and interests.

Rousseau's educational program in *Emile* was to shield the boy as long as possible from contact with society. The tutor's job is mainly negative, allowing the body to develop inner strength before the inevitable clash with society. The student was not to hear of religion until age fifteen; his first love affair was not to occur until age eighteen. His companion was to be Sophie, the perfect woman who had never broken with nature. At the end of *Emile*, the tutor hands his charge over to Sophie with the hope that the young man will retain through the woman a connection to nature.[16] In a subsequent novel, Rousseau acknowledged that the program would not work. Sophie ends up promiscuous and unfaithful. Emile becomes a complete solitary but as happy as he can be in his isolation.[17]

Rousseau's successor in the twentieth century is Freud rather than Dewey. Although John Dewey is sometimes associated with

Rousseau, he is quite critical of Rousseau.[18] For Dewey, the revolution had already occurred: democracy meant that there need not be a conflict of individual and society. Dewey constantly speaks of education as a social process that addresses the social needs of "man." At least until the 1930s, Dewey was brightly optimistic about social transformation and the ability of schoolteachers to lead the charge. "The primary business of school is to train children in cooperation and mutually helpful living; to foster in them the consciousness of mutual interdependence; and to help them practically in making the adjustments that will carry this spirit into overt deeds."[19]

While "society" became the frame for individual life, its meaning was to be influenced by another development in the late nineteenth century: the enormous growth of the business corporation. When the United States was formed, there was little attention to this possibility. An association of partners to form a corporation was expected, but the resulting arrangement would be "a summarizing device for contracting partners."[20] When Tocqueville described the country, he found the tendency of the citizens to "form associations" one of the most striking features. The business association did not especially stand out. "They have not only commercial and manufacturing companies, in which all take part, but associations of a thousand other kinds."[21]

The country was unprepared for the dramatic expansion of the (business) corporation. These societies within society became centers of overwhelming economic power, unregulated by any effective rules of conduct. Regulation was supposed to happen at the state level, but states began competing to see which one could have the *fewest* rules and thereby attract the most business. New Jersey led the way until it was outdone at its own game by Delaware. One district judge said that if Delaware were a person it would be indicted.[22] Individual workers felt helpless before the power of the company until labor unions provided some leverage for bargaining: one corporation talking to another.

In the rapidly advancing technological world, some individuals inevitably fell behind. They needed help to adjust to a world of complex organizations and technical skills. The progressive movement at the turn of the century addressed the problem of the displaced individual. Just about everybody agreed upon being "progressive," but there were two widely divergent means for achieving progress: apply scientific principles for the management of individuals or treat individuals with compassion and humanize the workplace.

For the first kind of progressive reform, a new science (Taylorism) was applied in factories, breaking down work into units that required simpler skills.[23] The same principles were advocated for the schools, which had to turn out reliable workers. As Nathan Bishop, the first superintendent of schools in Boston said of school reform, the same principles apply "as in any manufacturing or business enterprise."[24]

The other kind of progressive reform also found its way into the schools, making them kinder places, more understanding of academic deficiencies. Progressive education eventually tipped to the side of this second progressivism. John Dewey remained a complex combination of both kinds; hence his alienation in the 1930s from the movement he is credited with starting.[25]

The compassionate progressivism that dominated the schools did not penetrate very far into the factories. Compassion for slow learners and enthusiasm for group discussion did not sound like the way to make the best profit. If there was to be help for individuals who did not fit the modern job market, it would have to come from private agencies or from the government. Thus, progressive politics was the main opponent of progressive business; they agreed only on the fact that there were individuals who did not fit.

Throughout a century of discussion about government welfare programs, the terms of the dispute have altered little. Almost everyone is progressive and liberal—in the nineteenth-century sense of valuing the individual. We have two political parties that might be called conservatively liberal and liberally liberal. These parties have never been models of logical design. Both profess the need for welfare reform; they differ on the means but not the goal. Comparing today's reform proposals to the Works Progress Administration (WPA) of Roosevelt, James Fallows writes: "The goal would be the same now: to reinforce the idea that the society runs on work, and that individuals are finally responsible for themselves."[26] If any politicians disagree with this sentiment, either they do not speak up or else they are not heard.

If it is true that "individuals are finally responsible for themselves," then the government's role is temporary and as minimal as possible: get the individual worker back on his or her feet to join other individuals in the "society [that] runs on work." For those people who believe that more help is needed, the alternative has been "social responsibility." In the early part of this century, the business world ridiculed the idea. In recent decades, it has often been a good business move to express concern for social responsibility. However, social responsibility remains mainly a government activity that is to complement individual responsibility but not substitute for it.

The terms "social" and "individual" are not going to disappear; they serve many useful purposes. But they are extremely limited for expressing the idea of responsibility. "Social responsibility" could conceivably mean being *responsible to* society. That is, an individual human being's or a corporation's general responsiveness to obligation could be called "social responsibility." Unfortunately, *responsible to* was all but disappearing just as "social responsibility" came into common use. What the phrase instead suggests in the twentieth century is that an agent named "society" is *responsible for* activities such as housing the homeless. As numerous poor people would testify, society does not seem to care.

Throughout the twentieth century, Christian moralists have called for the development of "social ethics" to cope with the large and powerful institutions that fill the landscape. It is regularly said that the church does well with "individual ethics" but that its "social ethics" is deficient. One of the best-known ethics books of the twentieth century is *Moral Man and Immoral Society* by Reinhold Niebuhr. The title was catchy, even if the thesis is difficult to make sense of. Where does the immorality come from? In the book, the total contrast of "man" and society is never explained. For example, in attacking hypocrisy, Niebuhr indicates a continuity: "Naturally this defect in individuals becomes more apparent in the less moral life of nations."[27] In the second edition of the book, thirty years after the first, the author acknowledges that "the title 'Moral Man and Immoral Society' suggests the distinction too unqualifiedly." But the title "is nevertheless a fair indication of the argument."[28]

Niebuhr's thesis that individuals are good, society is bad has been a favorite theme of staunch defenders of the individual against "mass society," throwing together government, business, universities, mass media, and every other place in life where the lonely individual confronts intimidating power.[29] The classic educational example of this mind-set is the book *Summerhill*, a description of a school founded in England at the beginning of the century. The founder and longtime head of the school, A. S. Neill, says at the beginning of the book: "That society is sick no one can deny; that society does not want to lose its sickness is also undeniable. It fights every human effort."[30] The school's philosophy is to develop strong individuals who would never be able to reform society but who would keep their individuality intact. The book had great success in this country during the 1960s when young people were protesting against "the system," which included the schools they were in.

Given the premise that individual responsibility is obvious and good, but is it enough, the debate becomes whether there is a need for social responsibility as well. At most, defenders of social responsibility can make the case that it will help and not undermine individual responsibility. Given the history of "society" as an aggregate of individuals, whatever success social responsibility has is measured by the multiplying of individual responsibility. Thus the equation: individual responsibility plus social responsibility equals individual responsibility.

The split of individual and social becomes especially problematic when the question of "guilt" arises. As I have previously noted, responsibility and guilt often slide together. To assign guilt is to assume someone's responsibility for actions. And when guilt is assigned it usually assumes a world of individuals in which one of those individuals is guilty and others are not. What happens, however, when horrible crimes seem to be the product of a large group, such as the modern nation-state? Especially during the last half of this century, the question has been a haunting one. In this chapter, I address only the present aspect of the question. In the seventh chapter, the question is expanded to include the past.

Whenever the phrase "collective guilt" comes up, the predictable response begins: "I don't believe in collective guilt, but . . ." and what follows is indeed a version of collective guilt. Wasn't Nazism a collective evil? Wasn't the German nation implicated in Nazism? Not being clear about how to fix guilt, we let it float free in vague, conspiratorial accusations. When a terrorist explosion happens, whole countries, ethnic groups, or religions are painted with guilt. Not "Hamas," or some identifiable group, planted the bomb on an Israeli bus but "Muslim fundamentalists" or perhaps "Muslims" are guilty. At the time of a vicious killing of Jews in a van on the Brooklyn Bridge, Mayor Rudolph Giuliani rightly calmed the city by insisting: "This act of evil is not the act of a people, but it's the act of a person or persons."[31] A question nonetheless remains of how we relate persons to organizations and groups.

One strategy is to separate "the people" from the government; it was not the Iraqis who were guilty in the Gulf War but the Iraqi government. If the government is not democratically elected but is run by a dictator, the guilt gets easily assigned: Saddam Hussein did it. Allan Bloom claimed that when he asked students to name something truly evil, they could only come up with one word: Hitler. And since Hitler is an aberration, there is little else to say about evil.[32] Jimmy Carter was elected president in 1976 on the promise to provide the country "with a government as good as its people." It is flattering and comforting to "the people" to be told they are blameless. But unless the government can be reduced to an individual ("Nixon's the one"), then assigning guilt to a government is almost as problematic as saying the country is guilty. The difference is that several million instead of several hundred million are guilty.

Attempts to find a way out of this problem are usually better at criticizing the inadequate concept of "collective guilt" than providing an alternative. Victor Frankl writes: "As for the concept of collective guilt, I personally think it is totally unjustified to hold one person responsible for the behavior of another person or a collective of persons."[33] The first thing Frankl denies is holding one person responsible for the behavior of another, which is not usually the question at issue. The second thing he denies is that a person is responsible for "a collective of persons." If the "collective" is simply a grouping of individuals, then the individual person does have a share in the guilt; if the collective is not an aggregate of individuals, then who *is* responsible for the behavior?

A favorite example here is a lynch mob. A group of people do something horrible that an individual would not do. Who is guilty of hanging the accused? Frankl's book is about life in a concentration camp, not too far a cry from a lynch mob. Surely he implies that there was something at work here other than individuals being guilty. But his strongly individualistic psychology provides no language for analyzing who and what was responsible.

The distinguished contemporary philosopher Jürgen Habermas says in an interview: "There is no collective guilt. Anyone who is guilty has to answer for it as an individual. At the same time there is something like a collective responsibility for the intellectual and cultural situation in which mass crimes become possible."[34] Habermas helpfully moves from guilt to responsibility, which is a more flexible term. However, saying that there is "something like a collective responsibility" does not do much to clarify a person's relation to the intellectual and cultural situation. The first link to that situation is being *responsible to* it. If that is not affirmed, then "something like a collective responsibility" will blur right back into collective guilt.

The intellectual and cultural situation is always a set of overlapping communities and organizations that shape one as a person and provide the corporate context in which a person accepts responsibility for certain deeds. The choice is not between individual responsibility and collective responsibility. Actions are both personal and corporate. The degree to which I am responsible for corporate activities will indicate if I should feel guilty for misdeeds.

Communities and Organizations

In arranging the description that follows, I employ several ways to distinguish among corporate forms. One crude division is by size, a factor not of itself decisive but never entirely to be neglected. A personal sense of responsibility certainly feels different when the corporation is four people rather than four million. However, once it is a sizeable organization—whether four thousand or four million people—differences in responsibility do not primarily depend on size. The shape and purpose of the organization and one's relation to its internal structure are more important than size.

Even with a very small group, a variety of structures is possible. In a dinner party of four, the waiter is attentive to how the check is to be made out. Not only are some ways more bothersome than others, but the waiter can probably guess the size of the tip by knowing the arrangement for the payment of the bill. If the group wants four separate checks, that is a collective form of payment: collect from each of four people who happen to be at one table. However, the group might say: put everything on one check and we will figure out what each of us owes. A further coalescing would be indicated by their saying: give us one check and we will split it evenly into four parts. Or, finally, one of the people may be a business executive with fellow workers. In the last case, an expense account attached to an official position may effortlessly swallow the bill. The waiter's tip is likely to rise in the above progression from first case to last.

The smallest conceivable group is two people. Ordinarily the word group is not used because we imagine that the two can directly communicate without organized procedures. We are often mistaken about the ease of "interpersonal" exchange and then are shocked on discovering misunderstandings and conflict. Even two people who seem perfectly matched for what they are doing, whether marriage, stage acting, tutoring, or apprenticeship, operate in an environment of natural and artificial beings, including language with all its ambiguities.

Action by two people can be entirely separate, shared equally, or be exercised through an instrument that is distinguishable from the two parties. State law recognizes such distinctions in the way bank accounts and small corporations operate. Several decades ago I was a member of a group of people who founded a nonprofit educational corporation. Over the years the members drifted away until I and a friend remained not only as the sole officers but as the whole corporation. I find it sometimes helpful to be the president of a corporation when I talk to other corporations. I sign legal documents, including checks, in the role of president, distinct from other roles in life that I play. The privileges I receive are entirely legal and, although the procedures are minimal, I am aware of being tied to larger corporate entities. Similarly, a married couple is not incorporated as a legal corporation, but they are a corporate reality. The persons are responsible to each other, and for some activities, such as buying a house or filing a joint tax return, they are responsible for the corporate act.

Our sense of responsibility for actions develops through personal interaction with one and usually with more than one but still a small group of people.[35] If "community" is used for a union of humans that differentiates persons as it unites them, then the fundamental community is restricted to a few people. If we look first just at numbers, a group that clearly deserves the term community would have an upper limit of a dozen or less. Students of group interaction often cite eight to eleven as an ideal number.[36]

The reason for the limit can be seen in the formula for the number of combinations in a set. To be a community means interacting with each person, that is, one can listen to and answer to each person. The number of combinations (x) in a set of (n) elements is 2 to the n power minus 1. When n=5, x=31; when n=6, x= 63; when the set goes from 10 to 11 the number of combinations increases by 1024; when one is the twenty-fifth person to enter a room, one carries 33 million combinations. If being a responsible member of a group entails interacting with the whole group, growth in size quickly makes community a mathematical impossibility. Multinational corporations or federal governments need established impersonal structures of listening and answering. So do organizations of fifteen people.

The heading of this section is community and organization. Rather than these two terms standing for opposed entities, the meanings shade into each other, with "community" emphasizing a simpler human-to-human exchange, and "organization" bringing out impersonal arrangements and a concern with objects. As already noted, communities have some organizing, and organization can connote groups that range from those that try their best to be personalizing and communal to groups that try to eliminate the personal touch.

An overly sharp contrast of community and organization is traceable to the 1890s.[37] "Community" was the usual translation for the German *Gemeinschaft*, which was opposed by society and organization. Community was given a nostalgic meaning, the small town where everyone knew everyone else. Society and organization became associated with large cities, modern business, and powerful government.

Community is often imagined as a defense against the lonely and heartless world of mass society and its impersonal bureaucracy. And, indeed, most people do value communal experience in the family, neighborhood, friendships, and local religious groups to provide a personal tone that they do not usually meet at the post office, the supermarket, or the Department of Motor Vehicles. Exceptions, however, do exist; some people get their communal experience at the post office, the supermarket, or in jail.

Community suggests a degree of reciprocity in personal exchange, the possibility of having intimate knowledge of a person's life history. In our mobile world with media of instantaneous communication, there is nothing unusual about a person not knowing who lives in the next apartment, while at the same time maintaining a close relation with a person three thousand miles away. Many people live in a set of fragmented communities, but everyone has some sense of communal relations in their lives.

A person's life can be profoundly shaped by responsibility to someone whom they speak with only once a month or twice a year. People can feel kinship with a writer whom they have never met. The books, the ideas, perhaps organizations that partially embody the ideas can be an object of personal response. A person can be responsible to an entity that is not itself responsible for actions. A person can be inspired by a great cause that is not a corporate actor. Someone might, for example, respond to the ideal of humanity, even though humanity does not do anything on its own.

At this point it will be helpful to describe the corporate responsibility of communities and organizations, starting with the family community and ending with the business organization. In between are numerous groups that can be more or less communal, including urban, national, religious, and professional groups. The natural person has to listen to the artificial person thereby accepting personal and corporate responsibility for actions. Depending on their kind, corporations have to listen to single persons and groups of people, including a wider public than the people within their organization. Then when the corporation acts, it has to do so through a mechanism that can establish personal and corporate responsibility.

The family is for everyone the first and for nearly everyone the most lasting experience of community. There is endless debate over how to use the term family. At the far end today in the United States, a family can be any two or more people who declare they are. The tendency simply to invent what family means has a long history in the United States. In the seventeenth century, the Puritans distinguished between the natural or biological family, which did not much interest them, and the Christian family that had undergone conversion. The adult converts *chose* to become a real family. Children were always anomalous because they were not yet converted.[38] The married couple were the family; everyone else, including the children, were out at the blurry edges.

Although the conversion experience did not typify later immigrant populations, other conditions conspired to identify family as mainly the small household. Marriage as a contract between two parties has always been held in high regard; children, especially after economic changes in the nineteenth century, are something of a luxury.

Frequently today one hears a comparison of "traditional family" and today's scene. More often than not, the context is a dire warning about the disintegration of the family. When it is said that only 5 or 10 percent of households are traditional families, the assumed model includes father at work, mother at home, and three or four children. Obviously some things have changed. However, in other ways there is striking continuity from the seventeenth century to the present. The Synod of Boston in 1679 was certain that the family had completely disintegrated; every generation since then seems to have thought the same, but a replacement of the family has never appeared on the horizon.[39]

The three-generation household is not typical today, but neither was it in the colonial period.[40] Grandparents were important then and still are. (Grandparents like to be close to their grandchildren, but free to go home.) Today more than 95 percent of children under age fourteen live with one or both parents; that is as high as ever. Most one-parent families make heroic efforts to stay together.[41]

For thousands of years the chief characteristic of the family has been the relation of parents and child. In most of history, family also included other relatives. I admit that the term family has some arbitrariness, but I think it makes sense to concentrate on the parent-child relation as the main note of what a family is. At least for the purpose of discussing responsibility, the relation of parent and child should not be treated as a peripheral extra, a tendency that is unfortunately too common in writing in the United States on the family.

With the primary meaning of family being the parent-and-child relation, other relatives surround the central unit. Nonfamilial groupings may deserve protection and encouragement, but they should be distinguished from the family. A couple who do not have children should be able to get tax benefits, insurance, and inheritance provisions. A gay couple should be able to receive the same recognition. But a couple constitute a different kind of corporation than a family.

Such a distinction has in fact found recognition in recent decades, mainly by the avenue of divorce law, not ideally the way to go about this issue. Divorce courts can recognize that two twenty-year-olds with no assets constitute a different kind of reality than a couple married for twenty years, who have three children, a house, and longstanding social relations. Personal and corporate responsibility differ in the two cases.[42]

Family responsibility means that family members are responsible to each other. That responsibility lies heaviest on the parents to listen to each other. The quality of the parents' interaction is the chief influence on whether children listen to their parents.

The parents' responsibility to their children is greater than the child's being responsible to parents. Parent and child move in the direction of mutuality, but it takes years to get there. During infancy, the parent is responsible *for* most of the actions of the child. This responsibility should continuously lessen as the child gets older. At the end of life, the positions sometimes reverse; the adult son or daughter may have to take over responsibility for many of the actions of an aged parent.

Can the family function as a corporate unit with responsibility for its actions distinct from individual family members? The answer is yes, but how such commitment occurs is in a state of transition. The government in its 1990 census eliminated the category of "head of household" because many people complained that it was an anachronism. The assumption that the father is the head comes down to us from centuries past. Father had the power; father "made the decisions." Today this is often not the case, whether or not there is a father in the household. Nonetheless, families do decide things, big and small, from buying a house to choosing tonight's video tape.

Families do not need a set of externally imposed rules to decide things; they do have to work out new ways to share in the deciding. "One person, one vote" is not an adequate principle, at least not all the time. Very young children need *protection from* equality of rights, even though they should start exercising many rights at an early age. They sometimes want voice but not vote. A sloppy and inappropriate democracy will lead to frustration and chaos. A "responsible family" will have parents who listen to each other and listen to their children. When decisions occur, whether by father, mother, or children, the action will represent the whole family's interest as far as possible.

This principle continues to hold even if the family unit is broken by death or divorce. When parents die, one child is likely to be executor of the will. The good of the family ought to remain paramount. When divorce occurs, the parents have to continue to be responsible *to* the children. And so long as the child is an economic dependent, the parents remain responsible *for* the child's welfare. Most of the time today (but not necessarily in the future) that means the father supplying money to the mother, who is caring for the child. The irresponsibility of divorced fathers is frequently bemoaned. Divorce courts and ordinary speech have not helped to fix the responsibility clearly. "Alimony" is not the right way to discuss financial arrangements in divorce cases. The child's welfare ought to be the centerpiece. How much does it cost to care for the child? Who can pay it? Who is going to pay?[43]

Families and households are small communities embedded in political communities and organizations. A city or a nation is not the family writ large. It cannot duplicate the intimacy of the family; its dealings are not governed by love.[44] It can, however, have communal qualities, a respect for persons, a celebration of human freedom. The alternative to being a family household is not a business bureaucracy. A city ought to be a place with pride in its history; a place of good talk and creative art; a place for people to experience a community more diverse than family or household can provide. As Aristotle said, "similar people cannot bring a city into existence."[45]

Cities provide benefits to their inhabitants; in turn the citizens have to be responsible to their place. No number of police can make a city law-abiding if the citizens have no respect for its texture and do not cherish what the city makes possible. The United States has always had a problem with cherishing and supporting its cities. Already in 1647, William Bradford was complaining that people were moving out of downtown Plymouth: "The town was like an ancient mother grown old and forsaken by her children, though not in their affections yet in regard to their bodily presence."[46] Not everyone has to live in big cities but the problems of living in a political community travel to the suburban mall, rural village, or seaside resort.

Cities and towns provide the space for corporate activities of every kind. A city expresses itself not only through its government but also through its artists, religious communities, civic associations, business firms, professional groups, sports teams, universities. All of these groups have to work together in a climate of cooperation. The urban government has to be sensitive to the life pulse so that its decisions represent the best interests of the whole city. Municipal governments have legally determined structures to exercise corporate decisions. Included in the government ought to be the protection of minority views and convenient access to the means for expressing disagreement.

The dominant political community for most people is the nation. It should have the same principles as the city, although the size and complexity of national governments are bewildering. If you do not wish to be responsible for (in a small way) what a city is doing, you can usually move. But for most people, changing their national citizenship is impossible; and one's native tongue shapes the personality. What one listens to as a child in Spanish, Chinese, English, or Russian is the basis for how the person answers in specific actions.

The idea of a nation suggests a common family tree; it is not that all are brothers and sisters, but they are supposed to be cousins. The relation between national or ethnic groups and the state is a great unresolved problem in the contemporary world, likely to generate a continuing string of civil wars. The United States had a head start on this problem, always having been a "nation of nations." Its sharp racial division nearly ended its brief history, and the problem has not been fully resolved. Its ethnic composition is so diverse that a split into two camps (similar to Canada) is unlikely. The danger for the United States, and by reverberation the rest of the world, is the submersion of the political diversity into a powerful myth. As the historian Richard Hofstadter put the problem: "It has been our fate as a nation not to have an ideology but to be one."[47]

The responsibility of each country on the world stage has to be analyzed in relation to its history and its internal structure of law. The United States has always had a special relation to a myth born in fifteenth-century Europe. The myth was given a name in 1507: America. From then until now, the term "America" has had mythical/religious/ideological meaning as well as a continental meaning. When the United States was founded in the 1780s, it deliberately identified itself with the myth America (and thereby also laid claim to the continental America: north, south, and central).

The whole story of the effect of this identification cannot be told here. The relevant point is the extreme difficulty of the United States' accepting corporate responsibility for its action when the name of the political actor is confused with the name for a myth or religious dream. Whenever a politician or an op-ed writer starts talking about "America's responsibility," it is all but impossible that anything clear, practical, and ethical will follow. Similarly, when left-wing critics the world over denounce "America," the attack is neutralized by their being swept up into the myth. Any effective criticism has to name the United States, the government of the United States, specific agencies of the United States government. Whoever is responsible for sending the marines or waging a trade war, America did not do it.

That is not to say America does not exist. It has been a powerful idea for more than five hundred years, and it continues strong as ever. People in the United States are responsible to the idea; elsewhere, people are attracted or repelled by the idea. The danger both within and without the country arises when people cannot distinguish the idea from the country behind the idea.[48] Millions of immigrants have come expecting to find America and have been disappointed to find the United States. Those who stayed have often come to appreciate that the country is a partial embodiment of the dream of liberty and wealth.

No president is likely to stop saying "God bless America." Every president in history has wielded the power of America in support of programs of the United States government. Without America, a collection of immigrants in flight from various places could not have maintained a United States federation. England had the monarchy; the United States had America.

What is sometimes called excessive patriotism ("America is number one") should not be called patriotism at all. It is not a love of the *patria* or nation so much as a love of the *idea* of the nation. America has never lost a war because by definition it cannot. However, like every political actor, the United States has a mixed record in fighting wars, keeping treaties, and assisting other nations. Most people in the United States think of their country as extremely generous to other countries. America may be altruistic, but the United States is way down the list of countries in giving foreign aid (less than one-quarter of 1 percent of its budget).

A United States citizen has a share in responsibility for the country's actions, both good and bad. That will follow from being responsible to the country and its history, a responsibility that recognizes the good things that the country has provided. The final sentence of Colin Powell's *My American Journey* expresses that sentiment: "My responsibility, our responsibility as lucky Americans, is to try to give back to this country as much as it has given to us, as we continue our American journey together."[49]

The most obvious way to exercise national responsibility is by voting. Even in the most important elections, only about half of the voters exercise this right and obligation. Some people have big obstacles that prevent their voting. Some people proudly announce they do not vote because neither candidate satisfies them. That is not a defensible position; responsibility often means choosing the lesser of two evils. Voting, it is true, can be frustrating when the process leading to it is controlled by powerful economic interests. However, the proper response is in the direction of doing more than voting instead of proudly announcing one's purity of intention by doing nothing.

A responsible citizen contributes to the country by doing good work, political and otherwise. Most people do not have to be deeply involved in party politics; the system could not bear having most people active in political organizations. There are other things to do in life; one has to have trust in those who represent the community. However, on some issues of passionate interest the citizen has to speak up. If a nation is doing something immoral, one has a responsibility to protest by some means. If one does not protest, then one accepts responsibility for a share in the immoral activity. The Talmud warns: "Whoever can protest and prevent his household from committing a sin and does not, is accountable for the sins of his household. If he could protest and prevent his fellow citizens from committing a sin and does not, he is accountable for the sins of his fellow citizens."[50]

The protest, of course, may not be successful at preventing evil deeds. Usually one cannot tell until after protest has been attempted. When protest is unsuccessful, one's responsibility for the activity is lessened but does not disappear; it may be lessened to the point where one does not feel guilty. However, any sensitive citizen of the United States knows that the food on the table, the gas in the car, the clothes in the closet are not without ethical taint. Those who are recipients of a country that can get its way with power have to ask what their responsibility is. Wallowing in guilt does not do anyone any good; thanksgiving, generosity, civility, and a desire for greater justice would be appropriate qualities of response.

There are numerous corporate realities that people belong to within nations and some that cross national boundaries. Among the latter are religious and professional groups. Each of the world's great religions was a transnational corporation centuries before ITT or McDonald's came to be. A person is shaped by his or her response to the ideals and practices of a religious body. How much an individual person is responsible for actions of the institution varies according to the internal organization and the person's place in it. A Baptist has a different relation to the Baptist convention than a Roman Catholic has to actions of the United States Catholic Conference. There is a tradition of being

Jewish but no clear-cut central organization responsible for what Judaism does. Identifying oneself as Baptist, Roman Catholic, Presbyterian, or Jewish indicates an acceptance of some degree of responsibility for actions by the group. But a Catholic does not become guilty of every crime by every Catholic organization in the world.

Most religious people have some differences with policies of organizations representing the group. If a person finds himself or herself completely at variance with the corporate view, the responsibility is not so much to leave as to accept that one has already left. When one continues with a religious group, while dissenting on some important issues, one would be responsible for expressing protest in appropriate forums. For example, a Roman Catholic would presumably agree with Pope John Paul II in *Crossing the Threshold of Hope* that "irresponsible global population" is unacceptable and that "the right path is that which the church calls *responsible parenthood*."[51] The loyal Roman Catholic might strongly disagree about the interpretation of "responsible parenthood."

Once when I was giving a talk that I had been requested to give on the Catholic church, I heard myself say: "I am not an official of this church; I do not speak for this church." I stopped and reflected on my denial. I rephrased my stance by saying that "I *do* speak for this church, although in no official way." I have not only the right but the duty, according to whatever position I occupy, to speak to fellow Catholics and to people who are not Catholic about this corporation. If I were not willing at all to speak for the organization I should deny I am a member. I may have no more influence over decisions in the Vatican than do nearly all of the other eight hundred million Catholic people, but I have to take seriously the responsibility for whatever influence I do have.

Not surprisingly, a person's relation to his or her profession has similarities to religious membership. Professions have their historical origin in religious commitment. In modern times, professions have claimed privileges on the basis of special knowledge and service to the community. At their best, professions continue to be communities of skilled and dedicated people, willing to place an ideal of service above economic self-interest. At their worst, they are islands of privilege for the upper middle class, with a degree from a professional school being the gateway to power and money.[52]

The responsibility of the professional is not to let the ideal slip down into crass self-interest. Every profession has a code of ethics which calls the person to accept duties beyond ordinary ethics; the term responsibility is central in most of these codes.[53] In return the professional is given *license*, privileges that the nonprofessional does not receive. A professional will not take responsibility *for* his or her work unless he or she is first responsible *to* the ideals of the profession. The profession itself is not a responsible agent, but professional associations are a mark of modern professions. Medicine does not wield power; the American Medical Association does.

At least until recently, a professional association differed from a labor union. Because of the imbalance of power with management, the labor union had to use threats of disruption to gain benefits for the membership. The professional association took its case public by educational means; the members were engaged in work they believed in and believed to be of service to the public. A lot of blurring has occurred in recent years. For example, schoolteachers, who had never used the tactic of strike until the 1960s, have used it frequently since. The problem, in part, was that the professional association failed in the early part of the century, a situation that made the labor union route more attractive. The good side of the blurring is that some laborers now have benefits once reserved to professionals (better control of one's time and way of working). There remains the need for some kinds of work to be in the hands of skilled and dedicated people. Perhaps more gradations are needed rather than a single division between laborer and professional.

Can professional associations take corporate action? To the extent they represent the profession and have an established order of command, an association can act for the benefit of its members and the wider public. The ethical challenge is not the former but the latter. There is no reason why the American Medical Association, American Bar Association, American Psychiatric Association, and all the rest should not look out for their members. The professional life, however, is supposed to be a pull beyond self-interest.

It can be a responsibility of a professional person to speak out in criticism of the professional association if the organization becomes a defense against any public criticism of its members. If there is racial or gender bias within a profession (something that has affected nearly all modern professions), the professional body has to act, spurred by its members. In contrast to laborers, most professionals have some protection when they criticize. University professors, the gatekeepers to professions, have the most protection. They have a corresponding duty to criticize their own profession when it is deserving and to speak candidly about the ambiguities of professional power generally.

The business corporation is at the end of the community–organization spectrum, deliberately organized to channel its energies toward buying and selling products. Though at the end, the business corporation falls within the general category of corporations discussed in this chapter. Often when the question of corporate responsibility is raised, the assumption is that the business world is the only question, and no meaningful comparisons are possible. Business corporation equals corporation.

Although businesses are oriented to making a product and thereby a profit, they are also places of livelihood in the older sense of that word: a way of life and not just a way of "making a living." For a business corporation to sustain success over a long period of time it needs a degree of community. Detroit's automobile industry seems to have learned the lesson after a long decline. If you simply string workers along an assembly line that requires their hands but not their heads, the product as well as the people will eventually deteriorate. European and Japanese automobile makers were the force that finally brought some change to Ford, General Motors, and Chrysler.

If business corporations are aware of the value of community *within* themselves, that is a help when they look at their effect on community (familial, religious, urban) outside themselves. If the corporation is responsible to its own workers, one can hope that it will be responsible to the communities it interacts with and that it will accept responsibility for more than making money. It ought not to take responsibility for the lives of its workers, as the George Pullmans and Andrew Carnegies did in the nineteenth century.[54] It ought to take responsibility for its own actions that impinge on the lives of both workers and nonworkers in its orbit.

When business corporations are asked to do good in addition to their business dealings, the result is usually either dismissal of the idea as impractical or else displays of public relations. In an essay entitled "Do Business? Do Good? No. Do Both," David Bollier writes: "A growing number of companies are discovering, however, that real synergies can occur when moral idealism and traditional management are combined. This is not a tale of 'social responsibility' in business which focuses on philanthropy and community service. . . . Instead these communities combine doing real business and doing real good."[55]

I think there is room for skepticism about how much "real good" some businesses can do, but at the least they could reduce "real evil" they do and perhaps even do some good. More noteworthy in Bollier's description of corporate responsibility is the curt dismissal of "social responsibility." He is probably accurate in identifying this phrase's meaning in the business world as "philanthropy and community service." And while philanthropy and community service are welcome, that is not the main line of business reform. We do not need business people thinking profit plus social responsibility. We need them to be responsible to the total environment and responsible for the effects of their actions.

Today, practically everyone is responsible *to* large business corporations, and most people have some degree of responsibility *for* what these corporations do. James Coleman has a useful classification for measuring the natural person's responsibility for a corporation's actions. Someone may be: (1) customer, (2) employee, (3) neighbor, (4) member/owner.[56] The first two may have some limited responsibility for the company's actions; the third has no responsibility; the fourth ultimately holds most of the responsibility. Of course, there are further distinctions, especially in the second and fourth categories: employee and member/owner.

At least within the law, an employee's liability is strictly limited. An employee is not held responsible for actions that if undertaken on one's own authority are not criminal; an employee is held responsible for actions that are criminal, as defined by the law of the land. The fact that one was obeying commands to perform criminal acts is a mitigating circumstance but does not excuse.

Many people are part owners of business corporations, though they may not know it. Their pension plan or bank account is invested in the stock market. The multinational, multiproduct corporation is so complex that it would be a full-time job trying to avoid all involvement with products one considers irresponsible. One can easily avoid buying Philip Morris stock, but does one's pension plan have in its portfolio mutual funds that invest in a company that has cigarettes among its products? If one considers automobiles among the chief destroyers of lives and cities, how does one avoid all relations to the production, sale, and use of cars? Those who denounce big business as evil and proclaim their innocence of involvement do not have much ground to stand on. Perhaps there is space on the Amish landscape untainted by business. Most of us can only try to divest ourselves of what seems patently immoral and to support what seems relatively benign. Each of us lives with ethical compromises. A person could miss the big issues of responsibility if his or her whole attention is taken up with remaining free of any business evil.

Large business corporations have clear lines of authority and chains of command. The corporation acts through a board of directors and officials. If the corporation does some dastardly deed, it makes sense that the corporation should be held liable for punishment. What about individual officials? Reforms in recent years have been in the direction of "opening up" the corporation and making natural persons more liable to punishment. In such cases the question is whether the natural person initiated the activity, or, if not, could reasonably have been expected to have the knowledge and power to stop it.

The law and morality often part here. Officials of a company may escape indictment even when they are morally culpable. At the time of Watergate, many people were surprised to find out the continuous attention to preserving the president's "deniability," his insulation from guilty knowledge. The Watergate hearings were a textbook full of cases of culpable ignorance. Superior to inferior: "Get rid of this problem," and the unspoken condition: "Don't let me in on the details." The superior is always safe if he or she is willing to throw the inferior to the legal hounds. Richard Nixon violated the rules of this game when, according to the tape recording, he said to his two closest advisors that he would not cut them off. He sealed his fate that morning, brought down by some sense of community or friendship. Nixon had not invented the rules of the corporation for avoiding indictment. The rules were well known in the business world. Nowhere is culpable ignorance played so well as in the upper echelons of business corporations.[57]

Too much attention, however, can be given to the spectacular evil action that periodically hits the news media. Slapping a big fine on the company and indicting *someone* provides satisfaction to an angry public. But, as Peter French says in reflecting on Exxon's great oil spill in Prince William Sound, "our interest should not be in making the party liable for any particular oil spill, it should be in establishing the assignment of responsibility for general environmental protection itself."[58]

Yes, Exxon deserves a multibillion dollar fine; yes, the captain who was inattentive, incompetent, or drunk deserves punishment; both parties are responsible for the disaster. The bigger issue is how this failure functions to change the culture of the corporation. Will Exxon change some of its procedures and better monitor both its equipment and its people? One failure does not make a company bad; the big question is whether it is becoming a more responsible company by reflecting on past experience and incorporating adjustments.[59]

The artificial person that is the business corporation parallels the natural person in being responsible for more than it intends and more than an isolated act. Like an individual human being, a business corporation does not set out to do wrong; it seeks its own good. But corporations, like natural persons, have inner divisions and an unconscious (the company design) from which most decisions emanate. Most of the corporation's actions and their effects are not intended, at least in the sense of a living person having a conscious intention that the corporation perform a certain act.

Corporations, as much or more than natural persons, ordinarily live by habit, by doing what they always do. But there are people in the company—supervisors, managers, administrators, executives—who are paid to be conscious of what the company is doing. Even when a result is not intended, the company is responsible for the effect if it did know of the effect or could have known. Sometimes officials hide knowledge from the public; tobacco executives are not the only ones who have hid studies documenting the lethal effects of their product. Much more often, officials hide themselves from the knowledge. What they do not know they are not—legally—responsible for.

A main moral reform of business corporations would be to change the patterns of *responsible to*. A bureaucracy is designed to channel information downward in the most efficient way and to *prevent* information flowing in the other direction. That is, *responsibility to* means reporting to my immediate superior. Most information is filtered out along the way so that it will not reach the top. The enemy for the man at the pinnacle is excess moral information.

Some corporations build in alternative routes of information to cope with unusual situations. But to go around or over the head of one's superior is not usually a career enhancing move. Taking one's case to the news media is an almost certain trigger to finding a new job. The term "whistle blower" was coined a few decades ago for moral heroes who reveal the company's dark secrets to *60 Minutes* or *20/20*. The world will probably always need such people who risk career, reputation, and life in being responsible to a moral ideal beyond profits.

Serious reform also requires change in the design of the company itself. James Coleman offers examples of what he believes are post-bureaucratic reforms. For example, each section of an assembly line would have the authority to accept or reject the product of an earlier part of the line.[60] *Responsible to* takes on a clearer meaning here with personal and communal qualities. I think it is unlikely that bureaucracy is about to disappear. But the physical design of a building, as well as ordinary rituals of the workday, can either facilitate or obstruct the flow of *moral* knowledge. A person in a communal setting is likely to be truthful. An individual in a noncommunal setting (the classic bureaucratic arrangement) cannot tell the truth. Not mainly because people lie. The inferior's knowledge is piecemeal, and the superior can only hear a fragment of that.

Companies do bad things not because they are composed of bad people who deliberately sacrifice moral goods to high profits. Companies do bad things mostly because they are composed of self-divided people who are expected to block out what is irrelevant to the company's purposes. Not enough in their immediate environment engages their full range of listening. They cannot hear their own bodies, their co-workers, the ambiguities in their product's effects, their desire to be integral human beings. To exercise their personal and corporate responsibility they need to feel that they are working in an organization so designed that it does not suppress the best part of themselves.

CHAPTER 6

HUMANLY RESPONSIBLE

This chapter is in some respects an extension of the previous one. The field of responsibility broadens here beyond the human world. The last chapter moved from interpersonal concerns to interaction with the largest corporations. If "corporation" refers to any organized body, then one could speak of the world itself and all the great forces of nature as corporations that human beings interact with. We readily speak of the ocean as a body of water and, though it has been less common in modern times, the earth has traditionally been imagined as the mother's body from which we all come.

The responsibility discussed in this chapter, therefore, certainly has a corporate character. The caution that I need to express immediately is that the movement to extend ethical concerns beyond the human is not merely an extension to larger objects or more objects. "Environmental ethics" is not a coda to regular ethics, nor is it one more practical application of ethics. Instead, the last three decades have seen the beginning of a challenge to what ethics has been assumed to mean. No one is sure where this will lead us, but we are confronted with rethinking the most basic ideas we have used to categorize experience.

The distinction used in the previous chapter between natural person and artificial person suggests there is more to say about person. But environmental concerns do not seem to fit within this distinction. They do turn our attention back to the meaning of natural person and the relation of human beings to a natural (in the sense of nonartificial) world around them.

What the humans invent as artificial persons are necessarily at a remove from natural beings. The business corporation, in particular, interacts with the environment mainly on the basis of *use*. No one expects Exxon's relation to the earth's oil to be one of friendship, won-der, and tolerance. The humans create artificial persons to engage in use and control. That is not immoral, but it expresses only one attitude of the personal. The practices of the business corporation need a context in which natural persons encounter "natural nonpersons" in ways other than control, use, and exploitation.

The fundamental connection between human and nonhuman is found in responsibility: the humans have to be responsible *to* the entire nonhuman world. And subsequent to that, in being responsible *for* their actions, they have to study the consequences of those actions throughout the nonhuman world. Unfortunately, this is not the language that is prominent in the ecological movement. In the topics of the previous chapters, "responsible" was almost ubiquitous. That does not apply, however, to ecological literature.

We are in a confusing situation in which everyone seems to agree on the need to preserve the environment. Once past that principle, however, very little is agreed upon in economic and political policies. Underneath this confusion is the lack of agreement on an ethical basis for the ecological/environmental movement. Until the term "responsible" is more prominent in the discussion and the meaning of the term clearly developed in this context, the gap between protestation of concern for the environment and serious damage to the environment will continue to widen.

In recent centuries, the ethical problem with the nonhuman was the incapacity of the humans to recognize its existence in an ethical context. Among the five rifts in modern ethics that this book addresses, the one in this chapter is different because it has seldom been named as a rift at all. Modern ethics has been built around how humans should treat one another and how they should use property. The division of ethics into individual and social exemplifies and solidifies the bias. When liberal thinkers try to correct the narrowness of an individualistic ethic by looking at human groups, the nonhuman world is still not rendered visible.

A rejoinder to this complaint is that ethics is *in fact* and of necessity a human affair. The humans are apparently the only ethical or moral beings; they are the ones faced with ethical decisions. And is not the term "nonhuman" that I rely on in this chapter reflective of a human bias? If dolphins, redwoods, or mountains were categorizing the world, presumably human/nonhuman would not be the primary divide. I do not claim to give an argument that is not biased in a human direction; the argument is not based on the claim that all of us are equal. Still, the humans are related to the nonhuman world; to talk about human interaction assumes some relation to the nonhuman. We can only know what the word "human" means by a comparison to what is not human.

Throughout history humans have always made such comparisons. During most eras, the comparison has yielded a string of ways in which we are alike, another set of characteristics where we seem to differ. What has distinguished the period of modern Western ethics has been a conclusion, mostly implied rather than explicit, that we are so different from nonhumans that we are barely alike at all.

This movement of disjunction from the nonhuman world coincided with the full emergence of "humanity" and "humanism." The early humanists are rightly admired for wishing not to exclude any human being from the concept of the human—whatever the race, nationality, or religion of the individual. (They were not so good at sexual differences.) To be recognized as a full partner in humanity was the necessary step to dignity, respect, and an ethical life.

What these early humanists could not see was that they were unwittingly creating a deeper split between human and nonhuman. One of the most celebrated lines in modern literature is Montaigne's "Nihil humanum a me alienum puto" (I think that nothing human is alien to me). Stephen Toulmin points out that, although regularly quoted as a sign of liberality, it is a restrictive statement.[1] Everything human is not alien implies that everything nonhuman *is* alien.

Montaigne and other early humanists should not be indicted for affirming their openness to all things human, while calling the nonhuman world alien or other. But in the absence of affirmations of kinship and similarity with the nonhuman world, "alien" quickly became a morally loaded term.[2] Marx found it a readily available term to describe laborers separated (alienated) from the product of their labor. Early psychologists were called "alienists," people concerned with the patient's separation from a healthy self. In discussions of immigration policy, "alien" is not a friendly category. And unfriendly visitors from another planet are not unexpectedly called "aliens."

Throughout the twentieth century there has been a current of philosophical thought that has attacked "humanism." This line runs from Nietzsche to Heidegger to Foucault and beyond.[3] For most people who identify themselves as "humanists," any criticism of humanism is

totally incomprehensible. They had assumed that their only opponents were fading religionists who found humanism to be antireligious. And indeed humanists such as Marx readily admitted that
humanism required "taking back what heaven had stolen from earth";
that is, the expansion of the human was at the expense of the divine.
But the post-Nietzschean attack on humanism has arisen at the heart
of the secular world. Having won the battle with heaven, people
began questioning the meaning of "humanism," which had long
seemed secure.

It was easier to invent the *concepts* of humanity and humanism than
to devise political and economic arrangements that would allow
everyone to experience a *human community*. It is also easier for us in the
twentieth century to see blind spots of the seventeenth, eighteenth,
and nineteenth centuries in their perception of the human. The most
telling bias was a failure to explore the relation of men and women.
Early modern humanists did not invent the bias; it was centuries old.
However, it is surprising that in the context of trying to encompass all
of the human, there was not more attention to this central question.
And the twentieth-century critics—Nietzsche, Heidegger, Foucault,
and their descendants—have not been in the best position to offer a
new language for man–woman relations.

This whole complicated story of humanism is relevant to this chapter in that confusion and conflict *within* the human inevitably rever-
berates in the world of the nonhuman(s). In the previous two chapters,
I said that a split between individual and collective could only be
addressed by rethinking each side of the split; problems reside within
the notion of "individual" and in the vagueness of "collective." Something analogous applies in this chapter. In the question of relating
human and nonhuman, there are conflicts hidden in the abstract
notion of the human; there is also the need to name, at least occasionally, the nonhumans within the nonhuman.

I do not propose to substitute new terms for human/nonhuman.
Actually, they are already a reform of the language bequeathed to us
by the seventeenth century, namely, the language of "man and
nature." Any attempt to work out a new, comprehensive relation
within man/nature is doomed to failure. The two abstractions are
locked into a historical relation that offers almost no alternatives
except conquer or surrender. "We are always conquering Nature,
because 'Nature' is the name of what we have, to some extent, con-

quered."[4] It is not impossible, of course, to retrieve an older and wider meaning of "nature," but that is unlikely to happen so long as man/nature is assumed to be a comprehensive pair. I find it astounding that the word "nature," (or the phrase "natural world") in the vast majority of cases, still means the world of the nonhuman. No complex relation of the human and nonhuman can be worked out until this meaning of "nature" is admitted to be inaccurate.

As noted above, human conflict has usually spilled over into the nonhuman world. Wars are not only deadly to human combatants but scorch the earth and its nonhuman inhabitants. The man who beats his wife is not going to be gentle with animals. Cut-throat competition between fishing companies eventually wrecks the fishing beds. The trees, dogs, and fish are used to bearing the brunt of intramural human squabbles.

What is a genuinely novel development in the late twentieth century is a human attempt to apply to its relation with the nonhumans the supposed *solution* to human problems. For many people, progress in human affairs has gone on under the banner of "equality." And some of those people are convinced that the next logical step is to extend that ideal to the nonhuman world. The ideal of equality is often joined to the more particular claim of rights. In the span of a few decades, the phrase "animal rights" has gone from being incomprehensible to being the name of a well-established movement that is casually included with other movements demanding equal justice. More than ten million people in the United States belong to some kind of animal rights group.

Many people concerned with law are skeptical about this extension of rights language. Before tying up the courts with a new world of questions that courts are ill equipped to handle, we have to look carefully at the idea of rights itself. Human rights, besides being a protection of individuals against oppressive governments, were an assertion of what distinguishes human from nonhuman. One should at least notice the paradox of now trying to extend (human) rights to nonhumans. Extending such rights without limit would at some point evacuate the term of meaning. Even advocates of "animal rights" do not mean to extend rights to every animal organism. A theoretical and practical line is drawn somewhere, perhaps at mammals. No one can even imagine a judicial system enforcing the rights of all animals.

I should acknowledge here that there are individuals and religious groups who, taking equality and rights in some broader and nonjudicial sense, profess to include all *life* in their ethical concerns. Such people are often admirable in their commitment, challenging the rest of us to examine our attitudes.[5] They may have a lesson to teach that the human race will eventually have to learn. Nevertheless, the jump from valuing *human individuals* to valuing *life* involves a dangerous leap to what seems even more abstract than "humanity."

If one applies the test of responsibility, it is clear enough to speak of being responsible to the dog or responsible for feeding the dog. Human beings are indeed responsible for preserving the life of this redwood or the cleanliness of this pond. Is it clear what it means either to be responsible *to life* or responsible *for life*? I do not mean to dismiss the issue with a rhetorical question. Ethics may in large part be an attempt to answer this question. But unless "life" is concretized in living beings that we respond to and respond for, ethics disappears into a mist.

One of the most famous "life philosophers" of the twentieth century is Albert Schweitzer. He was not an armchair philosopher speculating on life while benefiting from "man's conquests of nature." After a career as a biblical scholar, Schweitzer followed a personal call to go to Africa and care for the sick. His *Civilization and Ethics* is a great work of ethics, foreshadowing developments of a half century later. His words ring strong today: "The time is coming when people will be amazed that the human race was so long before it recognized that thoughtless injury to life is incompatible with real ethics."[6] I have no problem endorsing that sentiment, but I am left unclear about his use of responsibility. He writes that "ethics, then, is subjective, extensively and intensively limitless responsibility for all life within his sphere. . . ."[7] That seems to overstep what the human is responsible for, especially in the case of animals. Human responsibility is never limitless; it is limited by the responsibility others have for themselves.

Schweitzer believed that he had discovered the needed fundamental principle of morality: "It is *good* to maintain and cherish life; it is evil to destroy and to check life."[8] Can humans live without "checking life"? Would the attempt to avoid destroying or even checking life lead to a homogenized vision of life, while ethics still involves sometimes taking sides? Schweitzer and other religious figures in history have tried to shake people out of their mindless trampling under foot the beauty and the vitality of the world. Behind his fundamental principle of morality is reverence, the attitude that would infuse all ethics. Schweitzer figured out what this attitude required of him. I would be cautious about carrying the political language of equality into the ethics of ecology. Equality has problems in settling human disputes; when applied to the nonhuman world, in the form of respect for all life, its limitations become more obvious.

Equality and Inequality

I wish to argue here that "equality" is not adequate to the task it is being asked to handle. Its limitations should be noticed in the intramural struggles of politics before it is put to use for a wider purpose. It would be stupid to attack the word "equality." But one can respect all the great achievements done in the name of equality while still arguing that equality can only deal with certain well-defined problems. The attempt to expand its proper sphere of operation gets us into bitter, unresolvable disputes. I do not wish to argue that we need more inequality and less equality. We need a way of speaking with other available choices than equal/unequal.

"Equality" has its most obvious place for use in mathematics. Two factors or elements are equal when they are the same. The language of equal or unequal makes most sense if an object is measurable and the dimensions can be expressed numerically. If a judgment pertains to *qualities* of things, then equality does not apply.

The term equality can be and has been stretched beyond its etymological meaning. We can say that the artist's use of red in this painting is the same or equal to the red in another painting. We can say that the team's performance was the equal of its best performances. We may say of two children that they are equally gifted. If pushed to clarify such statements, we would say that in the factors most relevant to our judgment, the two cases seem to be very similar; the admitted differences are not what interest us.

As a rough way to measure what cannot be quantified, we use equal/unequal. So long as there is some awareness of what we are doing, the effect is not reductionistic. R. H. Tawney, reflecting on the work of physician or schoolteacher, notes that "equality of provision is not identity of provision."[9] I think a clearer contrast would be that "equality in the care to provide is not the same as (equal to) equality in what is provided." The word equality, outside a mathematical-like setting, cries out for the phrase "in regard to what?" To say that two people or two cities or two nations are equal would be meaningless without an explicit or implied specification. Two people can be equal in height; two cities can be equal in population; two nations can be equal in gross national product.

In modern times, the empirical and mathematical sciences have provided a firm basis for many judgments of equality/inequality. Probably more influential has been modern economic theory and the way economic metaphors influence modern politics (starting with the word "economics," originally meaning household now meaning numbers). A favorite metaphor of twentieth-century politics is "the marketplace of ideas." The *quality* of ideas is subsumed under market power and market price. Is one idea qualitatively better than another? What is its selling price?

Equality need not always be expressed in dollar values, but its effectiveness is closely tied to measurable quantities. One of the most famous statements of an argument is Thomas Jefferson's "all men are created equal." Taken in isolation, it would not be a false statement but an unintelligible statement. Simply to say that "all men are equal" is—literally and precisely—meaningless. Jefferson, of course, neither started nor stopped with the phrase on equality. He began with the statement "we hold these truths to be self-evident." Then followed several dependent clauses, the first of which is that all men are created equal. The second clause gives a rough account of the way they are equal: "that they are endowed by their creator with certain inalienable rights, that among these are life, liberty, and the pursuit of happiness." Jefferson made appeal to a creator who sees that all men start out equal in regard to having human rights. The rest of the document is about the long and painful efforts to "secure these rights." Jefferson was certainly aware that in regard to almost anything measurable in history, inequality has been the condition of most men, and even more so most women.

How can we tell when "equal rights" have been secured? For the basic rights of not to be killed or imprisoned, we have reasonably good indicators. Amnesty International publishes annual statistics on how many people are being killed, tortured, imprisoned by their own governments. Each nation has its own story about those numbers (the United States has a lot of explaining to do about its per capita prison population); but the numbers themselves speak loudly. Some nations are renegades, systematically in disregard of fundamental rights.

When one looks at a particular situation to determine equal rights, there are often precise, measurable signs. If Rosa Parks could sit in row twenty-four on the bus but not row two, that is a measurable insult whose remedy is obvious; everyone has an equal right to every seat. If "Denny's" took fifty minutes to serve African American customers and ten minutes to serve white people, the legitimate demand is: equal service. The hamburgers should take equal time whether the eater is black or white.

It is not surprising that "equality" has been a word of great rhetorical power throughout modern times. Jean Bethke Elshtain writes: "American society is, perhaps, unique among nations in that from the first, equality ("all men are created equal") has been one of the touchstones of its national identity and political culture."[10] That touchstone of equality is a mark of great national pride for the United States. It is also the reason why, in the absence of other ethical language, the country is so contentious and puzzled by its own problems.

Elshtain's book is itself a reflection on the seemingly intractable nature of our present problems. She places her hope on a defense of equality that does not mean sameness. For example, she says "in education and the academy, the equation of equality with sameness led to a muddleheaded assault on any notion of distinctiveness or value." Similarly, she writes of liberal critics of policies confining equality to legal recognition: "Rather than challenge the equation of equality with sameness, many critics implicitly embraced the idea: the more we were the same the better."[11]

I find this line of argument unpersuasive. "Equal" *does* mean sameness, applicable to two cases where the length, width, size, or some measurable category is the same. Equality means submitting to an impersonal, objective standard so as to escape from discriminating, subjective judgment. That is the strength of the term and the value that it has had in history. Even if one could change the equation that equal equals same, which is unlikely, the result would not be an improvement. We need a language of both sameness and difference for the peculiar combination of these two in human life. Equal does very well when the issue is sameness; it cannot bear both same and different.

Elshtain seems to want equality to be the one main player. Any challenge to the ideal of equality becomes an attack on democracy. She describes a feminist conference that she attended where women invoked a "discourse of difference." They were suspicious of the word equality because they believed it was biased by male history. Elshtain writes: "The rush to eliminate equality from our political aspirations struck me as daft."[12] Certainly, anyone trying to eliminate equality from the political idiom would be as Elshtain concludes "not too keen on constitutional democracy itself." Perhaps that is what the particular women at that conference were doing: choosing difference to the exclusion of sameness (equality). However, what one finds in daily news stories and books, as well as innumerable conferences, is people groping after a language that can identify in what ways "we" are the same and in what ways "we" differ. The "we" can be races, nations, genders, or a reference to humans and nonhumans.

There were several movements of the 1950s and 1960s that flowed like tributaries into the environmental river. The Negro civil rights struggle marched under the banner of equality at least until the 1970s. If you have started off by being counted as three-fifths of a person, the indispensable step is to get recognized as five-fifths. If you have been a slave with no legal rights, you want equality before the law. The chief symbol of political equality is at the ballot box where "each one shall count as one." The court can step in to see that the majestically impersonal law is applied without discrimination against selected groups.

The Supreme Court finally did its part in 1954, striking down school-segregation laws. The decision began a long struggle to change the way the nation thinks about race. The court had to admit that its decision in the late nineteenth century had solidified the dominant white power. The court could not undo the ensuing history; it could only take away obstacles and restrain some evils. The doctrine of "separate but equal" had worked out badly even though "separate but equal" is a logically coherent idea.

In the regular condemnations since then of "separate but equal," the impression may have been generated that "together and equal" is the only desirable alternative. However, just as separate does not necessarily entail unequal, neither does together guarantee equal. More basically, an exclusive concern with equality was not adequate for the long-term changes in race relations. The court's job is to eliminate gross inequalities regarding opportunity; it is not equipped to say how experience of racial difference might enhance people's lives.

Any oppressed group in modern times when asked what it wants is likely to reply: freedom and equality. Compassionate and justice-seeking individuals outside the group may help the group to change the laws. Then a moment comes when, great progress having been made and equality almost achieved, prominent members of the group say: "Maybe equality is not what we most need." What is meant, though it can be lost in charges and countercharges of disloyalty, sellout, and ingratitude, is that equality is indispensable for a space to live in, but then one has to live with a much more complicated language of personal and corporate relations.

A key test is the meaning of the term "discrimination." If one consults the *Oxford English Dictionary,* one could never guess that discrimination has a negative meaning.[13] Through centuries of use, the word has expressed one of the greatest human powers: to discriminate means to think carefully, to judge with concern for quality not just quantity. Of course, it has always been possible to discriminate *against* someone, which is the opposite of discriminating *for* someone. But discriminate itself simply means a human exercise of the power to judge. To make the word discrimination a totally negative term is to place all hope in equality, a term that does not ask for discriminating choice, only for quantitative measurement.

The conflict between equality and discrimination is painfully evident in the most recent history of African American struggles. "Affirmative action" has been the attempt to look for qualified people in unaccustomed places. The government tried to nudge the academic and business worlds to recognize the existence of black talent, to think of a person's black race as a possible enhancing quality when the person is as qualified as anyone else. In other words, the school or employer would have to discriminate, think with qualities in mind.

Affirmative action could have been a way to challenge the reductionistic use of quantitative criteria, especially in the academic and professional worlds. How about caring for one's community as a test of professional competence? But if one cannot discriminate, the alternative is numbers. Opponents of affirmative action programs complain that it is a quota system, and that is in fact a vulnerable spot. If discrimination (complex thinking) is outlawed in favor of equality, then a quota system is almost inevitable.

Some day people will probably marvel that race was ever a question. Imagine a visitor from Mars trying to figure out what all this talk about race inside the human race is about. The humans divide themselves with a half-dozen color codes, *none* of which is accurately descriptive. At the present and for well into the next century, equality is not going to be adequate to the problems of overcoming current injustices. Nevertheless, equality remains a meaningful standard here because racial differences are not among the most interesting ways that human beings differ. Emphasis upon sameness is appropriate.

Sexual differences, in contrast to race, do seem profound. That there is some important difference between male and female, men and women, goes back to our origins and continues to be a crucial fact in daily life. The contemporary women's movement got its impetus in World War II but emerged in the wake of the black struggle in the 1960s. An earlier *woman's* movement also had affiliation with the racial struggle. At the end of the nineteenth century and the beginning of the twentieth century, race and sex were placed in the same conceptual world. Emphasis was upon equality or sameness (despite the fact that the woman's movement itself was afflicted with a good bit of racism).[14]

Anthropologists led the way in emphasizing that there were no essential differences between the races; this was in opposition to a crude application of Darwin's ideas that made blacks inferior to whites. The emphasis became even stronger when Nazism proclaimed its doctrine of superior and inferior races. Sex got included in this insistence on equality.[15] The one thing that the woman's movement (also given the name "feminism" in the 1910s) agreed upon was the vote. Women should be equal to men, and enfranchisement was the symbol of that equality.

The women's movement of the 1960s began with a renewed demand for equality. The difference between men and women had been used to women's disadvantage and for segregation from public life. The demand seemed clear at first: an end to "house arrest," access to the workplace where the power and money are, equal rights of employment, marriage, credit cards, insurance, and every other sphere where contractual rights hold. For a decade, the women's movement struggled to get a hearing, to be taken seriously.

Then, just as real progress was evident, some women began saying: "Maybe equality is not the main thing or the only thing we want." Perhaps we are different and should be different in significant ways. Thus began in the late 1970s a much more contentious phase of the women's movement, in which the disputes are as much between women as between men and women. Katha Pollitt coined the phrase "difference feminism," which she thinks represents something regressive. Since feminism has been so associated with equality, the phrase "difference feminism" is almost self-contradictory.[16]

The emergence of these debates within the women's movement parallels debates within ecology. What I take many women to have discovered is that equality in regard to x, y, and z is indispensable. But to say that "men and women are equal" would obscure the ways women have differed from men and may wish to differ in the future.

For thousands of years there have been two approaches to this issue. The first opens with the statement that "men and women are the same." In response to the protest that the statement is obviously not true, the statement is modified to "men and women are the same, except for x." Plato in the *Republic* says that men and women are the same—"except for birth and begetting."[17] Plato wanted a military in which men and women would be equal. The United States military is probably coming closer to Plato's ideal than has any group in history. Men and women are now treated equally, starting in boot camp (except that women do fewer pushups). Some people consider this elimination of difference to be progress.

The second approach is to say "men and women are different." To the cries that this is not true, the statement is modified to "men and women are different, except for y." Rousseau says that in what pertains to sex, men and women are completely different; he adds that in what pertains to their humanity they are the same.[18] His emphasis is on the difference between the sexes for the sake of complementarity. The woman's equality in humanity tends to disappear into the shadow. Complaints about a lack of equality for women are met with the banter that equality would lower women. In 1991, the Ninth Circuit Court of Appeals ruled that in cases of sexual harassment against women, the standard of judgment is not the "reasonable person" but the "reasonable woman." Some people consider this recognition of difference to be progress.

The relation between men and women (and less overtly the relation in same sex love) has always been intertwined with human/nonhuman relations. I noted in chapter 4 that the self-dividedness of the person is somehow related to sexual division, though the relation is more complex than man=active, woman=passive. Some kind of dialogue occurs within men and within women, making possible more complicated and interesting relations of men and men, women and women, men and women. (Plato's myth of the androgyne has all three of these possibilities.)[19] It seems to me that the premise which has to be used today is: men and women are the same in important ways; men and women differ in important ways; we are sure about some of the sameness and some of the differences. We have to listen some more and study some more to discover which differences should stay and which should go.

Ecology

The environmental movement is sometimes given its symbolic point of origin at Earth Day in 1970. The movements that preceded it (black, feminist, gay) had long histories of lonely individuals struggling for justice before the rise of a media-supported movement. The environmental movement had a history too, although even in the late 1960s only a handful of people had ever heard the word "ecology."

The environmental movement seemed to be the most comprehensive one imaginable. It also seemed to be the one that triumphed immediately. Earth Day in 1970 was experienced by many people as a victory celebration; everyone spoke in favor of the honored guest, earth. No Martian protesters appeared on the scene to denounce solar system discrimination. What particular human groups had so long struggled for—equality and justice for all—was truly to include "all" without restriction to the human. The *New York Times* proclaimed: "Conservatives were for it. Liberals were for it. Democrats, Republicans, and independents were for it. So were the ins and outs, the executive and legislative branches of Government."[20]

In subsequent decades it is becoming apparent that victory celebrations should be postponed until the battle lines are clearer and progress is secured. The hope is eventually to go beyond the metaphor of battle and struggle, but longstanding conflicts have to be recognized before they can be transcended. In the past, "nature" has been portrayed as a vicious competitor with "man"; nature had to be conquered, subdued, beaten into submission.[21] Today "nature" is spoken of as what "man" should be in harmony with. Nature means balance, unity, peace; all we have to do is recognize our place as "simply one group of many in a greatly expanded biotic community."[22] A biotic community sounds like a place where all that political infighting is resolved and no species claims superiority.

Sexual attitudes in the seventeenth century are glaringly reflected in the way "nature" was approached by "man." The metaphors for the new science were explicitly sexual with the scientist portrayed as a gallant suitor. "Let us establish a chaste and lawful marriage between mind and nature," said Francis Bacon. The new science can expect a fruitful issue from this furnishing of a "nuptial couch for the mind and the universe."[23] Nature was passive, ready to be taken; all man had to do was climb on top. Bacon in one place draws a comparison between science and the inquisition of witches. "Neither ought a man to make scruple of entering and penetrating into these holes and corners, when the inquisition of truth is his whole object."[24]

If today one cites such expressions of sexual/ecological relations, it is likely to draw gasps from an audience. How crude to think "man" is on top of nature, looking down as the superior who dominates the inferior. How lacking in an egalitarian spirit. "Man" has to give up his pretensions and reoccupy the position he broke out from within the harmony and unity of nature.

One of the essays that helped to spark the environmental movement was a brief piece by a historian of science, Lynn White, Jr. In "The Historical Roots of Our Ecological Crisis," White traced the problem to Christian arrogance that placed man over nature. He allowed that there was one exception in Christian history: Francis of Assisi. Over the last three decades, Francis of Assisi has been hailed as the patron saint of ecology. Francis is certainly an admirable figure, but White's characterization is misleading: "The greatest revolutionary in Western history, St. Francis, proposed what he thought was an alternative Christian view of nature and man's relation to it: he tried to substitute the idea of the equality of all creatures, including man, for the idea of man's limitless rule of creation."[25]

The statement is wrong on both counts. Francis did not propose man's equality with all creatures, nor was man's *limitless* rule of creation an idea that had to be opposed. Francis, like nearly all orthodox Christian theologians, believed in a hierarchy of God's creating in which the human being has a special responsibility to and for creation. Since human power is one of listening and answering, the attribution of limitless rule is absurd. White's contention that in Christianity "no item in the physical creation had any purpose save to serve man's purposes" misses the point that the purpose of every item was to glorify God. The human being was the high priest of creation; all things were related to, taken up into the human, as the greatest expression of the glory of God.[26]

My purpose is not to write an apologetic for Christian doctrine nor to deny that Christians in practice violated their professed beliefs. But the strong strain of anti-Christian (and anti-Jewish) writing in ecological literature is an obstacle to exploring new ways of thinking that might be linked to very old ways.[27] A wholesale condemnation of the Bible on the basis of a verse in the first book of the Bible ("Fill the earth and subdue it; and have dominion over the fish of the sea and over the birds of the air and over every living thing that moves upon the earth") presumes that there is nothing to be learned from studying the actual history of both Christian and Jewish religions.[28]

Lynn White, Jr.'s essay was somewhat different in his trying to find a redeeming feature in Christian history. But in contrasting Francis of Assisi's "democracy of all God's creatures" to the standard Christian view, he compounded a problem that was already severe enough. He fed a romantic, overly simple idea into a movement whose temptation was to romanticize equality and avoid discriminating judgments. One author, in a careful study of Francis's view on this matter, writes: [The Bible] asserts the belief in divine creation, organized according to a plan that is hierarchical and unchanging, with all parts having their established positions and dependent on divine will and action. This was the most fundamental basis for Francis's conception of the natural world."[29]

Serious study of Francis would throw light on how language and attitudes are drastically different today, but those differences could shake us into discovering where indeed there might still be sameness. For example, despite Francis now being hailed as the patron saint of nature, he never used the word "nature" in his writings. How could he have got along without the word? He did not deal in such abstractions. G. K. Chesterton writes that "St. Francis was a man who did not want to see the wood for the trees." He did not respond to nature; he was responsible to particular beings that we abstract from with our term nature. "He did not call nature his mother; he called a particular donkey his brother or a particular sparrow his sister."[30]

As to his responsibility for the nonhuman world, Francis showed unusual respect for animals and inanimate objects. He could praise

God for them; he engaged in listening and speaking to animals. Like any mystic, Francis believed that there is one respect in which creatures are equal: they are all equally nothing apart from divine creation. Within the hierarchy of what God has created, the humans are the morally responsible creatures. The humans have a power (on loan and in humility) that the other animals do not have. "After his preaching to the birds, for example—an act which stressed hierarchy and community at the same time—Francis gave the birds permission to leave."[31]

One response to Lynn White, Jr.'s portrait of Christianity was an essay by René Dubos, asserting that the true patron saint of ecology is Benedict of Nursia, the founder of the Benedictine monks. The Benedictines, both in the development of farming and the copying of manuscripts, have a sizeable part in the origin of Western civilization. The Benedictine rule, writes Dubos, is inspired by the second chapter of Genesis "in which the Good Lord places man in the Garden of Eden not as a master but rather in a spirit of stewardship."[32] Dubos's recounting of this strand of Christianity was helpful, although pitting Benedictine against Franciscan traditions was somewhat unfortunate. Each tradition was an exercise in responsibility, bringing out different but legitimate responses to the needs of the time. The last line of Dubos's essay could include Benedictine, Franciscan, and dozens of other Christian strands: "Reverence for nature is compatible with willingness to accept responsibility for a creative stewardship of the earth."[33]

One testing point for the direction of ecology, the one that receives the most attention in the news media, is the human attitude to nonhuman animals. Extraordinary changes for the good have happened here. Public awareness has dramatically changed in the last two decades. The only drawback is a skewing of the larger movement into using a political language which can be misleading here. Since the publication of Peter Singer's *Animal Liberation* in 1975, the category of "animal rights" has come into common use. Singer's adoption of the term "speciesism" has not been very successful, but the idea behind it has spread rapidly.[34]

That idea is that beyond racism, sexism, ageism, classism is the ultimate bias, namely the claim that humans are superior to other species. As with previous -isms, court action can be required to protect the right to life, liberty, and the pursuit of happiness of all species. The courts have in fact been helpful in preserving the existence of some species that were threatened with extinction. The ethical principle underlying these legal forays remains cloudy.

In a blistering review of Roderick Nash's *The Rights of Nature*, Mary Midgley notes that "'rights' is a legal term, describing the privileges of each contractor. It is a competitive, confrontational term (they have rights against one another), not a term which helps at all to arbitrate these clashes."[35] Our ecological problem is in part a lack of categories beyond rights and equality. For thinking of whales or apes, the principle that "each one shall count as one" may be of service. What are we to do when we think about the two million species scientists have so far named among what may be one hundred million species?

When the Endangered Species Act of 1973 was passed, not many in Congress realized what they were doing; no senator voted against it and only four members of the House. The snail darter, the spotted owl, and a few hundred other species received a right to life. The list has gotten longer over the years; for each species removed, thirty new ones have been added. But over the last two decades several hundred thousand species have become extinct.[36]

Is the only possible response to this fact a more aggressive attempt to extend equal rights? Or is the idea of equal rights subsidiary in a world where humans have to listen and then answer. In a book critical of the approach taken by the Endangered Species Act, Charles Mann and Mark Plummer conclude: "Crying 'no more extinctions,' produces a noble sound, but it does nothing to stop extinction. And it has the potential to worsen the plight of biodiversity, because demanding the perfect can prevent us from obtaining the merely good. To do better, we will have to accept the responsibility that comes with being human at this time in history."[37]

We seem to be only in an early stage of developing an ethical language rich in distinctions for responding to our animal kin. The human race has had various distinctions, for example, between animals as pets and animals used for food.[38] We intuitively distinguish between our relation to horse or dog and our relation to mosquito or cockroach.[39] Does each housefly have the same importance as each whale? The more one asks such questions, the more enticing becomes a single principle: equal justice for all. But a pronouncement that all nature has rights and that all life is to be revered could be an escape from our responding to nonhuman beings with whom we have actual contact, and deciding what we are responsible for in our actions that affect the world of nonhumans.

The most fundamental ethical category relating to animals should be "care" rather than rights. Care of varying degrees and kinds can be directed toward the entire animal world. Care would lead to responsibility toward animals before we decide what actions to perform. Responsibility toward krill and plankton is of a different order than responsibility toward the family dog. One has to respond to personal experience of nonhuman beings, experience that includes information about their place in the universe.[40]

There clearly are occasions when individual animals try to communicate with us. Only if someone cares, will he or she bother trying to understand. Elizabeth Thomas writes: "Our kind may be able to bully other species not because we are good at communication but because we aren't. When we ask things of animals, they often understand us. When they ask things of us we're often baffled. Hence animals frequently oblige us, but we seldom oblige them."[41] The issue in these instances is not best handled by equality/inequality. When there is mutuality in relations, a different scale is at work, one that respects the relative autonomy of each party and tries to work out acceptable compromises.

Aldo Leopoldo in *A Sand County Almanac*, one of the founding books of the environmental movement, wrote that "all ethics rest upon a single premise: that the individual is a member of a community of interdependent parts."[42] That might be an acceptable principle, but the phrase "interdependent parts" requires clarification. Interdependency signifies that we are not talking of a part to whole relation. Community is composed of beings that become themselves by and in communion. Each being is responsible to all the others.

The humans are *morally* responsible to all the rest because of the power to perfect or to do damage to the community. The humans are the ones who have partially broken out. Their order is a restored order in the finding of their place. They are killers, not only in meat factories and fur farms but in bulldozing to build a house, walking across the grass, or breathing the air. For this human characteristic they need rituals of thanksgiving and forgiveness, as well as determination to avoid causing unnecessary suffering and to reduce suffering.

The humans are also the great producers; they make things not seen before, even by fellow human beings in previous eras. What the humans make they have a right to use. Ethical questions have mostly revolved around ownership rights: which human has the right to use which piece of property. Laws exist to sort out what belongs to whom. When ownership is extended to land and other natural beings, rights are easily abused. If rights and obligations flow from within responsibility, then the ownership of land means to listen to the land and care for it.

The idea that one should take care of what one owns has not worked out well with what humans call "waste." Since no one owns waste, who is supposed to take care of it?[43] The solution to the problem of waste starts with one simple premise: there is no such thing as waste. Living bodies consume in the sense of using up. "They do not produce waste. What they take in they change, but they change it always into a form necessary for its use by a living body of another kind. And this exchange goes on and on, round and round, the wheel of life rising out of the soil, descending into it through the bodies of creatures."[44]

Hierarchy and Uniqueness

The image in the last quotation—a hierarchy of unique beings in a cycle of interdependence—suggests the direction for an ethical language that would properly bridge human and nonhuman. The language of equality is powerful though not fully adequate to racial problems; it is more markedly incapable of handling sexual interdependence. Ecological interdependence includes relations between humans, and human interdependence with nonhumans. Equality here is mostly irrelevant.

In a cycle of interdependence we might say that each is equally important to the existence of the cycle; with one missing link there is no chain. That seems to be what people mean by saying that all species are equal. But there is life beyond merely existing. The image of a chain is somewhat misleading. If one imagines a cosmos, a three-dimensional sphere, then all elements are necessary to the whole, but some are more central than others. Equality is a two-dimensional term, exact in its judgments about height, area, population, and anything reducible to quantity. The meaning of life, the beauty of the world, and the significance of human action are not measurable by equality/ inequality.

Human responsibility is a three-dimensional term. It is conceivable that one can measure the response of a tuning fork or even the response of a dog. And Pavlov in his famous experiments showed that humans share with other animals in patterns of stimulation followed by response. But *moral* responsibility signifies the way in which humans differ. They can listen at various degrees of attention, they can evaluate their previous responses and then commit all or some of their energy in their answering activity. The humans, as Martin Buber said, are "the center of all surprise in the world."[45] People even surprise themselves, sometimes in disappointing ways, but often in accomplishing good things they did not know themselves capable of doing.

Does that mean humans are more important than other species? If "important" is a question of meaning, value, and significance, then humans are *immeasurably* more important, that is, important in ways that are impossible to state as a measurement. I am unpersuaded by scientists who, after surveying the skies or looking into a microscope or studying the archeological record, declare that "man" is an insignificant speck who should stop trying to assert his importance. Such statements from individuals who spend their waking hours trying to achieve status, reputation, control of data, power of persuasion, money, breakthrough in knowledge, the Nobel prize, and endless other marks of achievement do not ring true.

The humans, as far as the humans know, are the center of meaning. Without the humans there simply are no judgments of meaning. It could be, as religions claim, that there is a greater mind, consciousness or source of meaning, in which humans only participate. That would not lessen human meaning but enhance it. No scientist can pronounce with certainty on that matter. What scientists could do is to stop telling (other) people that they are not really important.

If one sticks to measurements of size, then the human being is a barely visible speck. Modern astronomy was not needed to tell us that. As G. K. Chesterton said, "it is quite futile to argue that man is small compared to the cosmos; for man was always small compared to the nearest tree."[46] Human greatness depends on the ability to take in the entire universe in the form of knowledge and then respond in ways that reverberate without fixed limit. Aristotle saw intellectual knowledge as the human ability to become other than itself without ceasing to be itself. This mysterious human power invites endless inquiry and scientific data, but nothing can eliminate the mystery within this fragile animal.

Frederick Turner, acknowledging that measured in time and space human kind is a tiny speck, adds: "Measured in a more fundamental way, by density and complexity of information, we are already the largest objects in the universe."[47] This statement turns against itself to try to shake up the understanding. Measuring the humans as the "largest objects in the universe" is a metaphorical way to go beyond mere objects to "density and complexity."

The statement relies on the word "information," which has become a favored word in the computer age. At least until recently, information was that aspect of knowledge reducible to quantity and measurement. The computer screen can provide a number for exactly how many bits of information are stored there. Many writers today are using "information" with a richer meaning, signifying (human) density and complexity. They may succeed, given that the term's etymology does not confine the word to the superficial, mechanical, and impersonal meaning it has recently had.

For the present, however, I would be resistant to saying that "responsible to" is all a question of information. There are "well-informed" people who lack moral depth. There are other people who, though lacking the requisite material to play Jeopardy, are knowledgeable in morally complex ways. That is not a glorification of ignorance and lack of information. Rather, it is a denial that education consists in acquiring information and that the person having the most information is the best educated. Alfred North Whitehead criticized a view of education as preparing someone to some day read off answers to the universe. A better view, thought Whitehead, was that education was what remained after you have forgotten all (the information) you had learned.[48]

Since all of our language implies spatial imagery and measurements of some kind, we can never entirely escape from physical models with shape and size. For imagining an organizing of elements, our language in recent centuries has been dominated by pyramids of power. The language of organization and moral discourse reflect each other. The superior is above, the inferior is below. To have *high* ideals is desirable because a person should strive to go higher in life. In Lawrence Kohlberg's scheme of moral development, it is assumed without question that higher is better. The "man" who can abstract to a higher and higher level will be motivated by *principle*, not dragged down by his body, his feelings, his family, or his friends.[49]

A morality of responsibility, when it has to use direction, would trust more to depth than to height. For the morally mature person, judgment comes from deeper down. Of course, depth can be taken in a two-dimensional way, "down" being a linear path. Responsibility needs a three-dimensional, organic movement, which can include movement to the depths and then rising, to a within and then outward, to a circling about a center that gathers in the periphery.

When imagery is confined to a triangle or pyramid, then change is limited to a form of leveling. Modern political revolutions have been intent on getting rid of class structure, of changing human relations from status to contract. The individual would be freed from the domination of aristocrats and nobles. But even in the United States we end up with an upper class, middle class, lower class; the pride of the country is that the middle class is large and can keep expanding. People who would like to get to the top may feel resentment toward those who are there. Did they really earn their way up there? Does the top deserve their power and wealth, or is it at the expense of the bottom and middle?

Except for a very few people at the pinnacle, rebellion in the name of egalitarianism sounds desirable. Despite the supposed liberty of the individual, people experience their work life and much of the rest of life as caught up in pyramids of power over which they have no effective power. One can count on applause when the politician delivers the line: Let's get government off the backs of the people.

It is not surprising that, in the absence of any other imagery and language, ecological literature absorbs this rhetoric. Faceless bureaucrats have built a pyramid of privilege on the backs of the (equally) oppressed. The surprising part in an ecological application is that the oppressive bureaucracy is the human race. All the other species play on a level field. The humans—apparently because they were told by the Bible—broke out of the pack and declared themselves sole rulers and owners. Their brief period of delusion now coming to an end, their task is to climb down from the heights in their picture of the universe and recognize what they have always been: one of the millions of species that populate the earth. Join the democracy of all creatures in which equality reigns. Life will be more harmonious when "man" finds his place in "nature."

The one word that is used to summarize what is wrong is "hierarchy," an ordering of elements according to rank and importance. It is difficult to find any uses of "hierarchy" with a positive meaning in contemporary writing.[50] Even people in business and government who are trying to reform organization say they are opposed to hierarchy, apparently having a pyramid in mind as the only possibility for hierarchic arrangement.

A profile of Arthur Sulzburger, Jr., publisher of the *New York Times*, quotes him as saying, "for the *New York Times* to become all it can and for it to flourish in the years ahead, we must reduce our dependency on hierarchy in decision-making of every sort."[51] One gathers from the article that Sulzburger wishes to encourage open discussions in the newsroom and on retreats, better employee–management relations, more equitable treatment of blacks and women. While the publisher can say "we are trying to become more egalitarian," the newspaper is surely one of the most precisely structured organizations in the country; it carefully prepares people years in advance to take the next step into key positions at the paper. A *New York Times* without any kind of hierarchy is simply unimaginable.[52]

Similarly, in the complicated centers of government, power is channeled by organizations that determine order and importance. Elizabeth Drew, in a description of the Clinton White House, quotes one advisor: "The president doesn't want hierarchy. . . . He wants all kinds of advisors swirling around him constantly." She also quotes cabinet secretary Robert Reich's explanation that those close to the president are products of the 1960s "who when young were in reaction to the hierarchical society we inherited."[53] The president may want advisors "swirling around him constantly," but there is some process by which those few dozen or hundred got chosen to be those advisors; and "swirling" has a rhythm and order to it; otherwise, listening and answering by someone in the middle cannot happen.[54]

Hierarchy is a word that means sacred order. An objection to the sacred part (hier-) would be understandable, but when people dismiss hierarchy they seem to be rejecting the order of either human design or the natural world of patterns that rank elements within a whole. The attempt to reject the order in hier-archy can only lead to an-archy, a chaotic transition to some new hierarchy. All "men" are not equal in all ways. Some have bigger bodies than others; even more important for establishing their kind of order, some men have more guns.

The term hierarchy goes back to a pseudonymous Syrian monk in the sixth century, whose writings had profound effect in the Middle

Ages. The character known today as Pseudo-Dionysius wrote a treatise on hierarchy, the sacred order of the universe.[55] He imagined a world similar to that described in the first chapter of the book of Ezekiel: circles within circles. As in nearly all religious traditions, the imagery is circular and spherical. God was not imagined as a CEO in an office at the top of a skyscraper but as the ultimate power at the still center of the universe. The humans in this image were not at the top (there was no top), but somewhere near the center. Humans were not the most important creatures; angels were superior to them. Angelology plays a key role in Thomas Aquinas's *Summa Theologica*. Perhaps there is some significance to the unexpected and widespread reemergence today of angels.

Whether or not there are beings superior to the humans, men and women played a central role in the hierarchy of creation. Everything was oriented around the center, and that is where human kind was imagined to be. In that sense, everything was *for* the human, but only a very small part of the world could and should be *used* by humans. The world was there for being blessed, listened to, appreciated, cared for. By entering human life, things were further exalted in their importance.[56]

Everything in the hierarchy had its place, although the humans were not so arrogant as to think that they knew the place of each thing. Standing in the middle of a small clearing, the humans cannot see over the heads of the giraffes, the whales, the dolphins, the bears, and their other close kin. Eventually, they developed a looking glass to survey the sky and another to see creatures invisible to the human eye. They must still listen deep within themselves for the voice of each creature, somehow present in the human, the "workshop of all creation."

I think that this imagery is not irrelevant to the organization of the *New York Times* or the White House. The place to listen is not at the top but in the middle. Knowledge needs to move in a community exchange rather than up a single line from individual to individual. Of course, a pyramid is sometimes the best ordering if a task is precisely defined and the aim is to assemble a product. However, as a *comprehensive* basis for organizing political, religious, or educational communities, the pyramid is disastrously confining. Even in the business world today, advances in technology or the production of a good newspaper require another form of hierarchy than a pyramid.

In the nonhuman world of organization, we usually do not have to design circles within circles; they are already there. Magnificent cyclical designs surround us, most of them beyond our view or comprehension. Throughout history, humans have tracked their way through these designs, never seeing a complete picture of the cycles they were interfering with. Conflict and pain are part of the cycles of nature. Humans cannot eliminate the pain, but they should try to avoid adding to it.

On regular occasions, I hear a bang on my window as a bird flies into it, usually knocking itself unconscious. I know that shortly afterward a cat will come by and will proudly display to me the live bird in its mouth. As I go out to try to revive the bird and let it fly away, I am aware of being in the slightly absurd position of stopping a cat from doing what cats naturally do. However, since my window seems to be built on an ancient flight path, I also feel it is my interference (or the house builder's) that has brought this bird to its current plight.

Much of ethics today is not much more effective than temporarily saving one stricken animal, a gesture ridiculously disproportionate to the sea of violence, suffering, and destruction all about us. But responsibility requires responding to the situation we are in. Devoting one's time and energy to the care of one small being is the basis for any universalistic claims. Small gestures have to restrain grand visions.

The loss of a hierarchic principle would not bring humans closer to the rest of the world. Denial of hierarchy is simply an evasion of responsibility. The humans are superior in receptivity; their superiority is an obligation, a burden. Humans are the best at suffering, the basis for their glory and also the reason for their fears. It is because they suffer the world, that is, receive it into themselves, that their lives are richer in quality than are other species. They can also foresee their deaths and suffer not only in dying but in thinking about dying. Other animals can suffer painful deaths, but only the humans get the news six months in advance so that they can start experiencing a long process of dying.

Suffering is the basis of human uniqueness. The humans are the most unique of all the animals; they are the most different of animals because they are like all the animals. The term "unique" offers one possibility for dealing with the issue of same and different. It is a quite commonly used word but one whose paradox is seldom noticed. "Unique" is one of the most unique words in the language.[57]

As a start to exploring the meaning of "unique," one must acknowledge that grammarians often insist that terms such as more, very, or most cannot be placed before unique; either a thing is unique or it is not. But people regularly say "very unique" or "most unique" because they sense that unique is *always* a comparative term. When people say "very unique" they mean "very nearly unique" or closer to unique than another. "Unique" means different from all others. But since a thing cannot be different from all other things (they are at least the same in being things), uniqueness is a way of describing a process of increasing difference.

There are two directions that this process of increasing difference can take. One is a process of exclusion, the other a process of inclusion or at least the power to include. In the sequence 333M, 33M, 3M, M, the last element in the set can be seen as the most unique. It has the *fewest* notes in common with the other elements. It is almost totally different by way of exclusion. In an opposite direction, with the sequence a, ab, abc, abcd, the last element can be called the most unique. It is different from all the others by having the *most* notes in common and by being the most inclusive.

In neither case is the last element finally and totally unique. In the first set, the last element has one note, but it is still the same as the other elements in being an element. In the second set, there is the possibility of an element abcde following in sequence. No being can have no notes in common with all others; no being, so long as history endures, can have all notes in common with the others.

Uniqueness by increasing exclusiveness belongs to the two-dimensional world. As one slices up space, or time imagined spatially, one can approach a uniqueness of exclusion: "this was a unique event." The Greeks thought there were atoms, so named because they had no characteristics except their indivisibility. We now know that not only can atoms be split, but a new, complex world is inside. Atoms have lots of common notes with others; protons or electrons have fewer. When humans try to make themselves unique in this way, they look for a characteristic that no one else has; the result is usually eccentric and unsuccessful. There are only so many notes to establish such difference. Adolescent fads in rebellion against authority produce a depressing sameness: the clothes, the hairstyle, the drug. A haircut cannot be totally unique; it cannot even be very unique once a few other people start imitating it.

The specifically human uniqueness can only be achieved by *not try-*

ing to assert one's unique property. The paradox, which every post-adolescent should have learned, is that the formation of the self comes about by communion. One has to let go and become unique by letting the whole world flow in. What we discover is our kinship with everything and everyone. The I becomes utterly distinctive, humanly unique, because of its incorporation of human and nonhuman life.[58]

A nonhuman animal has a degree of uniqueness based on a process of openness to the other. A dog or a horse can have a distinct personality, different from all the others. But the human being's *nature* is *to be* unique; its nature is an openness to all other natures. The human being is born unique; its vocation is to become more unique. Born with little or nothing that can be called instincts, the human is the most open to development. Being less programmed at birth makes for more excitement, joy, and fear. Becoming unique requires a constant process of being responsible to the world and responsible for one's actions.

Some recent thinkers have come to the conclusion that there is no self. The human self having been "decentered," it is now declared "fictive."[59] This stream of thought is badly in need of both feminist and ecological movements. The self needs a recentering, but it cannot be the dictatorial self of early modern thinking. A self that listens to men, women, children, animals, trees, and rocks will be able to relax and let conversation and organic flow carry the burden. "Such a self," writes Jane Flax, "is simultaneously embodied, gendered, social, and unique."[60]

The experience of the contemporary person is often one of suddenly finding no one who will give orders: neither a father in heaven nor a father on earth and no stern, rational rule-giver within the self. Too narrow a focus on fathers and sons left us unprepared to deal with "mother nature." The man who had thought nature was under his feet and was totally under control may now feel engulfed by nature. Peaceful surrender may seem preferable to a hopeless attempt to conquer, but it means the disappearance of moral responsibility.

If one begins with the question "to whom and to what am I responsible," then today's ecological upheaval holds the possibility of regrounding politics, business, ethics, religion. Neither Christianity, Judaism, Islam nor other major religions are necessarily opposed to ecology. Religions, in fact, are needed sources of the imagery, language, and attitude needed today. In turn, Christian, Jewish, Muslim, and other religions need to rethink their doctrines in light of our new awareness of human–nonhuman relations. It is not an exaggeration to say that the chief religious movement in the world today, especially after the fall of communism, is ecology or environmentalism. But it is badly in need of conversation with older religions that have more experience with directing passionate feelings into at least harmless and possibly productive expression.

CHAPTER 7

RESPONSIBLY PRESENT

This chapter on how responsibility is related to past and future divides neatly into two parts. In fact, the division may be too neat and requires some initial resistance before past and future are discussed. In this fourth of the five modern splits that responsibility can heal, what is the temporal split? Are we dealing with a split between the past and the future, or between the past and the present? Or could there be a three-way split of past, present, and future? That we experience some kind of temporal rift is clear enough, but there seems to be ambiguity about naming the division.

In a split between past and present, the future seems neglected; and these days no one wants to be accused of neglecting the future. In a split between past and future, the present seems to disappear; and surely the present is where we are. If we take all three names of time, then the present might be imagined as the bridge between past and future.

That conclusion—the present is the bridge between past and future—may seem like a truism. Isn't that the common sense view which practically everyone lives by? But there are different ways one might imagine a bridging. In the dominant image that centuries of clock ticking have given us, the present divides but does not unify past and future.

In this modern image, the present is a point that is always disappearing. The past is behind our backs; the future rushes to meet us at the rate of sixty seconds a minute. The present is always here, but when we try to grab it, it has always just gone. There is also a peculiarity about the way we speak of the future, as if it were a realm of existing time and indeed, for some people, the most important time; but it does not exist at all as a location. Any kind of bridge that the present could offer is not between two shores with the same reality to them.

These paradoxes that we encounter as soon as we start thinking about time come from the image we have of it as a series of points constituting a line. Edward Hall calls this image "monochronic," one thing after another, scheduled in sequence; it is like lining up for the store clerk.[1] With this image, the point in the middle is the present; the points to the left are the past; those to the right are the future. A contribution of the Watergate era to contemporary speech is the phrase "at that point in time." Critics often say that the phrase is redundant. Someone saying "at that time" would mean the same thing. The popular redundancy is nevertheless revealing. When asked to think temporally, people go for *points* of time.

I wish to argue in this chapter that time imagined as a series of points leaves no place for responsibility. If the first moment of responsibility is listening to, then responsibility has no place in a line of temporal points. Where is the human self to stand if the past has disappeared, the future has not arrived, and the present disappears under one's feet?

In the metaphor that I used in the previous chapter, time needs to be three dimensions rather than two. A two-dimensional view of time is especially hard on the present. At least the past and the future both get a *segment* of the two-dimensional world. The present is reduced to a mathematical existence of one dimension. In contrast, within a three-dimensional meaning of time, the present becomes all there is. With its breadth and depth, the present is able to include and preserve the past. The present can also open to and herald the future; in John Dewey's phrase, the future is "the quickening possibilities of the present."

It would be much easier to speak of responsibility if we had richer imagery and language regarding time. And indeed every novel, play, short story, or poem that challenges a meaning of time without breadth and depth helps to create the context for responsibility. Movies can be especially helpful in playing with time, resisting the image of a single series of points. But there are on the other side relentless pressures to keep time marching along in proper sequence. Our economic system does not deal kindly with those who forget that "time is money" and that one must keep the money moving to have a sound investment in the future.

While it would be a great advantage to have rich images of time before discussing responsibility, the opposite movement is more likely. The cultivation of responsibility joins with artistic expressions to enrich people's sense of time. The past becomes richer in and by the act of listening to it. The future is grasped in the responsible actions of our present lives rather than in just peering forward. The present is the focus of responsibility, a present that has bodily depth and spiritual character. A person who lives out responsibility the best he or she can has a sense of the unity of time. There are still some fragmenting and clashes of fragments, but the single process of listening and answering provides the center of temporal unity.

To test out this meaning of responsibility in time, I will examine the question of corporate failures in past history and the relation of people in the present to these past events. In addition, I will examine responsibility in the present to and for the future. The future does not exist as a reality to interact with, but we interact with corporations that will still exist in the future. And one special place where the future already exists is in children's lives. How do adults, especially parents, responsibly act in relation to children?

The Past as Present Memory

The heading for this section is taken from a statement by St. Augustine, one of the first great thinkers to reflect on the nature of time. For Augustine, time is a three-fold present: the present as we experience it, the past as a present memory, and the future as a present expectation.[2] This inclusion of the past in the present is a common experience for anyone grasping the nature of time from *within* time. When time is looked at as an external object, it takes on the character of a succession of points, the present disappearing into the receding past. That picture leaves out the self that experiences time. For the "time-full self," writes H. Richard Niebuhr, "the past and the future are not the no-longer and the not-yet; they are extensions of the present. They are the still-present and the already-present."[3]

For now, I concentrate on the past as the still-present and on what this conception of the past does to responsibility. In the modern world there is usually a denial of responsibility for anything that happened in the past. The individual's responsibility is limited to what he or she does in the present moment. But that has not solved the problem of responsibility, and it has led to vague feelings of generalized guilt. In an individual's life, something done ten or thirty years ago may fester just below the surface of the time-full self. Orders from the will to put the incident behind and get on with life do not succeed. The memory may have to surface completely before it can finally be accepted into a person's identity. "All that we have felt, thought and willed from our earliest infancy is there, leaning over the present which is about to join it, pressing against the portals of consciousness that would fain leave it outside."[4]

In the twentieth century, we have come to recognize this phenomenon, or at least we are not surprised by it, in the lives of the sick and the criminal. But more generally, anyone who reflects on the hidden chambers of one's own heart catches glimmers of, and is sometimes startled to a greater awareness by, the presence of the past in the present. As a William Faulkner character says: "The past is not dead. It's not even past."

The past that is in us seems to spill out beyond our individual selves. Does not my past include my mother's life and my grandfather's experience? No clear line can be drawn across the historical record to exclude all trace of the past from the time-full self of the present. That fact can be an enrichment of personal life, a gift from people that we have never known, who "lived faithfully a hidden life and rest in unvisited tombs."[5] However, it is also the basis of vague and generalized guilt that weighs upon personal conscience. In chapter 5, I examined the idea of "collective guilt" that spreads to all the individuals in an organization when crimes are done by the organization. Here I extend the question to crimes done in the past. Is a forty-year-old U.S. Christian responsible for the bombing of Hiroshima? For the seventeenth-century clearing of the land in Massachusetts? For the fifteenth-century killing of Jews in Toledo?

Before anyone attempts to give a yes or no answer to such questions, it is important to have an adequate image of how we are connected to the past. Likewise, a comprehensive and consistent idea of responsibility has to be brought to this question. One must keep in mind that responsibility begins with being "responsible to." The man or woman who is not "responsible for" events that occurred before his or her birth is not necessarily absolved of responsibility. He or she may have a strong obligation to be responsible to those events.

Before examining a few examples of such events, it will be helpful to reflect further on how we are related to the past. The realization that time has depth and that the past is still with us arises from intimate encounter with another human being. We become present to ourselves in the presence of another personal being.[6] Responsibility as a listening and an answering to someone establishes the person as time-full, with memory and hopes. When interpersonal exchange is not strong enough to sustain acceptance of the present, then a person clings desperately to some element in the past or scrambles furiously toward an imagined point in the future.

Ironically, when people's lives are a mess—whatever their degree of fault for the condition—they are often said to be too present-oriented. The poor, for example, are said to live too much in the present, not planning for the future. In fact, most poor people are desperately concerned with the future, while they cling to whatever they have of the past. That desperation prevents a full experience of the present. "Do you believe in the life to come?" asks Clov, a character in Beckett's *Endgame*. "Mine was always that," replies Hamm, "moment upon moment, pattering down, like the millet grains . . . and all life long you wait for that to mount up to a life."[7]

In the twentieth century we have a whole profession dedicated to helping people integrate the past in the present. The person of the therapist and the conversation between client and therapist provide the context for accepting the past as present memory. Sometimes the process fails when the therapist and the client traipse around in memories simply as past, as things to be collected, assembled, reconstructed. The focus has to be kept steadily on the present and the presence of the past in the present.[8]

A breakthrough often occurs between people when they simply stop wrangling over different interpretations of past events. All the talk, which may have been necessary to get to that moment, ceases. In silence, often accompanied by ritual, the past is accepted as the past. Its reality is not denied; it is a fold in the present, forever there but not the sole determinant of what happens now. "To have character is to know that I move in a history I neither summon nor command, which carries consequences none the less for my choices and conduct."[9]

The link between the individual person and the larger history is found in the idea of *tradition*. We do not live as one drop in an ocean of time; we live as a thread of personal life interwoven with the larger fabric of history. Nearly everyone today lives in a cross-stitching of several traditions. One of those traditions can have a liberating effect on another. Then, too, the effect can be confusion rather than liberation when one tradition overlaps and conflicts with another. It helps to recall that a single tradition itself always has conflicting elements, even though people entrusted with the preservation of a tradition try to hush up the disagreements. "Traditions, when vital, embody continuities of conflict."[10]

The tragedy is that those who try to preserve tradition as a single, monolithic way of thinking and acting give a bad name to the very thing they are trying to save. They try to "pass on the tradition," whereas tradition is itself the passing on. What has to be passed on is the sense of vitality, reverence, and openness. When people try to pass on tradition, they succeed only in passing on the inert remains of a tradition. The enemy of a living Tradition is dead traditions.[11]

Tradition means "to hand on." The metaphorical basis of the word is tactile: human hands touching human hands. Tradition runs into conflict with speech that has been codified in writing. The oral/aural metaphor of responsibility often joins with tradition's tactile nature to resist written conclusions about how things have to be. Tradition inspires a rereading of statements from a different perspective on life. Tradition is often the best friend of the radical reformer who knows the limits of human nature's changeableness.[12]

The term conservative is often used of people who are obsessed with an image of a good world fifty years ago or who know the truth because of a text from the fourth or the seventeenth century. The term conservative would best apply to people who love the whole tradition, listening to the disparate voices that challenge faddish ideologies of the moment. "Tradition is the democracy of the dead," writes G. K. Chesterton, "the extension of the franchise to that most obscure of all classes: our ancestors." Tradition refuses to submit to "the small oligarchy of those who are walking around."[13]

In modern times the term tradition is closely linked to religion. We speak of "traditional religions" or "Buddhist tradition" or—the peculiar abstraction invented for the twentieth century—"Judeo-Christian tradition." In this usage, tradition is usually taken to be a drag upon progress, the chief opponent of a rational improvement of society. The sixteenth-century Protestant reformers attacked *traditions*, particular accretions of the medieval church, while speaking positively about Tradition.[14] Later reformers were not always as careful to distinguish. In the eighteenth-century Enlightenment, Protestant Christianity was sometimes spared the attack directed most specifically at Catholic and Jewish traditions. But all religion eventually suffers when tradition becomes a negative term, one designating the dead weight of centuries past.[15]

The struggle against tradition, in large part successful, has not proved to be the great boon that the eighteenth century optimistically looked forward to, when "the sons would be liberated from the prejudices of their fathers." Along with religious traditions, other forms of tradition also lost out. There was an educational tradition in the West, rooted in the classics of Greek and Roman literature; it was overthrown in the name of a more functional, relevant, up-to-date education.

In John Dewey's earliest writings on education, the great opponent was "traditional education." A progressive movement was needed to modernize education and base it on the new psychology. In the 1930s, Dewey still describes the conflict as progressive versus traditional, even though by that time the traditional was in tatters. Dewey was by then unhappy with the progressive revolution, but his opposition of progressive and traditional left him no alternative except to push on: more scientific method is the only hope of the future.[16]

Recent decades have seen some softening of the assumption that modern equals good, tradition equals bad. Tradition can turn narrow and reactionary, but some form of tradition is unavoidable. A particular way of doing human acts is passed on to each newcomer in the race, starting with the way parents care for children. Each family in turn is linked into some composition of ethnic, political, and religious history. The particular language that each of us first learns shapes our way of life far more than we are usually aware.

The human memory is not a record of events in the past, stretched out behind us, but the history of myself and my people alive in the present. In our memories, what happened twenty years ago may be closer to the present than what happened last week. Indeed, something that happened centuries or millennia ago may continue to be a living memory, exercising considerable influence on today's actions. On the Jewish sense of tradition, Yosef Yerushalmi writes that "memory flowed above all through two channels: ritual and recital."[17] Whatever terrible things may have happened in the past, they have to be remembered if only for the purpose of forgiveness. Adam Michnik said that while he was in prison "I thought up the formula that one has to be for amnesty and against amnesia."[18]

Amnesty and forgiveness are needed both for the bad treatment visited on my people and the bad treatment that they gave to others. The second, involving the asking of forgiveness, is often the more difficult part because it is unclear to whom the appeal can be made. This is where vague feelings of guilt circle about us. We deny any kind of collective guilt for the sins of our great-grandfathers, but we are aware of enjoying the fruits of lands seized, people enslaved, investments made. J. R. Lucas writes that "as we enter into the inheritance of our predecessors, we undertake some responsibility for what they did in the process of producing those goods we now enjoy." This statement does *not* say that we are responsible for what was done by our predecessors; it refers to undertaking a responsibility to do something now "to make reparation for what was done in the course of producing those benefits."[19] That does not seem feasible without acknowledgment of traditions and corporate realities that link us with our ancestors.

Some Examples

A business corporation can be held responsible for a crime that occurred many years ago. The corporation can be responsible even though none of the officials was alive when the event occurred. The law thereby recognizes that a corporation's responsibility is not just a collection of individual responsibilities. People in the corporation may seem to be unfairly stigmatized by such an attribution of responsibility, but as present officials they have a responsibility *to* the past. That can include learning not to make the same mistake again as well as to make whatever restitution is possible in the present. Corporations, including the business kind, have traditional cultures or ways of humanly doing things; they possess a set of beliefs, rules, and rituals. To go to work for a corporation is to agree that it is a tradition one wishes to be associated with and that one's personal reputation is affected by that association.

The business corporation, however, is only a small slice of the problem. The more common form this question takes is our responsibility as a member of a national, racial, or religious group for actions in the distant past.

During the last decade, the world has experienced a succession of wars rooted in ancient ethnic or religious conflicts. Whatever crimes were committed, they often go back long before the birth of any of today's combatants. Each side has its interpretation of who is responsible for the bloodshed, but there is little agreement on any of the facts. The person who grows up in the maelstrom has a responsibility to listen to the voices of the past, not just the ones that prop up self-justifying explanations for today's deeds. The past may be so buried in myth and fiction that there is never going to be agreement on responsibility for actions in the past. What contemporary leaders are at a minimum responsible for is not to inflame the situation with irresponsible accusations.

Northern Ireland is a case in point where officials traded unhelpful accusations for decades. Then, partly inspired by South Africa's example, the two (or more) sides began to use their words more carefully, along with restraint on violence. In February, 1986, the BBC broadcast "At the Edge of Union," an interview with Michael McGuiness, the reputed IRA leader. The Thatcher government, contrary to tradition, tried to block the BBC from showing the program. In that interview, McGuiness said: "Every death in Northern Ireland is the responsibility of the British government." Margaret Thatcher's response was that "the IRA is responsible for over two thousand deaths" (that number included killings by police, the British army, and the Protestant paramilitaries). To any outsider, it seems highly unlikely that either statement could be true.

The beginning of a breakthrough toward peace did not come from any agreement about who was really responsible. After various feints and gestures, the IRA declared a cease-fire and published a statement in August, 1994, saying: "A solution will only be found as a result of inclusive negotiations. Others, not least the British government, have a duty to face up to their responsibilities."[20] That second sentence is still aggressive in asserting that it is the British government that has to face its responsibilities. When the so called "Framework Document" was published in February, 1995, a balance was struck, even if "responsibilities" is left vague: "Both governments expect that significant responsibilities, including meaningful functions at executive level, will be a feature of such an agreement."[21]

If the British and the Irish can find a way to work out these "responsibilities," there may be hope for Northern Ireland. One could also imagine hope in several dozen other civil wars that seem to go on endlessly. It would be hopelessly simplistic to suggest a formula for Bosnia, Somalia, Rwanda, Palestine, and conflicts still to come in the former Soviet Union. Nevertheless, it can be said that clearer, cleaner lines of how to talk about responsibility are a step.

The responsibility is *to* the past and *for* the present action. In a form to be described later in this chapter, there is also responsibility to the future. The fighting stops when key people are shaken out of their insistence on a strict accounting for past misdeeds and they take a good look at their present. The gesture of a single person at the opportune moment can break through a paralysis of wills. Or if there is response to the children on both sides, then the terms of the dispute change. A lot of unresolvable disagreements over the past can become simpler when the focus is on the question: What kind of world do we want for our children?

The fiftieth anniversary of the end of World War II reawakened some unresolved feelings about who was responsible for what. In this case, some of the people responsible for World War II decisions were still alive. The question is of a different kind for the population born since the 1940s. Between the United States and Japan there were some bruised feelings about accepting responsibility for the events of more than a half century ago. In U.S. speech, "Pearl Harbor" is an implied accusation; in Japanese speech "Hiroshima" imputes a crime against humanity to the United States.

The internal struggle of the Japanese to come to grips with responsibility for the war boiled over into public rancor at the time of the emperor's death in 1988. The emperor "had been formally responsible for everything, and by holding him responsible for nothing, everybody was absolved, except, of course, for a number of military and civilian scapegoats."[22] Thus when the mayor of Nagasaki, Hitoshi Motoshima, said, "I do believe that the emperor bore responsibility for the war," it started a furor that was hard to understand from outside the country.[23]

Among the letters in support of Hitoshi Motoshima was one from a retired mechanic who wrote as follows: "It is our responsibility to history to analyze scientifically the mechanism which has shaped popular consciousness since the Meiji period and led to war . . . only then can the question of our leaders' war responsibility be fully resolved, not by 'victor's justice,' but by the Japanese people themselves."[24] This statement distinguishes between responsibility to the past and responsibility for the past. The duty to respond *to* the past lies upon the whole population, whether or not they were alive during World War II. Those who were alive bear some responsibility for war actions, depending on their age, knowledge, place in the military or government, and how they followed their consciences. Responsibility for present action includes educating oneself and others about mistakes in the past that should not be repeated. The political theorist Maruyama Masao has called the prewar Japanese government a "system of irresponsibilities—the Shrine, the Official, the Outlaw."[25] That system has been changing since the end of the war. The full acknowledgment of Japanese responsibility (including the part before Pearl Harbor) has still to be completed. But after a long struggle in the Japanese parliament in 1995, Prime Minister Tomiichi Murayama was able to offer an apology in the form of denying the principle that "the military elite, not the nation as a whole was responsible for wartime atrocities."[26]

United States responsibility for its war activities is especially focused on the dropping of two atomic bombs on Hiroshima and Nagasaki. In March, 1995, Hitoshi Motoshima in a speech to foreign correspondents said: "I think the atomic bombings were one of the two greatest crimes against humanity in the twentieth century, along with the Holocaust."[27] At the time of the bombings, the vast majority of people in the United States approved the action. Since then, occasional voices have been raised in criticism of the bombings as unnecessary and immoral. The U.S. government has shown no inclination to apologize. Among the monuments from more than 150 nations in the Peace Park in Hiroshima, the United States is conspicuously absent. The Smithsonian Institution had planned for 1995 an exhibition entitled "The Last Act: The Atomic Bomb and the End of World War II." Although historians tried to give what they thought was a balanced view of the history, a bitter dispute broke out. In January, 1995, the Institution's secretary, Michael Heyman, announced cancellation of the exhibit.

Especially for veterans of World War II and for many others of their age, any criticism of the bombings seems disloyal and naive. It was a brutal war, and the undeniable fact is that the war quickly ended after the atomic bombings. The only alternative, it is argued, was an invasion of Japan. That step could have involved more deaths, both Japanese and U.S., than the atomic bombs caused. Estimates of what would have been the number of casualties vary wildly.[28]

Behind what appears to be a dispute over numbers lies other issues not quantifiable. It is sometimes said that the United States would never have used the bomb against a European city, that part of the motivation was racial.[29] Was the United States engaged in an act of vengeance for Pearl Harbor? In the minds of many Japanese, their country became a victim, or at least there is a symmetry of immorality: we brutalized Nanking, you obliterated Hiroshima. Any suggestion of symmetry infuriates many vocal U.S. citizens.

The solution to this dispute may come in another generation or two when the people who are most emotionally involved have left the scene. The question will then have changed, but it will not go away. Time does *not* heal all wounds unless it gets some help. Bitter feelings can be lodged in the souls of the next generations even when people of those generations are mostly ignorant of who started what and who did what to whom. Historians have to keep doing their best to piece together the data and to form the most accurate record they can. In this case, accurate history will not be the decisive element in the dispute, but it at least provides some ballast and some limits for arguments.

The moral problem for a U.S. citizen is not to judge the Japanese but to take some moral stand regarding actions of the U.S. government. It is neither necessary nor helpful in this case to try to create a calculus of immoralities, to prove that whatever we did they did worse. Undeniably in war one horrible deed is met with what is as bad or worse. There is a useful body of literature developed in the Middle Ages that insisted on moral restraint even in war. This writing is tragically and obscenely referred to as "just war theory." Wars are massive concatenations of injustice.[30] Neither side can escape with clean hands, but there nonetheless remains a need to restrain injustice even in the midst of warfare. Those who dismiss any moral concerns with the slogan that "all's fair in love and war" are cultivating the ground for the next war in the souls of their enemy.

People who defend the bombing of Hiroshima seldom bring up Nagasaki. Even if one could make a case for Hiroshima, the second bombing would remain indefensible. Of course, the shock of the first bomb so numbed both sides that the second could not have the same effect. That is the way with morality. As the Talmud says: "One good deed leads to another good deed and one transgression leads to another transgression; for the reward for a good deed is another good deed and the reward for a transgression is another transgression."[31]

One vicious act makes the next vicious act more smoothly possible. Bombing Hiroshima in August did not seem such a big jump from the firebombing of Tokyo in March, 1945, or the bombing of Dresden a few weeks before that. And indeed Hiroshima stands out not for being entirely different from what had preceded it but for being the same in most respects, though bringing the evil of war into a culminating act. The V-2 bombing of London was unique; Dresden was more unique; Hiroshima was still more unique. Nagasaki was the most unique.

The fact that Hiroshima/Nagasaki was a case of atomic rather than "conventional" warfare made the moral step a profound one. Things could have been different; another country might have developed the bomb and used it more recklessly. The simple fact remains, however, that the United States is the only nation to have used such a weapon against a civilian population. The United States has to bear that responsibility. The scientists who developed the bomb, President Harry Truman and those of his advisors who decided to use the bomb, and the military men who dropped the bombs have a greater responsibility than do other citizens. The young need to hear this acknowledgment from their elders. The reason for being responsible *to* these events is not so that we can wallow in guilt, but so that the deliberately vague sign in the Hiroshima Peace Park holds true: "Let all souls here rest in peace; for we shall not repeat the evil."

The distinction between "responsible for" and "guilty" is crucial to maintain here. That the United States, its government, and specific officials were responsible for the deed is beyond doubt. What kind of guilt, if any, to assign to particular individuals may be impossible to judge. That assignment of individual guilt is not what the rest of the world expects or needs. It is rather some assuring sign that the United States and its citizens can recognize a corporate responsibility for past actions because they are responsible to their own history. It is most important that those born since the 1940s be able to distinguish guilt and responsibility as well as responsible to and responsible for. Responsibility does not disappear simply because you were not in on the deciding action, in fact had not been born. (A Gallup Poll in 1995 showed that almost a fourth of the population knew virtually nothing about an atomic bomb attack.)[32]

Every day at the museum in Hiroshima, bus loads of school children arrive to go through the exhibit. It is disconcerting to be a spectator from the United States surrounded by a sea of Japanese children. I had the urge to start screaming "I didn't do it. I'm not guilty. I was your age when this happened." Being driven into screaming denials of guilt would not have been morally helpful to me nor intelligibly helpful to them. However, a little moral disconcertion never hurt anyone, especially if one is challenged to see a moral issue from the other person's point of view. Ian Buruma, describing a visit to Hiroshima, expresses resentment "when schoolchildren approach you, prompted by their teachers, to ask what you think of peace."[33] Whatever the motivation of the schoolteachers, it is still a good question for a child to ask an adult.

The corporate act of the United States that is still painfully present just below the surface is the disaster of the war in Vietnam. The war was divisive when it was being fought, and many of the cast of characters are still ready to bring out their arguments. The young men who fought the war (their average age, nineteen) carry their horrors with them in middle age. Everyone else, whatever agreement or disagreement they expressed at the time, carries unresolved feelings. Today's young are uncomprehending but sense the bitter aftertaste in the country. Today, a prosperous-looking Vietnam, angling for economic cooperation with the United States, sends a mixed message: what the United States did could not have been so bad if they are looking so good, but also, what was the point of the whole fiasco that slaughtered three million people?

Bitter feelings were rekindled by the publication of Robert McNamara's *In Retrospect: The Tragedy and Lessons of Vietnam*.[34] Ironically, McNamara's reason for publishing the book was to cure the country of the cynicism engendered by the war. The book seemed to do the opposite; both sides felt worse. One must credit McNamara with the courage to acknowledge his mistakes in the execution of the war. But in accepting so much responsibility for it being "McNamara's war," the responsibility of many other people might be obscured. More important, as nearly every reviewer and interviewer pointed out, the confession of fault stops at the most crucial moment when McNamara failed to oppose the war.

One of the most crucial sentences in the book is a statement of dizzying logic. As to why he did not resign and criticize the war, McNamara says: "I believe that would have been a violation of my responsibility to the President and my oath to uphold the Constitution."[35] Note the unusual use of "responsible to." I have said repeatedly in this book that the question is seldom asked "to whom and to what am I responsible?" Here McNamara does ask the question but he responds with tragic narrowness and confusion. A secretary of state should not publicly oppose the president he is serving. But the point was to resign so that he could disagree. Responsibility to his country and its constitution, responsibility to thousands of young men he had started on the way to death, responsibility to a war-ravaged land and its people would seem to demand opposition to the war. That McNamara could not see that in 1968 is not surprising; it would have required great wisdom and courage. That McNamara in 1995 still could not see the point made the rest of his confession seem hollow.[36]

When one grapples with responsibility to and for the past, the case of Nazi Germany is perhaps the most dramatic and most complex case of the twentieth century. Despite the complexity, the same rules of grammar for responsibility apply. An adequate image of time is indispensable as the precondition for discussing responsibility. The time-full present does include the past which does not disappear behind our backs but is layered within our bodies and within the earth. When Ronald Reagan was criticized for going to Bitburg in 1985, he replied: "I don't think we ought to focus on the past. I want to focus on the future. I want to put that history behind me."[37]

Reagan should not be severely judged for articulating what is so widespread a notion of time. Nonetheless, the straight line into the future is an image that invites the shirking of responsibility to the past, confused accusations of collective guilt, and a failure to grasp the implications of one's present actions. The only morally responsible way to "focus on the future" is to look deeply into the past that is embodied in the present.

Most Germans alive today were born after World War II. Clearly, they are not responsible for any atrocities of the war, including the Holocaust. Nonetheless, there is a German nation with its history, culture, and language that are powerfully formative. Hitler and Eichmann are part of that history as well as Goethe and Beethoven. A young person in Germany has to accept himself or herself as heir to that history, both the good and the bad. Being responsible to that history includes trying to understand the roots of World War II, acknowledging that one does not get clear of association with vicious stereotypes by a simple act of the will.

Dangerous sentiments, including anti-Semitism, have not entirely disappeared. Who or what is responsible for their origin need not and probably cannot be agreed upon. More important is acknowledging their presence in a wider culture than the skinhead fringe where they surface. A calm admission of this fact, together with thoughtful reflection on the past, would be more effective than harangues about evil youth. Officials today do have a responsibility for immediate condemnation of neo-Nazi sentiments and for clamping down on violent action under the banner of such ideology. The government can restrain evil; it cannot provide a total cure.

Immediately after the war, the allied victors did assign guilt to individual Nazi leaders. The presumption of the winner is always that the loser was in the wrong. In this case, however, certain activities of certain leaders did seem to cry out not for "victor's justice" but for a moral judgment that transcended national law. The legal basis for the Nuremberg trials was shaky. Aware of what he called the victors' "inescapable responsibility," Justice Robert Jackson made the case with admirable restraint in his opening statement: "The privilege of opening the first trial in history for crimes against the peace of the world imposes a grave responsibility. . . . That four great nations, flush with victory and stung with injury, stay the hand of vengeance and voluntarily submit their captive enemies to the judgment of law is one of the most significant tributes that power has ever paid to reason."[38]

The appeal of the judges was to reason, humanity, or (the inadequately named) "natural law." One could justifiably be skeptical about the ability of such concepts to restrain monstrous evil. Any eighteenth-century optimism about the insuperable power of reason, humanity, and natural laws has been wounded, perhaps mortally, by events of the twentieth century. Still, if reason, humanity, and natural laws are not finally adequate, we should be capable of recognizing and condemning irrational violence, savage inhumanity, and the wholesale destruction of the natural. Humans may have to be responsible beyond reason, humanity, and nature's laws, but first they have to get that far.

Whatever the legal ambiguities of the Nuremberg trials, that is not the center of today's moral ambivalence about the Nazi phenomenon. The unease is centered in the transition of the generations. As I said of Hiroshima, time will inevitably shift the question; it will not necessarily heal the nation. Some coming to grips with the past has been evident during recent decades in Germany. Jewish insistence on remembering has kept the issue to the front. Various commemorations in the past decade have been occasions to acknowledge and accept the past. While a fanatical fringe continues in total denial, few people in Germany or elsewhere are taken in by the preposterous attempt to prove that the Holocaust did not happen.

Even the best-intentioned gestures at remembrance and acknowledgment can go awry. A painful case is a talk by Philip Jenniger on the occasion of the fiftieth anniversary of *Kristallnacht*. Jenniger was at that time the speaker of the West German Parliament. He tried to give a comprehensive assessment of Germany's responsibility for the Holocaust. He pleaded that memory should not die, even though the young should not be held responsible for something they had no part in.

In the middle section of his speech, Jenniger asked a series of rhetorical questions, designed to force reflection on what was in German hearts in the past: "As for the Jews, hadn't they in the past sought a position that was not their place? Mustn't they now accept a bit of curbing? Hadn't they, in fact, earned being put in their place?"[39] For a speaker to ask ironical questions is always a dangerous strategy. In Jenniger's case the result was explosive and disastrous. The press around the world reported his speech as an attack upon the Jews. Given the occasion for the speech and the credentials of the speaker, such an interpretation is astounding, but it hounded Jenniger out of office. Obviously he should have tried out his emotionally charged words with some colleagues to test whether such words could be heard on this occasion.

Unfortunately, mistakes of this kind lead future speakers to be more cautiously bland. Some generalized responsibility is placed on the table but without a probing of what ordinary people were responding to and what we can learn from the past. Non-Germans today are not the ones to tell Germans about their history; Germans have to work through their particular past. Other nations cannot be judgmental because it is not clear that any nation is unstained by the past or that any nation can say with certainty: it can never happen here. The Holocaust is a past event centered in Europe; in the time-full present, its effects are still reverberating. I think it is a sad irony that the very first thing one meets on entering the United States Holocaust Museum is a bomb detector—not for German bombs in World War II but for today's bombs of deranged individuals who wish to eliminate memory.

An aspect of the Holocaust that opens it beyond German responsibility is the part that Christian doctrine—and Christians—played. The problem here, as it is so often, is an assumption that the choice is between a blanket indictment and a denial of any responsibility. A fair and honest appraisal lies elsewhere. It seems safe to say that Christian doctrine was not directly responsible—the cause—of Nazism. At the same time, Christian language and attitudes regarding the Jews formed part of the background for the rise of Nazism. If there is any truth at all to this second proposition, then Christians have a serious responsibility for examining their current speech about Jews and Judaism.

Victor Gollanz, in *What Buchenwald Really Means*, attacked the British press for holding all Germans responsible for the Holocaust. His complaint had merit, but his explaining of the matter was dreadful. He said that "collective guilt" was an Old Testament idea from which the example of Christ should have liberated us.[40] To use a typical Christian stereotype of "Old Testament" versus "Christ" in this context is remarkably insensitive to Christian responsibility for Jewish stereotyping. In recent decades Christian scholars have been digging at the roots of Christian anti-Semitism.[41] Their work has provided salutary changes, but the problem is nowhere near resolved.

The single most dramatic event in this rethinking of Christian language was the Second Vatican Council of the Roman Catholic church. Its document on Jews and Judaism set a direction for Catholic–Jewish dialogue that has continued despite occasional bumps in the road. A succession of popes and numerous committees have wrestled with the language of Christian–Jewish relations, not with entire success but with evident good will that most Jews and Jewish organizations appreciate. The Vatican's refusal to recognize the state of Israel was for a long time a nearly insuperable obstacle to communication. A resolution of that obstacle suggests more cooperation in the future.

At the heart of Christian persecution of Jews over the centuries was the contention that "they crucified the Lord." The director of *Shoah*, the long documentary film on the Holocaust, had no trouble finding Catholics today in the shadow of the Auschwitz camp who explained the suffering of the Jews with the same epithets used by medieval peasants. Obviously the education of Christian church members has a long way to go. At the level of historical scholarship there is probably more agreement than disagreement between Christians and Jews in answering the question "Who killed Jesus?" Roman authorities with the collaboration of Jewish individuals and groups were responsible.[42]

Even by the time the New Testament was written there were mythical and abstract ways of speaking that would taint all future Jews with an act they could not have been responsible for. The church cannot repudiate its own founding documents, and it has a right to elaborate a theology that interconnects all creation in a single grand vision. The tension between a statement of historical fact and a theological interpretation can still be confusing. *The Catechism of the Catholic Church,* published in the 1990s, takes pains to separate out individual Jews at the time who bore some responsibility for the death of Jesus. But then the document suddenly jumps into another language: "The church does not hesitate to impute to Christians the gravest responsibility for the torments inflicted on Jesus, a responsibility with which they have all too often burdened the Jews alone.[43]

Anyone concerned with a grammar of responsibility has difficulty making sense of this statement. How could Christians be responsible for killing Jesus when no Christians yet existed? Perhaps in some atemporal vision, the sins of Christians cause the sufferings of Jesus. If the Catholic church wishes to continue to say that (as it has throughout history), it would be better to leave the Jews out of the statement entirely.[44] A historical-minded Jew could read the sentence as saying that Christians are willing to take over the gravest part of the responsibility, a responsibility they have given to the Jews *alone*. But since the Jew knows there were no Christians living at the time, a profession of responsibility for the event seems like a rhetorical flourish to hide the fact the "the Jews" are *still* responsible.[45]

The Christian composer of the sentence would probably be insulted that anyone could interpret the words that way, but longstanding Jewish suspicions have not been completely allayed. The problem here is not blatantly bigoted statements or even thoughtless stereotypes. What we have is a muddled grammar of responsibility that helps neither Christian nor Jew. If Christians state clearly what they are responsible for, it would clarify what Jews are and are not responsible for. Catholic theology might be more effective in a catechism if it asked "to whom and to what are we responsible?" A Christian who is responsible to the suffering of Jesus might be led to respond to the sufferings of others, not least the Jewish sufferings from Christian persecution. But a Christian who is told that he or she is responsible for Jesus' suffering on the cross is lifted outside any historical give and take.

As for Christian complicity in the Holocaust, churches and individuals have a mixed and not very good record. There were moral heroes who tried to rescue Jews. There were some organized efforts, including the town of Le Chambon, inspired by its Protestant Christianity. There were protests by church leaders within Germany and without.[46]

One person who has come in for special criticism is Pope Pius XII. His predecessor, Pope Pius XI, had prepared an encyclical condemning Nazism, but he died just before it was completed.[47] Neither Pope Pius XII nor his cardinals took strong public stands in defense of the Jews. Would papal leadership have made a difference? Perhaps not, but the pope was in the position of being responsible for trying. Whatever behind-the-scenes efforts Pope Pius XII made, Jews still express bitter disappointment at his public stance.

One should note carefully that the accusation is not a general complaint about Christians or about popes. Jews expect a lot from the papacy and are disappointed when the papacy fails. That may sound peculiar, but throughout history persecution at a local level was usually countermanded by papal intervention. When Catholic theologian Rosemary Ruether painted an unrelievedly bleak picture of the history of Christian–Jewish relations, Jewish historian Yosef Yerushalmi took exception. The statute on the purity of blood in fifteenth-century Toledo was a forerunner of Nazism but not the same thing. The most striking difference, says Yerushalmi, is that in 1449 Pope Nicholas V condemned the statutes and excommunicated the perpetrators. Thus, Yerushalmi concludes, the complaint about Pope Pius XII is that "he *broke*, in essence, with the tradition of the medieval popes."[48]

The Future as Present Expectation

This section on the future is shorter than the previous one on the past. In a grammar of responsibility, there is immeasurably more to say about the past than about the future. The past and the future, despite the linguistic ease of coupling them, do not exist in the same way. The past has a solidity of accomplished actions for which some persons are responsible. The past is also there as voices to be listened to, and from which we might learn what should not be done. At first glance, both responsibility to the future and responsibility for the future seem to be mere figures of speech without any solidity at all. How can anyone be responsible for performing an action that has not yet been performed? How can anyone get advice by listening to the future when those voices have not yet spoken?

We can only give answers to these two questions by digging down into the present. If the present is imagined as a disappearing point and the future is a series of such points that have not yet appeared, then there is no responsibility to the future as the basis of a responsibility for the future.

With the present as a disappearing point, a use of the term responsibility is possible, but it is in a language different from the one proposed here. I refer to the twentieth-century strand of thought that isolates the "will" as moral agent. In an almost exclusive concentration on the will, the future becomes obsessively important. The future has to be created by acts of the will. The future becomes the one great hope, but "man" has to invent it.

To invent the future, the willing individual need not listen to the present. What he or she needs is a *vision* of the future. The first step in this way of speaking is to decide what the year 2005 or 2050 should look like and then "make decisions" to get there. Although what shows up as the centerpiece is the willing to get there, the painted picture of the future has already been decided; that is, some individual or small group has already done the main deciding. Decisions about the future are governed by a vision of the future, but that future is already someone's decision. Some circular movement in these matters is unavoidable, but this circle is too narrow and it is especially dangerous when the circle is not admitted at all. Much of what is called "futurism" talks glowingly about individual freedom, but a rigid control of what we are exhorted to do is the futurist's vision of the way things should be.

Accompanying visions of the future, therefore, are programs to control and predict the future. The future is the great hope but only if we know what it is going to be and we can aim straight toward it. The person as listener/answerer disappears to be replaced by scientific data. The result, writes Alan Borgmann is "we vacate our first person place and presence in the world just when we mean to take responsibility for its destiny."[49]

Those who are uninterested in all of this predicting and planning get criticized by the forward-looking visionary as irresponsible. Some of these improvident people probably are lacking in responsibility. Gustave Thibon distinguishes between the improvidence of the saint and that of the decadent man. The saint does not worry about the future, according to Thibon, "because he carries his treasure within." The decadent man does not think of the future because he is the plaything of the moment. The decadent man shares the same understanding of time as the visionary; but, despairing of the future, the decadent man tries without success to disappear behind the present moment.

The person Thibon calls the saint has a different understanding of how past and future are related. The phrase "he carries his treasure within" could be misleading, conveying the sense of a private, inner world cut off from political and organizational reality. That is a common caricature of the "saint"; it is Weber's ethic of pure intention (which for Weber is the opposite of responsibility). Here, however, the treasure within is a depth within the person that resonates with the depth of the present. The person who lives in the depths of the present *cares* about the future, but he or she does not worry about it. He or she has come to terms with the unpredictability of the future. One cannot *take* responsibility for the future, but one can calmly *accept* responsibility for present actions that have future consequences.

The consequences of one's actions include economic and political repercussions in other people's lives. Even in simple, peasant societies, a sense of the future is not lacking. The person who plants crops knows there is an unpredictable future before harvesting. Two people who marry are acting both for their own happiness and the future of the tribe in the unpredictable lives of their children. As society has become more complex, we are pressed to think more about the future and to try to control it. The frightening fact about contemporary life is that the future is more unpredictable than it has ever been. A leak in an oil barge or in a nuclear power plant can upset the plans of tens of millions of people.

Because of this possibility of terrible disasters from the irresponsibility of one person, the world now depends more than ever on the human capacity to promise. Trust is a fragile basis on which to deal with the future; nevertheless, it is the specifically human way. One person promises; the other person trusts in promise. Hannah Arendt draws a comparison between forgiveness as the remedy for the irre-

versibility of the past and promising as "the remedy for unpredictability, for the chaotic uncertainty of the future."[50]

The modern idea of contract was designed to replace a handshake of
understanding with a legally air tight document. Contractual obligation is a helpful clarification, indispensable for the interaction of artificial persons. It has not replaced and never can replace the element of
trust. As Albert Hirschmann notes, market exchange involves a time
element as well as limited information. Whatever may be printed on
the label of the product, every trip to the supermarket involves life and
death trust in other human beings.[51]

People die every day from someone's unwashed hands at the meat
factory or someone's failure to tighten a screw on the steering wheel.
The detailed plans for the future disappear in one unpredictable
moment. Books that go on for hundreds of pages describing the future
seldom mention that the individual dies. Why devote all one's energies to future generations when my lot is to die? As Robert Heilbroner
pointed out in an essay on the theme "What has the future ever done
for me?"—we are at a crucial moment when the bond between the
unborn, the living, and the dead seems to be coming apart.[52] If the only
question is "what's in it for me?" all the talk of the future increases
despair and a desperate defense against the one predictable thing
about the future: the fact of my own death. In Simone Weil's phrase,
every human being, threatened by death "secretes falsehood" as a way
of avoiding mortality.

The ultimate denial would be the claim that we are not in fact mor-
tal. Surveying the present scene in *The Imperative of Responsibility*, Hans
Jonas writes: "Death no longer appears as a necessity belonging to the
nature of life, but as an avoidable, at least in principle tractable and
long-delayable organic malfunction."[53] The convoluted qualification
in that sentence means we may postpone your cancer indefinitely,
though of course you could still get hit by an out-of-control bus five
minutes from now.

The premise of Jonas's statement that "death no longer appears as a
necessity belonging to the nature of life" is found a few pages earlier:
"The difference between the artificial and the natural has van-
ished. . . ."[54] If that were true, I cannot imagine a worse calamity.
Human life exists in the tension between the natural and the artificial.
The strength of the artificial is that it does not die; it is indeed our way
to the future. The greatness of the natural is inseparable from the fact

that it does die. The natural person has to join with artificial persons to exercise responsibility to and for the future.

Spokespersons for various causes are always talking about our responsibility for the future. They usually do not say how we can be responsible for what does not exist. Peter French is able to provide the answer: "The responsibility relationships to future generations can be sensibly articulated through corporation-like entities."[55] People are what we most care about, especially our immediate descendants, but it is corporations (political, religious, business, educational) that are the necessary link. We are responsible to the past by way of corporate entities; we are responsible for the future by involvement with these artifacts. French notes the irony of this situation for the modern liberal: "The endurance of corporate persons, a prospect that terrorized the Enlightenment liberals, insures the projection of moral and cultural responsibilities in both temporal directions. Corporate juristic personhood acknowledges in law what is necessary to the ecology of rational agency."[56]

For the distant future, responsibility for those generations is responsibility for the actions of corporations that will still exist. There is a different kind of responsibility in relation to the *next* generation. Future adults already exist in the form of today's children. "How we treat children really tests who we are, fundamentally conveys who we hope to be."[57]

Today's adults exercise a responsibility *to* the future by being responsible to their children. Adults also have some responsibility *for* children, although this is a responsibility that is frequently overstepped. Even with the youngest children, responsibility for them is limited. And that responsibility has to decrease every year, every month, every day.

One can regularly read in the press that parents do not care enough about their children, that they are no longer willing to sacrifice themselves for their children's future. Such adults are plentiful enough. When time is seen as a series of points passing by, the forty-year old parents, who are supposed to be examples of adult maturity, may be out "grabbing for the gusto." The children are left free to fend for themselves, a freedom that can get drowned in drugs and violence.

The alternative urged upon parents is often a mirror image, within the same framework of responsibility. Instead of the mother working outside the home, she should go back to her proper place. Daddy should be the responsible breadwinner. The parents should be responsible for their children's actions.

In this line of thinking, children do not need freedom; at home and at school they should be told what to do. Under the guise of caring for the child, this set of assumptions places a terrible burden upon the child. The parent acts out his or her life by taking responsibility for the child. The tennis-crazed father who lives through his daughter or the stage mother who wants her boy to be a movie star are not the only problems here. Good and generous parents are constantly being encouraged to be responsible for their children's lives.

Hans Jonas's study of responsibility makes this responsibility of parents the center of his theory: "Here is the archetype of all responsible action, which fortunately requires no deduction from a principle because it is powerfully implanted in us by nature or at least in the childbearing part of humanity."[58] Jonas's other "archetype" is the statesman deciding about the future for the people he is responsible for. Both cases thoroughly distort the meaning of being responsible for. Because Jonas does not have a meaning of "responsible to," then the all-important future is placed in the hands of the visionary statesman and the instinct-directed parent. They have to be responsible for the rest of us.

A proper grammar of responsibility would be most intent on listening and then answering in a way that moves toward *lessening* the responsibility for others. Dietrich Bonhoeffer writes: "The responsibility of the father or of the statesman is limited by the responsibility of the child and of the citizen, and indeed the responsibility of the father and the statesman consists precisely in rendering conscious and in strengthening the responsibility of those who are committed to their care."[59] And in this framework one can say mothers as well as fathers, schoolteachers along with parents, politicians and religious leaders. Adults care for children by increasing the child's responsibility for his or her actions as quickly and as smoothly as possible.

Richard Farson's *Birthrights* in 1974 probably struck many people as outrageous and impractical.[60] It is a radical proposal for children's rights. The right, for example, to have a new set of parents at adolescence may seem extreme, but it is really a variation on what most cultures in the past have done. Apprenticeship was not just the acquisition of job skills, but interaction with a surrogate parent.[61] In more recent times schoolteachers were said to function *in loco parentis;*

they could be other significant adults in the child's life besides the parents. And Robert Bly seems to have convinced many men that what they lacked in childhood was not just a father but a brotherhood of elders.[62] Parents should not and cannot carry the whole burden of strengthening the child's responsibility. The child needs to be responsible to many adults in the process of becoming responsible for its own actions.

Farson also proposed the economic and political enfranchisement of small children. They would be responsible for money by dealing with earning, saving, and spending money. They would learn to vote more responsibly if the voting age were lowered to six years old. But wouldn't they vote for a candidate on superficial grounds? Yes, and so do a lot of adults. If adults had been respected as responsible persons at age six, their interest in politics might not be atrophied by the time they pass the arbitrary line of age eighteen. Lowering the voting age from twenty-one to eighteen did almost nothing to increase political involvement, because there was no logic at work.

In politics, as in most things, a child does not suddenly become responsible on the first day of adulthood. A young person has a degree of moral responsibility by age five or six. The task for adults is to see that the child's "responsibility to" continuously broadens and deepens. Concomitantly, the adult must reduce responsibility for the child's actions. Obviously, there are tasks beyond the physical or mental ability of a six-year-old; I would not want to see the age for driving a car lowered to six.

For admission into movie theaters, some rough classification system, similar to the present one, can be informative. However, the child's context of care will be most important in how the child reacts to scenes in the street or in the theater. Robert Coles, the extraordinary conversationalist with children, found a wide range of responses to the movies children see. Coles reminds us that even with the very young "the passive response is not the only one available." We very often underestimate the child's ability "to attend selectively, to summon a sense of proportion, to call upon human and common sense, to assume a varying or even quite insistent critical distance from the subject under scrutiny in the film."[63]

Children have to be allowed a kind of padded cell to try out the actions they wish to be responsible for. Some quiet time is part of that. David Elkind writes that "the child who sits quietly doing nothing is learning how to withdraw from the world without antagonizing it."[64] Trying out different masks is an indispensable part of growing up. "Hypocrisy" got a very bad reputation in the eighteenth century; sincerity became the one, great, solemn virtue.[65] Hypocrisy meant playing with different masks to discover who you want to be. Children need such play and the development of an inner self to sustain the play of turning one face or another to the world. Which is the true self? Only by testing out his or her actions against the outer world can the child discover the self.

Garrison Keillor, in one of his television specials, complains of the fact that children now take "mental health days" when they don't want to go to school. When I was a kid, said Keillor, I would say that I had a sore throat when I wished to skip school. My way was better, claimed Keillor, because "lying is a way to take responsibility for your life."[66] The response to his punch line was an embarrassed laughter of recognition.

Everyone lies as a child, but it is assumed to be an evil deserving of condemnation. Only with the moralistic tone of Keillor's voice is one allowed to admit that as a child "lying is a way to take responsibility for your life." That is, getting to the point where one is capable of lying and pulling it off is a sign of achievement for moral responsibility. One now has an inner space to listen and decide for oneself. My mother, as many mothers, used to say to me when I was a child: I can read you like a book. I let her think so, and she was indeed perceptive. But as soon as I could, I established a place inside where no other human being enters uninvited.

I would add a footnote here to the child's trying out versions of the truth with the adult world: this relation is asymmetrical. An adult has the greatest responsibility for telling the truth when the receiver is a child.[67] Adults sometimes assume that it is more acceptable to lie to children; if "it is only a child," the truth can be stretched or avoided. The morally responsible adult does not lie to a child. It is sometimes difficult to find the way to convey the truth. The blunt facts of a situation are not always the best way. Children eventually sense who are the truth tellers. It is precisely because the child plays with the truth and sometimes tries hiding behind deception that he or she needs an adult standard of truth telling.

The parent's task is to be *responsible to* the child while gradually ceasing to be *responsible for* the child. The child, like the future that he or she embodies, is unpredictable. The parent who would try to predict and to control the child's future only undermines what is accomplished by care and guidance. "Every realistic mother is reminded continually as to how much of her 'product' is beyond control. In child-rearing, she is facilitator and mediator, not 'maker'. *Outcome* is not an accurate term in reference to human beings who as long as they live provide surprises and demonstrate potentiality."[68]

I referred above to the phrase *in loco parentis*, one that was used of the school's responsibility. The phrase is seldom used now; unfortunately it may have been abandoned without our thinking through when, where and how it might have a legitimate meaning. Asking a university to play the part of parent is generally inappropriate. But for a nine-year-old, the school and its staff do have a responsibility that overlaps that of the parent. Schools teach insofar as they are communities and institutions; they continue the "socializing" that the parents begin.[69]

The relation between the parent and the school's teachers is a reciprocal one. Both are teachers of the young; they can learn about teaching from each other. This fact is obscured by the use of "teacher" to mean only the professional schoolteacher. Everyone is accustomed to statements about the parent as teacher, such as the following praise of the past: "The idea that the parent is the first and foremost teacher was taken seriously: teachers acted for the parents as trustees of children's education."[70] While trying to praise the parent as teacher, the author denies that the parent is a teacher at all; the second half of the sentence contradicts the first half. This standard way of speaking prevents conversation between parents and schoolteachers on the topic of teaching. The responsibility of each differs as to what is taught and how it is taught, but parental teaching and schoolteaching are a joint responsibility. Both are limited by the child's responsibility for itself, with the schoolteacher more limited than the parent.

A professional schoolteacher may have many more tasks to perform than to teach in the classroom. Functioning as monitor at the bus stop or in the cafeteria, the schoolteacher may be responsible for enforcement of safety regulations. As athletic coach, counselor or band director, the schoolteacher may be confidant, adviser, disciplinarian, friend. Depending on the age of the student and the nature of the school, the schoolteacher's responsibility can expand or contract. However, in no circumstances is the schoolteacher responsible for the student's life, or even for the student's learning.

The professional literature for schoolteachers during the last century has been afflicted with inflated rhetoric and impossible expectations. Such unrealism can produce frustration and cynicism. John Dewey, in his Pedagogical Creed of the 1890s, proclaimed that "the teacher always is the prophet of the true God and the usherer in of the true kingdom of God."[71] If Dewey had really meant *teacher*, and not *schoolteacher*, the statement would be defensible. The great revolutions in history are indeed ushered in by teachers: Moses and Muhammad, Newton and Einstein, Jefferson and Lincoln. But John Dewey is one of the culprits for our conflation of teacher and schoolteacher. Asking schoolteachers to usher in the kingdom of God—along with correcting last night's assigned essay—is asking too much. Dewey, I think, recognized that fact later in life although his rhetoric did not sufficiently change.[72]

What a schoolteacher should be held professionally responsible for is schoolteaching. Far from being the only form or the prototype of teaching, classroom teaching is a very peculiar and restricted form of teaching. Mostly what is at issue is words and numbers. The teacher in that setting has to show people how to engage in writing, reading, speaking, and computing. If one is consistent in the use of "teacher," then, of course, other people besides the professional schoolteacher teach in classrooms. A six-year-old can be a teacher there; in fact, one test of schoolteaching is that sometimes the schoolteacher and the pupil reverse their roles.

A teacher's responsibility is for teaching; a learner's responsibility is for learning. There is a single process of teaching–learning, as well as a clear distinction between the activities of teach and learn. Schoolteachers are constantly told that they must be responsible for the child, responsible for the child's learning. As one writer puts it: "Teaching occurs when one person consciously accepts responsibility for the learning of another."[73] It seems to me that no teacher, including a schoolteacher, has the right, not to mention duty, to take responsibility for the learning of another.

One leading writer on teaching, criticizing an individualistic view of education, writes that "to develop that sense—that I must be responsible for others as I am for myself, in order for me to have a world in which I would like to live—is a complex job."[74] I think that the ideal presumed for the schoolteacher here, "be responsible for others as I am for myself," is more than complex; it is an impossible burden for a schoolteacher and not an ideal at all.

Another leading writer in addressing schoolteachers says: "By accepting this obligation to foster these desirable outcomes, the teacher assumes moral responsibility for the student."[75] But no teacher can "assume moral responsibility for the student." And to ask schoolteachers to do that is to perpetuate the inflated rhetoric that infects the literature on schoolteaching.

The paradoxical result of loading on the schoolteacher's back the responsibility for the child's life and learning is a distaste in educational literature for the act of teaching. The logic in this paradox is clear enough. If teaching means taking responsibility for someone else's life, then it is an act that becomes immoral when the person can take responsibility for his or her own life. Thus, teaching is equated with big people telling little people what to think and how to behave. As soon as the little person is big enough to rebel, then teaching has to cease. Not surprisingly, both "moral education" and "adult education" literature have a strong animosity toward teaching and try to avoid the term.[76]

One influential writer in this area is Carl Rogers. His *Freedom to Learn* is a rejection of the idea of teaching. Before launching his attack, Rogers writes: "I am simply going to speak personally and raise the question that I would ask myself if I were given responsibility for the learning of a group of children."[77] Instead of asking what it means to be responsible for *teaching* a group of children, Rogers is asking what it means to be "given responsibility for the learning of a group of children." He assumes the two are the same and he concludes that teaching is oppressive. In his view, teaching becomes one of the chief obstacles to learning. *Freedom to Learn*, like so many books on education, sees the task as getting rid of teaching as far as possible so that students can be responsible for their own learning.[78]

Teaching cannot be appreciated as a fundamental human activity so long as "responsibility" is misunderstood. More particularly, the work of schoolteachers cannot be properly appreciated when the problem of "being responsible for the student's learning" is compounded by "teacher" and "schoolteacher" being equated. An exalted rhetoric surrounds the work of schoolteaching, which only frustrates dedicated schoolteachers. Why cannot we just say: teachers are responsible for teaching; students are responsible for learning. In a classroom, the professional schoolteacher is responsible for one very specific kind of teaching; the student is responsible for a corresponding kind of learning. That would lead to more reflection on the nature of teaching, including the activity of classroom teaching.

CHAPTER 8

RELATIVELY RESPONSIBLE

This concluding chapter addresses the question of a universal ethic, one that transcends national, racial, religious, and cultural differences. No one today is in a position to write such an ethic. The deficiency is not an individual failing. The ground for something approaching a universal ethic would have to be prepared for by longstanding cultural exchanges. This preparatory stage has not happened. Jet planes, financial markets, computers, movies, sports, television programs, rock concerts, and other international phenomena may be hastening the arrival of a worldwide culture, but human beings need time to develop working relations, not to mention ease in living together as relatives.

Any individual or small working-group that proposes a universal ethic has to state it in a particular language. German, French, English, Spanish, or another language has built-in strengths but inevitable limitations. Each language bears traces of philosophical, religious, political, and scientific debates that have occurred in that language. Translations into another language can convey the literal meanings, but the new house of meaning has distances and ambiguities not in the original.

If individuals or groups try to leave behind the cultural peculiarities of their own life, they may succeed in writing a *general* ethic but not a universal ethic. A general ethic abstracts from all individual cases in search of a highest (or a lowest) common denominator. Such an ethic offers guidance to no one, not even the people who have composed it. Mary Midgley has said that "the sad little joke about universal languages is that almost no one speaks them."[1] I would qualify that statement to say "languages that have claimed to be universal." We do not have any universal languages, just someone's attempt to invent a universal language.

Gottfried Leibniz in the seventeenth century believed that his attempt would produce a universal language that "will be very difficult to construct but very easy to learn. It will be quickly accepted by everybody on account of its great utility and its surprising facility, and it will serve wonderfully in communication among various peoples."[2] Leibniz, despite his genius, was taking on more than one expert can accomplish. Similar attempts down to Esperanto in the twentieth century have not been successful either.

The most likely candidate for approaching universality at the end of the twentieth century is English, which is far removed from the logical and simple way of communicating that Leibniz had in mind. If English ever does spread everywhere, it is unlikely to replace native languages. As a second language, it is already spoken in strange dialects that may create more than one English. Even the military and economic might of the United States, as successor to the British Empire, cannot control how people will develop the "American heritage of the English language."

A truly universal language would enhance not suppress local particularity. The movement from individual to general is by way of abstraction. But the movement from particular *toward* the universal is by deeper immersion into the particular. At least for now, and probably forever, the universal is available only by being glimpsed in the particular; it cannot be captured. To hope for a fully formed universal language is unrealistic.

The arts, throughout the centuries, have provided intimations of universal truth, goodness, and beauty. Great works of art have universality in the sense that someone of any age or circumstances might be personally moved by the experience of the work. Northrop Frye, commenting on *Macbeth*, writes: "If you wish to know the history of eleventh-century Scotland, look elsewhere; if you wish to know what it means to gain a kingdom and lose one's soul, look here."[3] Macbeth, Faust, or Don Quixote is not everyman; but men and women throughout the centuries have discovered parts of themselves in great characters of literature or in great portraits on canvas.

This approach to universality suggests why ethical systems are impossible to carry off. The attempt to compose a system of rules for everybody to live by begins from an arrogant premise. Nobody wants to be a piece of someone else's system. Moral rules that attempt to govern human actions are experienced by some people at times as a prison. When there is rebellion against such confining rules, the response may be to lift the rules to the level of general principle. Acceptance of principles makes agreements easier, but principles do not have much effect on action. Practically no one opposes principles such as "people should be honest" or "people should be truthful."

In the present era, principles are often translated into "values." Agreement on the value of honesty is nearly universal. But what it means to be honest in a particular situation, let alone how to produce honest people, is unclear. We seem stuck with, on the one side, rules and codes that are not accepted; and, on the other side, we have principles and values that are easily accepted but ineffective in practice.

The twentieth-century alternative to this dilemma has been to deny the need for a universal ethic. It is claimed that each group of people has its own ideas of right and wrong. Therefore, we should live by whatever rules and principles make sense to us and not intrude our morality on other groups that have a different morality. These days, however, this alternative is having its own difficulties; both its logical consistency and its practical effectiveness are in question.

The argument of this book is that a grammar of responsibility offers a corrective to this twentieth-century alternative. Responsibility is on the side of a denial that there are any absolute standards which could dictate a universal morality. However, responsibility is also a denial of the sufficiency of a relativism that dismisses the question of universality. Responsibility is rooted in the particular, but that does not preclude a movement toward a more universal ethic than any that the world now possesses.

Responsibility thus functions as a bridge for the fifth and last division in this book: absolute versus relative. Any help that responsibility can offer here presumes the previous four discussions. That is, if responsibility bridges the divisions of is and ought, individual and collective, humans and nonhumans, past and future, then it encompasses a rich particularity to approach the issue of universality. In contrast, if responsibility is simply a principle or a value ("People should take responsibility for themselves" or "People should make responsible decisions"), then no one is likely to object to its inclusion in a general ethic for worldwide distribution, but it will remain one of many such abstractions.

Responsibility is not enough, as I have readily admitted from the beginning. I have argued that it is a promising entry point for how to speak ethically, no less and no more. Progress in moral language is not likely to lead to a system of morality, in a form that the eighteenth and nineteenth centuries envisioned. Nonetheless, a science of ethics on the model of seventeenth-century science still has nostalgic attraction. A science wants its truths to apply to all people at all times and in all places. But the claim to scientific precision in ethics is always threatened by groups who simply will not fit themselves into the system.

We cannot return to a premodern age, but the meaning of "postmodern" can include a rediscovery of premodern as a place we can learn from. The twentieth-century acceptance of a morality relative to each culture is in a way a rediscovery of ancient times. A school of philosophy was once a way of life with its own beliefs, rituals, and behavior. Similarly, religious communities were groups of people joined by the same *curriculum vitae*.[4] St. Paul did not write ethical treatises; he addressed communities in Galatia, Corinth and Rome. To understand the moral teaching in these letters, one has to know something about the culture of the cities of Galatia, Corinth, and Rome, as well as the history of the Christian movement in those places. As with the rabbis before him, Paul's moral directives were not universal rules of conduct, but insistences that people live up to what they had previously promised.[5]

Aristotle's ethics had more impulse toward a philosophical universality. His treatises, nonetheless, were addressed to people already living in ethical communities. His contention that the way to become virtuous is to grow up in a virtuous community can be ridiculed as circular thinking; but it says something profound about community, teaching, and the ethical life. Much of what Aristotle says about the virtues does not speak to us precisely because it was so relevant to the culture in which and for which he wrote. The details of a virtuous life do not travel well from one era to another, or even from one culture to another within the same era.

That fact does not mean that different eras or several cultures are incomparable. Each group does distinguish between what is good, exemplary, and worth preserving from what is bad, condemnable, and deserving of elimination. We may not know the proper ways to carry out a detailed comparison, but comparability remains a human possibility. Most philosophical schools and religious communities in the distant past presumed that their own *ethos* was the standard for comparison. Their own morality was an absolute or a near absolute to which the foreigner was compared and by which the foreigner was judged. This chauvinistic element in the standard of comparison should not obscure the fact that the comparison indicated acceptance of others as part of a human community.

It was a momentous decision in the sixteenth century when the Spanish authorities ruled that the American Natives had souls. The Spanish invaders of Mexico had been horrified at the Aztec practice of human sacrifice—and with good reason. Bernard Williams comments: "It would surely be absurd to regard the reaction as merely parochial or self-righteous. It rather indicated something which their conduct did not indicate, that they regarded the Indians as men rather than wild animals."[6] Comparisons were both possible and inevitable so long as one assumed that human nature was present.

A European thinker of the sixteenth or seventeenth century could hardly imagine that the natives of America, Asia, or Africa were morally superior to him. Some eighteenth-century thinkers were open to admiring particular traits and skills of primitive peoples. They were especially fascinated by the innocent side of the American native, what Europeans understood as "natural man." The Europeans recognized that something valuable might have been lost in the course of civilization. Nonetheless, "civilization" was itself a recently coined word to indicate moral superiority. As heir to Greek, Roman, Hebrew, Christian, and Arab influences, Europe had sprung ahead in its mastery of science and technology. Eventually, 85 percent of the earth would be under its control, before the tide receded. Its morality was assumed to be the standard or absolute against which any other claim had to be measured.

The first chapter of Paul Johnson's *Modern Times* is entitled "A Relativist World." It starts from Einstein's meaning of relativity, but it goes on to describe how Marxism and Freudian analysis undermined "the highly developed sense of personal responsibility, and of duty towards a settled and objectively true moral code, which was at the center of nineteenth-century European civilization."[7] That simple statement is a key to the confusion, uncertainty, and chaos of the twentieth century, not only in a science of ethics, but in every facet of life. Without a standard by which to compare, comparison seemed impossible; without comparison, intelligibility disappears. Starting with evidence from history and archeology that human nature is more diverse than had hitherto been suspected, many anthropologists and philosophers in the twentieth century went on to the conclusion that there is no such thing as human nature.[8]

This position is sometimes called "cultural relativism," although that phrase slides around in meaning. In the nineteenth century, the term "culture" had been synonymous with education. The most influential writer on this subject, Matthew Arnold, defined culture as "acquainting ourselves with the best that has been known and said in the world."[9] In the twentieth century, anthropologists taught everyone to use "culture" to mean a group's particular way of life. Evaluation of culture as good or bad, superior or inferior, became highly problematic. Some anthropologists looked for universal laws in these newly discovered "cultures." But as finding universals became less likely, a relativizing of standards set in. Each culture sets its own standards; the outsider has no right to pass moral judgments.

This attitude of tolerance has much to recommend it as superior to previous chauvinisms. Still, there is a near contradiction in saying that a position is superior because it refuses to deal in superior/inferior. The anthropologist's appreciation of culture embodies a distinct moral attitude. A European or North American visitor ought not to rush in on an African tribe or South Pacific island to start reforming it on the model of the "advanced world." Nevertheless, the simple refusal of a single, absolute standard was not an answer to how various cultures are to work out moral differences when cultures interact.

That is where the world increasingly finds itself at the end of the twentieth century: absolutes have crumbled while "relative," as a description of morality, suffers from a previous disparagement as less than absolute. Several forms of authoritarian government have tried to fill the vacuum of Europe's withdrawal from empire. Communism was the most durable of these new absolutes. It not only provided stability for a large part of the world; it also provided the opposition with a nearly absolute ideology of anticommunism. The savage competition between the United States and the Soviet Union (obviously there could not be two absolutes) led to the exhaustion of both. Neither of them could provide an absolute standard for the rest of the world, although "America" is sometimes put forward that way.

The end of the Cold War released new energies within the former Soviet empire. Some of that energy took the form of ancient religious and ethnic conflict. The criminal element surfaced to exercise its own absolute standard. The Russian murder rate quickly achieved parity with that of the United States. Disorder is more frightening when people have had a very orderly way of life. Struggles in the former provinces and the disaster in Chechnya proved disheartening.

What transpired in the former Yugoslavia with the collapse of the old system is especially frightening. Neither the warring parties nor outside forces seemed able to make much sense of the slaughter. Marshall Tito and Soviet power had maintained the artificial unity of a country that was not a nation but an assemblage of ethnic and religious groups. Perhaps with sufficient time and intelligent mediation some peaceful divisions might have been reached. Multicultural havens, such as Sarajevo, might have provided models of success for the future. The fragility of any new order was overwhelmed by a paroxysm of hatred, greed, and violence.

A Relational World

The chaotic condition in numerous places can understandably lead to nostalgia for an old order when the streets were safe, the trains were on time, and refugees were not crossing the border. George Bush's proclamation of a new world order can sound like a sick joke. Nevertheless, the world does not seem to have any other choice than to begin working toward a new order, governed not by one absolute to which all others are relative, but by all being relatives.

The term "relative" ceases to have a secondary or negative meaning if there is not an absolute standard of measure. In fact, relative then becomes one of the most positive words in the language. The moral choice is no longer between absolutist and relativist, the latter taken to mean no standards at all. The choice now is between withdrawal into isolation and a broadening, deepening relation to all. "A person is a fellow being before it is a being."[10] To be moral is to recognize our relation to all other creatures and to live accordingly. In this new order, there are numerous standards and discriminations one is called upon to observe in our relational endeavors. No handbook or set of regulations provides mechanical and certain answers for moral living. An educated conscience that listens and answers is the chief moral guide.

Many people would like to hold on to a secure footing while they try out a relational morality. But as Kierkegaard insisted, you cannot try floating on the waves while you keep one big toe on the ocean floor. There are rules of operation for the swimmer, but most of them are learned in swimming. We might wish we had more time to wade, but we have been pushed into Kierkegaard's "70,000 fathoms." The choice is to sink in search of a new absolute or else learn how to swim. Neither proposal is inviting but only the latter is life giving.

The moral rules of operation are aspects, objectifications, reminders of relations between human and human, human and nonhuman. We will be impelled to a common search only if we give up reliance on absolutes. As Gandhi said, "how can he who thinks he possesses absolute truth be fraternal?"[11] The trouble with most "fraternal" quests in the past is that they have smuggled in pseudo-absolutes that interfere with genuine reciprocity of relations. An absolutizing trend is present in the way language functions, lifting up one group or one ideal to the exclusion of others. Does even the term "fraternal" include all that Gandhi and other revolutionaries have intended? Does it not have to be a sorority as well as a fraternity of truth seekers?

This question is not smugly asked to imply that we now finally do have an all-inclusive language. Every statement includes and excludes at the same time. There are no absolutely inclusive statements that include all relatives. In a relational world, one must continually ask "who is now being included and who is now being excluded?" and "is this the best accommodation for these circumstances?"

In recent years, the phrase "inclusive language" has been narrowly used as if "gender inclusive" were the only issue of inclusivity, and as if there were a set of one-time corrections. The question of inclusive/exclusive is at the heart of language; it is not a problem to be solved by a few additions and abstractions. The attempt to make universal statements often leads only to general statements, whose breadth is at the expense of depth and concreteness. Poetic speech with attention to concrete detail has a high degree of universality. In contrast, bureaucratic statements are highly inclusive by being general: they flatten out all the differences.

If moral language is to be both concrete and inclusive, that can only emerge as particular men and women listen to human and nonhuman interlocutors. Any one act of listening, any one statement, any one action is morally circumscribed by its historical situation. A man may use his moral passion to get a street light installed for the safety of a dozen school children. Another man may expend his energy on cleaning out a channel of water so that a school of fish does not die of pollution. A woman may spend her early evening hours delivering sandwiches to homeless people in her neighborhood.

Is this any way to run a new world order? Yes and no. Any act of listening to one's immediate surroundings and taking the immediate action that seems demanded could be a diversion from seeing the big picture. Still, in the absence of what Pasternak describes as "the kind of heart that knows of no general cases, but only of particular ones, and has the greatness of small actions," the big reforms go awry.[12] Someone ought to be working to get homes for the homeless, but simultaneously someone has to help those who are currently homeless to get through the night. The two "someones" can be the same person; in fact, *in some way* a person has to participate in both cases. However, that does not mean that everyone must split his or her time down the middle. Talent and circumstance should help to decide the most intelligent use of one's resources.

Although the responsible act of listening and answering is always concretely embodied in one person, at one time, in one place, there is no inherent limit either to the distance of what is listened to or the extent of the reverberations in the answer. The oft-quoted slogan of former House Speaker Tip O'Neil that "all politics is local" contains an obvious truth along with disastrously misleading implications. Any genuine political act is located in a small group with one location. But unless the action is to be quickly corrupted, it has to draw some of its wisdom from beyond the immediate locality and it has to answer for actions that ripple outward to city, nation, and world. By being deeply local, all politics has to be as universal as possible.

People in small, like-minded groups find it easy enough to be responsible to each other and with each other. Responsibility does include responding to family members, friend, or lover. We learn to work at harder cases of listening while we refresh ourselves with the unstressful rhythms of friendship and love. Two people who intimately know each other can listen to one another though hardly any words are spoken.

In small enclaves based on a common note of religion, race, sex, ethnicity, and dozens of other bases, communication is similarly smooth.

No one has to say what everyone assumes as the basis of the community. What is heard and what is answered lie within the group's culture. By written or unwritten agreements, some things are just not said. What is said within the group is accorded the benefit of the doubt, that is, it is given a positive interpretation. The same statement from an outsider is heard differently. Humor is a main test: the insider's joke is an outsider's insult.

Some people may be longing for the day when all these insides and outsides disappear, to be replaced by a world of individuals without clusters of race, nationality, religion, and the rest. Such a dissolution is highly unlikely and would not be progress. The small enclave is the source of much trouble, but it is the basis of much of the richness of human existence. The uniqueness of the human being lies not in the one note of humanity but in the combination of innumerable qualities. The human race is a plurality of uniquenesses, each person the seat of characteristics for many groupings. Each group can become a closed bastion of defense against other differences. However, each group can earn the name "community" by interacting with other groups in the direction of a richer humanity.[13]

The key to community and responsibility is the willingness to interact, which assumes that groups remain distinct but not separate. Instead of assuming that each culture has a different morality, we can begin by affirming our own morality, and let differences emerge as they may. When differences are apparent, then is the moment for quiet listening and an effort to understand the world from a perspective different from one's own. We need not abandon our own deeply held convictions in the process of trying to understand people who seem to be in fundamental disagreement with us. Eventually, we might find some common ground, and then argument can be fruitful. If we cannot find an agreed-upon starting point, then arguing is useless.

It is often said that one should not preach to the converted, but that is exactly who should be preached to because they share a common set of beliefs. Preaching to the unconverted is ineffective and insulting. Rational argument, as Wittgenstein points out, is a kind of conversion.[14] Without a sharing of rational premises, neither agreement nor disagreement in words is possible. Long stretches of silence can be part of dialogue. Rituals indicating a let-live tolerance may be all that is possible for a day, a year, or a generation.

Transcultural Morality

Deep-rooted divisions undoubtedly exist in the world. When "culture" became such a common word early in this century, the chief division was between large parts of the world that had been isolated from each other for centuries. The "far East" (that is, far from England) was still a dark mystery to European traders and politicians. The religions of Asia were starkly different from the Jewish and Christian religions of Europe. Asia had not separated religion and philosophy into two neat packages as had seventeenth-century Europeans. Africa, too, was a "dark continent" with rituals and beliefs unintelligible to the first European invaders and colonialists. Christianity had little success at penetrating the Asian mind. Christian missionaries made a more concerted effort in Africa, and they obtained a foothold there. Still, the native cultures lived alongside or just underneath Christian attempts to "civilize" African tribes.

Much has changed in the course of the twentieth century, but not everything. The modern world has intruded almost everywhere; there are few places left to hide from it in Asia, Australia, or Africa. Religious missionaries are still at work, although these days they work with much greater sensitivity to the local culture. That has meant a reemergence of some ancient practices, not only in Africa but in Latin America and even in places such as Ireland.

The contemporary missionary, however, is more likely to be the rock star, the Hollywood movie, the sports hero, *Time* magazine, or the computer whiz. There now exists an international "pop culture" that has spread around the world, if not to every tribe and village. This culture is often looked upon with disdain by those who cherish an older meaning of (high) culture. Insofar as pop culture is driven by greed there is good cause for suspicion. At the least, however, it suggests that there are common links between cultures. The supposition that cultures are self-enclosed worlds, each with a moral system unintelligible to the outsider, is challenged by the way music, movies, clothes, sports, and television programs travel from culture to culture. Not all these things travel equally well. Some music remains distinctly local while a rock concert can attract tens of thousands, across a variety of languages. Humor usually has trouble traveling. The *Tonight* show would not play well in Tibet, but it also never succeeded in England.

The big drawback in this new missionary outreach is that it remains largely one-sided. The modern world still intrudes upon the premodern. Most of the Christian missionaries in the world come from the United States. The new missionaries of film and recording are just as heavily concentrated in the United States, especially in New York and Los Angeles. Cultural influence today is backed by economic power. A reciprocal cultural influence is difficult to achieve between large, rich nations and those nations struggling to get in on the money that circles the globe twenty-four hours a day. The powerful players in the economic game are often called the "West," a term that illogically includes Japan. Do Great Britain, Germany, Japan, and the United States have a common ethic? They apparently have much in common in the understanding of economic benefits, but cultural differences remain. Japan absorbed a lot of United States culture after World War II. But millennia of differences between East and West do not disappear in one, sudden burst.

In F. S. C. Northrop's great work of a half-century ago, *The Meeting of East and West*, he employed the terms "aesthetic" and "theoretic" to contrast Eastern and Western cultures. Rather than assume the two to be permanently split that way, he argued for the spread of Western scientific method in the East. That change has continued to happen throughout this century. In the other direction, Northrop argued for a recovery by the West of the aesthetic component of knowledge. In connection with this recovery, he argued that there had been a historical mistake at the beginning of the modern West. "The problem underlying the conflicting Western cultures is identical with the one involved in relating correctly the compatible cultures of the East and West."[15] That is, an opening to the East, far from being a rejection of the West, would heal the split in the West between modern and premodern.

Much that has happened in the ensuing half century supports this premise. The words "modern" and "scientific" can no longer be assumed without question to mean "superior." But for the West to turn its back on modern science would be to no one's benefit. Instead, perhaps real reciprocity is becoming possible. The aesthetic and ethical standards of various peoples, say the Maori of New Zealand, need not be judged either inferior or superior to the Pakeha (white people).[16] In reciprocal relations, the point is simply to listen to and to learn from each other.

The aversion to issuing judgments of inferiority does not require a group to keep silent on moral issues. In the face of what appears to be grave injustice, the outsider shows respect by disagreeing. It sounds tolerant to say that the morality of each culture can be judged only from within that culture. Suppose, however, that one culture's morality includes "we kill people who disagree with us." A tolerance for that kind of cultural difference would eventually lead to the end of tolerance. Somewhere there is a limit as to how far cultures can disagree.

No culture allows indiscriminate killing. No culture can permit indiscriminate falsehood. Those two principles may not seem to go far since the term "indiscriminate" admits of endless arguments. Nonetheless, argument is itself indicative that there is some underlying agreement. Cultures are shown to be morally comparable because in each of them governments and individuals are required to judge which cases of killing and falsehood are allowable. Every culture allows some killing and every culture allows some falsehood. Where a culture draws those lines can seem shockingly immoral to another culture.

For example, throughout history, infanticide has been a quite common practice. Under such and such conditions, the newborn's life could be ended. In some cultures, a deformed baby is judged to be not human so that killing it is not murder.[17] In many cultures, ending an infant's life may be preferable to exposing it to terrible sufferings. Today, infanticide is thought to be a terrible crime, although contemporary medicine is creating situations where it is sometimes judged better to let the newborn die. Direct killing would still be a crime, but similar to cases of dying in old age, the line between letting die and killing is not always clear.

People who consider abortion a terrible crime believe that in the future the line for allowable killing will be moved back. Animal rights advocates think the line should be moved beyond the human. The Jains, a religious group in India, think that plucking fruit from a tree or washing oneself is inadmissible killing.[18] Not only between cultures but within cultures there are sincere and genuine disagreements about where to draw the line between those killings allowed and those that are not.

As one moves outward from the proscription of indiscriminate killing and falsehood, the room for disagreement becomes greater. That people should not be tortured and that people should not be imprisoned without a due process receive almost universal assent.

However, judgments in a particular situation vary as to how such principles apply. If any kind of physical punishment is allowed, the exact conditions of who, how, where, and to whom have to be carefully stipulated. A parent spanking a child and a policeman beating up a suspect are worlds apart within the same culture.

Every culture needs ways to restrain wrongdoers, but a government's power to arrest and to imprison is always susceptible to terrible abuse. Our legal system may have become skewed away from reaching justice for the victim of crime; if so, careful reforms are called for rather than wholesale overriding of the rights of the accused. Cultures draw different lines on these matters, but the first thing to notice is *the existence of lines* and not just differences in where they are placed. Ethical differences between cultures can be compared and should be compared. How to carry out the comparing may require careful distinctions.

A particular case that has stirred up strong emotions across cultures is a practice in Africa called "clitoridectomy," "female circumcision," or "genital mutilation." How a moral issue is named is half the issue. Discussion of this issue raises questions of tribe, race, religion, and gender. Christian missionaries in Kenya were horrified at the practice; in the 1930s they preached against it but to little avail. The practice seems to have some strong cultural roots. That means to change the practice would involve many other changes in the culture. An outsider may not be able to grasp these interconnections.[19]

A number of people in the West (Alice Walker is one of the most prominent) have taken up as a cause the elimination of the practice.[20] The United States government has also become involved. In return, complaints of cultural imperialism have been raised: "Why doesn't the United States put its own house in order before telling Africans how to act?"

The question of responsibility that most interests me here is who does the listening and speaking. Can only Africans speak to this issue or are African Americans allowed? Or perhaps only African and African American women? Do white women have as much right to speak as black men? Or does neither qualify unless they are Muslim? Should the United States get out of the way and let the United Nations handle the question? But is not the United Nations suspected of being unduly influenced by the United States on such matters?

One is tempted to dismiss all such questions as irrelevant to moral law. However, if the world is to move toward a universal morality that arises from reciprocal exchanges, then who speaks and where they speak are indeed relevant questions. The principle needs defending that no one should be forbidden to express a view; there are no unbridgeable gulfs of understanding between genders, races, or nationalities. However, in any emotionally charged case there are some groups more appropriate than others for speaking in public forums. International women's groups have a right to protest cultural practices in places where women have suffered silently for centuries. In the present example, it would be helpful to hear Muslim spokespersons distinguish this practice from the practice of Islam. Groups of African women, perhaps with support from African American women, would seem to be the most appropriate groups to take the lead if protest is warranted.[21]

The mention of Islam's crucial part in this case should be broadened to a recognition of innumerable other moral situations where Islam can be of great help. One could never guess from news accounts in the United States that Islam is one of the great moral forces in the world and potentially is a much greater force. As a religion passionately held and deeply embodied, it almost inevitably has a fringe element that is dangerous. However, the overwhelming majority of Muslims lead upstanding moral lives. When Islam provides the first real basis of moral dignity for prisoners in the United States, that is considered a peculiar aberration. But providing moral stability is what Islam does throughout the world.

The assumption that people vary so much from culture to culture that a transcultural morality is impossible was challenged by Christianity as it moved from a corner of Asia across Africa and into Europe. Islam's immediate success was more spectacular in spreading through Africa, Asia and parts of Europe. This strongly moralistic religion continues to spread in all continents today.

Is Islam a bearer of "responsibility"? I have said that responsibility arose in a Jewish setting and was appropriated by Christianity. Islam is certainly compatible with the idea. Even more than Christianity, Islam is based on listening and responding to the spoken word (the Qur'an is a book not only dictated but one to be recited). And in Islam more than in Christianity, the response is always corporate. It is not a religion to be segregated to the privacy of individual life. Islam still has to contend with its crisis of modernity. Can it prosper not only in the

United States, Germany, and France but in Turkey, Pakistan, and Algeria? In a world where "modern" is no longer the last word, Islam could emerge from its struggles with modern culture stronger than ever.

I should note here in connection with Islam but also in relation to each of the great religions that the theme of this chapter—from an absolute to a relative morality—is not antireligious. On the contrary, the collapse of pseudo-absolutes is a liberating moment for religion.[22] The most fundamental and universal religious doctrine is: No thing in experience is absolute. No thing and no human individual should be confused with God. It cannot be denied that religions in practice do idolize; a text or an individual gets equated with the divine. However, a prophetic strain runs throughout Jewish, Christian, and Muslim religions. The prophetic voice is always one of de-divinization. Christians believe that Jesus is the supreme manifestation of the divine in an individual life. Muslims believe that the holy Qur'an is a divine dictation. Nonetheless, the Christian, Muslim, or Jew has to await the completion of history for the whole truth to be revealed. As the mystics in all three religions have said, the "word of God" is always spoken now.[23]

The Jew, Christian, and Muslim (as well as Buddhist, Sikh, and others) has to discover morality in relations. The responsibility to a final judgment has to be lived out patiently and discriminatingly. Morality is developed in the breadth and depth of corporate relations. The decalogue of Exodus or the commands of the Qur'an are indispensable guides in a Jewish or Muslim community. They are not universal rules that automatically solve moral dilemmas. Jews, Christians, and Muslims do make claim to following moral commands that embody universal moral truth. Their leaders are usually wise enough to realize that the commands as formulated cannot be imposed on others beyond the community. At the most, one can get at the universal truths only in negative form ("don't murder," "don't bear false witness"). Other peoples may also get close to these universals with alternate formulas.

The moral road for religion is either to try escaping from body, time, and matter, trusting in an experience or a thing that is outside language. Or else, the road is deeper immersion into the relations of the temporal and bodily, trusting that the divine is glimpsed in the totality of all relations. Responsibility is in principle to everyone and everything, although a tradition highlights the most helpful standards of judgment. Within the tradition, as well as beyond it, much of the struggle is against any standard claiming to be the absolute and final answer. In Christianity, for example, the "unique Christ" is found only at the end of history when all things are taken up into Christ. Nothing from the past and no rulings of today can be absolute. The supreme moral guide is conscience: the capacity to listen carefully and then to answer on the basis of the best available evidence.

A century ago, the movement of de-absolutizing morality was already occurring. It was mistakenly thought to be the victory of secular enlightenment over reactionary religions. Today no one is as optimistic as was the great classical historian, James Bury, when he wrote: "The struggle of reason against authority has ended in what appears now to be a decisive and permanent victory for liberty."[24] Within a year of these words being published, Europe was engulfed in the most widespread and irrational war in history.

What should be clear at the end of the twentieth century is that Bury's opposition of freedom and authority was tragically mistaken. Neither individual persons, nor nations, nor the world can get along without forms of authority. Persons are embodied elements within corporate structures. A person needs guidance from the past and opportunities for cooperative action in the present. People need to have some trust in the bodies governing their life and some hope of influencing them. The alternative to trust in one's neighbors, respect for authority, and engagement in political life is an external force to maintain order. Authority, as Hannah Arendt was at pains to point out, is not a form of violence but the opposite of violence.[25]

Responsibility as Transcultural

A good test case for this chapter is whether "responsibility" is an intelligible and central concept in Japan. I have earlier pointed out that responsibility arose out of a Western religious setting. And although Greek philosophy did not have the concept, Greek ideas of individuality, rationality, and freedom coalesced with the metaphor of listening and answering. Can responsibility serve as a link between Eastern and Western cultures?

Hitoshi Motoshima, as noted previously, stirred up a furor when he said that the emperor bore some responsibility for the war. In a subsequent interview, he said: "In Europe, people's feelings are based upon centuries of philosophy and religion, but the Japanese only worship nature. . . . In a world ruled by nature, the question of individual responsibility doesn't come up."[26] Perhaps significantly, Hitoshi Motoshima is a Christian; one of his critics said he "had not behaved as a Japanese." A Shinto priest wrote in criticism: "It is a common error among Christians and people with Western inclinations, including so-called intellectuals, to fail to grasp that Western societies and Japanese society are based on fundamentally different religious conceptions. . . . Forgetting this premise, they attempt to place a Western structure on a Japanese foundation. I think this kind of mistake explains the demand for the emperor to bear full responsibility."[27]

Although this exchange suggests a problem with "responsibility" being compatible with Japanese ethics, it should be remembered that it is a disagreement between Japanese speakers. It may be that the Japanese Christian is trying to import an idea that has been foreign to Japan and will remain so. One could speculate, however, that the difference lies *within* responsibility, that is, between two different meanings of responsibility. Hitoshi Motoshima's complaint is a lack of *individual* responsibility. But as I pointed out in chapters 4 and 5, the term "individual" may create a contrast with "collective" that clouds the fact that persons are always corporately responsible. Possibly the Japanese would not only find corporate responsibility intelligible, they might be a help in teaching its meaning to the United States.

It should also be noticed that the Shinto priest rejected attributing *full* responsibility to the emperor. Hitoshi Motoshima had carefully and explicitly attributed only partial responsibility to the emperor. In addition to the criticism being inaccurate and unfair, it suggests that responsibility is not necessarily the issue so much as an individualistic idea of responsibility in which one official is deemed to bear *full* responsibility for a complex event.

Ian Buruma, in *The Wages of Guilt*, is very hard on the Japanese. Whereas he thinks that the Germans have been coming to terms with World War II, he thinks Japan has refused to accept its responsibility. Buruma interprets this difference to be based on the fact that Germany has been influenced by Christian ideas of responsibility and guilt. Japanese culture, in contrast, is based on shame, not guilt. Shame leads to a withdrawal and to covering what is exposed. No doubt there are some cultural differences concerning guilt and shame, but it would seem unwise to conclude that there is an unbridgeable gulf here.[28]

Perhaps as the scholar Keiichi Tsuneishi has argued, Germany was surrounded by neighbors that would not let it forget the past, while Japan was surrounded by many nations who were imposing brutal regimes of their own and not interested in bringing up a discussion of brutality.[29] One should not overlook, however, the discussions of the Japanese Parliament in 1995, referred to in chapter 7; much of the argument was around the word responsibility. And although the ultimate acceptance of the term may reflect external pressure, it would seem extreme to continue to claim that "responsibility" is completely foreign to Japanese thinking.

World War II, still enveloped in strong emotions, may not be the best place to examine the question of Japanese responsibility. Current business practice may be a better test. The *New York Times* business section carried a study of business failure in the United States and Japan.[30] One scholar says: "We talk about Japan as a collective society, and yet individuals there quickly take responsibility for corporate mistakes. By contrast, Americans are considered rugged individualists, yet we readily try to evade responsibility for mistakes." This puzzle would be largely solved by understanding responsibility as neither individual nor collective. The Japanese have a sense of being *corporately* responsible, which is why they accept personal responsibility for failure. The U.S. businessman may call himself a "rugged individualist," but that fantasy means that failure does not fit in his self-image. When failure happens, he certainly cannot bear *full* responsibility, so he flees.

Another commentator on U.S. business today says there is "an absolute absence of shame. People used to be embarrassed about either doing a bad job or having to do bad things to do a better job. I don't see that anymore." What is rightly suggested here is that "shame" need not be the opposite of guilt or responsibility. Shame played an important part in Western educational theory from John Locke to Erik Erikson.[31] Like guilt, a little bit of shame goes a long way, and shame was overdone in educational theory and practice.[32] Nevertheless, the nearly total removal of shame from Western countries leaves reason with little emotional support for doing the right action. A person who does something wrong should feel ashamed. Instead of shame being an insuperable barrier to understanding Japan, perhaps Japan could help Western countries to relearn from their own history the need for a little shame in the child's upbringing.[33]

My suggestion that responsibility is an idea of nearly universal applicability is an ambitious claim to make for any moral notion. However, anyone who rejects responsibility is faced with proposing an alternate starting point. Especially since the 1940s, with the Universal Declaration of Rights, almost all the trust has been placed in the idea of rights. Although I have no objection to rights, much of the world resents the imposition of what is thought to be a concept of modern Western philosophy. Even when the concept is theoretically acceptable, many nations still cannot follow the logic of Western rights. Why, for example, is the United States obsessed with a right to uncensored speech while seemingly not concerned with a right of everyone to get adequate food or a right to walk on streets free of gunfire? There may be a logic at work here, but it can be a puzzling one to outsiders.

I pointed out in chapter 3 that responsibility is not a parallel to rights but a precondition. Because people are responsible (ontologically and morally), the mutually related ideas of rights and obligations arise. Governments should indeed recognize the rights of people, but they will do that only if they are first responsible to their own people and responsible to the example of other nations. Governments that begin being "responsible to" get pushed toward recognizing rights. After the Soviet Union signed the Helsinki agreement in 1979, human rights advocates (the so-called Helsinki group) within the country got a footing for their movement and exercised real pressure on the government.[34] One can see here some of the logic behind the United States' near obsession with the right to uncensored speech.

I am not optimistic that the United States shouting "responsibility" instead of "rights" at China, Singapore, or Iran would be any more successful than it has been. The important point is that the United States should itself be more *responsible to* such countries and encourage a process of responsibility within these countries. Such encouragement need not exclude economic and political pressures. However, such a response would arise from listening to voices from within the country and from detailed information about the country rather than from approaching every country with a textbook statement on human rights.

It would probably be unwise to push the term "responsibility." Whether or not the word translates easily into a language and culture, the idea can be nurtured by those who understand the grammar of the term. A nation that wishes to see other nations responsible can best exercise that influence by showing how it is done within its own borders. A responsible country is made up of communities that interact with each other and a government that is responsible to those communities.

Listening to the people is not a simple process, as the founders of the United States fully recognized and as emerging nations have discovered. A responsible government does not just act on whatever 51 percent of the population say they want at any moment. There has to be stability and continuity of law. A careful system of checks and balances needs to be in place to get at the deeper desires and more genuine wants. Electronic plebiscites, with everyone pushing a button on their T.V. remote, would not necessarily improve democracy. Moral responsibility requires depth as well as breadth. That depth is revealed in thoughtful, civic conversation between citizens who can agree to disagree.

Many commentators have bemoaned the decline of *this* culture in the United States. Its replacement is "interest groups" and opinion polls that do not look out for the good of the people as a whole. Despair at the possibility of a "multicommunity culture" leads to aggressive insistence on a "multicultural society." In this latter, the government is arbitrator among the numerous cultures. Given the language of the twentieth century, one can, of course, describe the United States (as well as England, Canada, Germany, Australia, and new places every day) as "multicultural." However, that fact does not dictate any single approach ("multiculturalism") to education, business, or government.

A "responsibility to" entails respecting differences. Sometimes it is better to disregard differences, but first one has to regard before one can disregard. Seventy-five years ago in the United States, efforts were made to suppress all languages except English. The effect was an irresponsible destruction of valuable cultural elements. The alternative, however, does not require schools to give full and equal treatment to every linguistic heritage. New York City has 175 language groups.[35] Its school system would collapse if it tried to provide instruction for each language group. The schools as well as other institutions could show respect for other languages, encourage *all* of the citizens to learn more than one language. Students could be encouraged to preserve and to cherish a language spoken at home, while at the same time they master English.

If curricula and textbooks try to attend to each "culture" in the United States, they may end by satisfying no one. The irony of attempts at a multicultural curriculum is that they invariably unleash complaints of groups being short-changed. If, for example, "African American" is one of a dozen or a hundred cultures studied, is that not subordinating the crucial part that blacks have played in the country since 1619? Is indeed African American a single culture or should one distinguish the urban culture of the North and the rural culture of the South? Are the urban cultures of Oakland, Detroit, Chicago, and New York the same culture? Are the South Bronx, Harlem, and Bedford-Stuyvesant the same New York culture? Within the South Bronx, do Christian African Americans and Muslim African Americans have the same culture? These questions are not asked flippantly. Once "culture" is taken to mean any group interest in competition with other groups, there is no logical stopping place. Given the number of characteristics cited as the basis of a culture (race, ethnicity, religion, gender, sexual orientation, and many more), and the possible combinations thereof, there are literally thousands of cultures in the United States.

If a concern for cultural plurality is not to disintegrate into chaos, some restriction on what "culture" means seems to be warranted. When "women," for example, are thought to be one of the players in the multicultural discussion, the issue of gender is given *less* attention than it deserves. As is often remarked, a group with 51 percent of the population is a strange minority. Including women with a dozen or several dozen minority cultures is not the way to face up to the relation of women and women, women and men, men and men.

Similar to the "gender issue," several other deep divisions in the country are only obscured further by the indiscriminate use of multicultural. If "culture" were restricted in meaning to divisions in which people differ by how they speak, how they get married, what stories they tell, what they eat, how they pray and how they are buried, then the plurality of culture would look very different. For example, one of the most obvious and most important would be the division between the North and the "deep South." More than a century and a quarter of time has not yet healed the wounds of war. However, one would have to search long in multicultural curricula for acknowledgment of this cultural division.

Overlapping the North/South division is one of the most obvious cultural differences people have: religion. From the beginning of the country, there have been intense religious differences. The nation was born of an uneasy alliance between an eighteenth-century deistic religion and a revivalistic evangelism. What held the two groups together was devotion to the religious ideal "America." Successive waves of immigrants have raised the level of complexity in this tension. Since the ideal of "America" is biblically based, Jews and Catholics could find a home in the United States. Muslims and other religious groups face a much tougher challenge.

In 1991, New York State published a guide for multi-cultural study.[36] In this study there is not a single sentence on religion. Culture is related to *cultus* or cult; religion is a primary shaper of culture. A curriculum guide that proposes to examine every culture in the country but has nothing to say about religion cannot be taken seriously. When religion is brought into the multicultural curriculum (as in California), the route is often the grand survey of "world religions." Few teachers, let alone fifth graders, are ready for the intricate detail of these surveys. While becoming informed about all of the world's religions would be worthwhile, the actual religious situation of the United States, past and present, remains a blank for most young people.

Almost everyone admits that the situation is messy and illogical. No one has a solution that would return us to simpler times or would produce a logical and fair society. What "responsibility" could do—an adequate grammar of responsibility—would be to open communication within people and between people. Listening to all the layers of oneself would reveal that one need not react as a member of one interest group or one "culture." What culture is an African American woman, who is Baptist, lives on Manhattan's East Side, and works at the United Nations? Like most people today, she is a confluence of multiple cultures. She is embedded in overlapping corporate structures that provide moral guidance. These guides can sometimes be divergent. Her response to a black issue may conflict with a feminist view. Her evangelical response may conflict with her urban openness. Her international interests may be in tension with her national citizenship.

There is nothing wrong with this woman. Indeed, the hope for the future rests on such people who are points of intersection between groups that are tempted toward separation. The rich uniqueness of her life has its problematic side in inevitable tensions and conflicts of ordinary life. That is the challenge and complexity of responsibility as the basis of moral life today. Responsibility is not a private virtue removed from the world of politics and business. It is a textured listening to all of the corporate structures of one's life and then acting before a cloud of witnesses, whether visible or not.

To take responsibility for our lives is an attempt to do more than is possible. Such an attempt brings on despair among the downtrodden, hubris among the well off. To accept responsibility for the next step in our lives, based on trust in our friends and fallible knowledge of our own selves, is both possible and necessary. Every responsible action makes possible a more responsible life. Every particular act of responsibility makes credible a universal responsibility. A morality thus lived is deeply relative and therefore increasingly universal.

NOTES

Chapter One

1. See W. Cantwell Smith, "Responsibility," in *Modernity and Responsibility*, ed. Eugene Combs (Toronto: University of Toronto Press, 1983), 79.

2. Paul Johnson, *Modern Times* (San Francisco: Harper, 1991), 10.

3. Pope John Paul II, *The Gospel of Life* (Washington: United States Catholic Conference, 1995).

4. *New York Times*, February 18, 1993.

5. Newt Gingrich, *To Renew America* (San Francisco: HarperCollins, 1995), 105. In direct opposition to this Republican vision, Gingrich posits the "countercultural left" and its all-powerful society. "In their view 'society' is always responsible for everything" (p. 38).

6. *Contract with America* (Washington, D.C.: Republican National Committee, 1994), 9–10.

7. Newt Gingrich, *New York Times*, March 9, 1995.

8. *New York Times*, January 2, 1995, 9.

9. See column by Anna Quindlen in *New York Times*, November 16, 1994.

10. Administrative Board of the United States Catholic Conference, *New York Times*, March 19, 1995.

11. *New York Times*, June 22, 1994. Mr. Garcetti did not prove to be prophetic on this point.

12. Arlene Croce, *New Yorker*, December 26, 1994, 54–55.

13. *Newsday*, April 21, 1993. On the White House's handling of this event, see Elizabeth Drew, *On the Edge: The Clinton Presidency* (New York: Simon and Schuster, 1994), 131–33; for a summary of the event and its aftermath, see Peter Boyer, "Children of Waco," *The New Yorker*, May 15, 1995, 38–45.

14. *New York Times*, May 6, 1995, 9. During the House hearings in 1995, Janet Reno stood firm: "I still reach the conclusion I did then. Faced with what I knew then, faced with the best information I could get at the time, I did not see another option." *New York Times*, July 31, 1995, A12.

15. Ian Buruma, *The Wages of Guilt* (New York: Farrar, Straus and Giroux, 1994), 294.

16. Daniel Callahan, *The Troubled Dream of Life* (New York: Simon and Schuster, 1993), 68.

17. A study by the American Hospital Association estimated that 70 percent of deaths in hospitals are negotiated; see *New York Times*, December 9, 1990.

18. Daniel Callahan, *Troubled Dream*, 68.

19. Sol Linowitz, *The Betrayed Profession* (New York: Scribner, 1994), 11.

20. *New York Times*, March 19, 1995.

21. *New York Times*, February 28, 1993.

22. Plato, *Meno* 80e.

23. The main polls over the decades have been the National Fertility Studies, Gallup Polls, and National Opinion Research Center surveys; for a summary of these, see Mary Ann Glendon, *Abortion and Divorce in Western Law* (Cambridge: Cambridge University Press, 1987), 41; see also *The Abortion Dispute and the American System* (Washington: Brookings Institution, 1983); E. J. Dionne, *Why Americans Hate Politics* (New York: Touchstone, 1992), 341–43.

24. Kristin Luker, *Abortion and the Politics of Motherhood* (Berkeley: University of California Press, 1984).

25. Carol Gilligan, *In a Different Voice* (Cambridge: Harvard University Press, 1982).

26. Alasdair MacIntyre, *Three Rival Versions of Moral Enquiry* (Notre Dame, Ind.: University of Notre Dame Press, 1990).

27. Ibid., 78.

28. See Wayne Dosick, *Golden Rules: The Ten Ethical Values Parents Need to Teach Their Children* (San Francisco: HarperSanFrancisco, 1995).

29. William Bennett, *The Book of Virtues* (New York: Simon and Schuster, 1994).

30. Ludwig Wittgenstein, *Philosophical Investigations* (New York: Macmillan, 1953).

31. John Wikse, *About Possession: The Self as Private Property* (University Park: Pennsylvania State University Press, 1977), 16.

32. As an example of such an attempt, see Council for a Parliament of the World's Religions, *A Global Ethic* (Chicago: Council for a Parliament of the World's Religions, 1993).

33. Jane Flax, *Thinking Fragments: Psychoanalysis, Feminism and Postmodernism in the Contemporary World* (Berkeley: University of California Press, 1990), 223.

Chapter Two

1. See Gertrude Himmelfarb, *The Demoralization of Society* (New York: Knopf, 1995).

2. Plato, *Republic* 428–49.

3. Aristotle, *Nicomachean Ethics* (New York: Penguin, 1955).

4. Hans Jonas, *The Imperative of Responsibility* (Chicago: University of Chicago Press, 1984), 1.

5. William Bennett, *The Book of Virtues*, 186; *The Federalist* (New York: Modern Library, 1941), # 63, p. 408.

6. *The Compact Edition of the Oxford English Dictionary*, II, 2514. An exception is a use of "responsible for" in David Hume, *Treatise of Human Nature* (Oxford: Oxford University Press, 1978), 411, where he refers to actions that may be blameable "but the person not responsible for them." For the earliest uses of the term in French and German, see Richard McKeon, "The Development and Significance of the Concept of Responsibility," in *Freedom and History and Other Essays* (Chicago: University of Chicago Press, 1990), 66–67.

7. Ibid.

8. Arthur Adkins, *Merit and Responsibility: A Study in Greek Values* (Oxford: Oxford University Press, 1960), 3. See the interesting treatment of Aristotle in Marion Smiley, *Moral Responsibility and the Boundaries of Community* (Chicago: University of Chicago Press, 1992), 33–57; Smiley develops a consistent political approach to responsibility for which Aristotle is helpful.

9. J. R. Lucas, *Responsibility* (Oxford: Clarendon Press, 1993), 11; see also T. H. Irwin, "Reason and Responsibility in Aristotle," *Essays on Aristotle's Ethics*, ed. Amelie Rorty (Berkeley: University of California Press, 1980), 117–55.

10. Plato, *Symposium* 210a–c.

11. See Bernard Lonergan, *Insight: A Study of Human Understanding* (New York: Philosophical Library, 1970).

12. Huston Smith, *The Religions of Man* (New York: Harper, 1958), 204.

13. W. Cantwell Smith, "Responsibility."

14. See Philipe Aries, *The Hour of Our Death* (New York: Oxford University Press, 1981).

15. Bernard Haring, *The Law of Christ* (Baltimore: Newman Press, 1953).

16. W. Cantwell Smith, "Responsibility," 83.

17. Martin Gritsch, *Martin—God's Court Jester* (Minneapolis: Fortress Press, 1983), 170.

18. Voltaire, *Philosophic Dictionary* (New York: Penguin, 1971), 386.

19. John Locke, *The Reasonableness of Christianity* (Stanford: Stanford University Press, 1958).

20. Ben McIntyre, *Forgotten Fatherland: The Search for Elisabeth Nietzsche* (New York: Farrar, Straus and Giroux, 1992).

21. Friedrich Nietzsche, *Beyond Good and Evil* (Hammondsworth: Penguin, 1973), 87, #168.

22. Fyodor Dostoyevsky, *The Brothers Karamazov* (New York: Signet, 1957), 538.

23. Friedrich Nietzsche, *Genealogy of Morals* (Garden City, N.Y.: Doubleday, 1956), 190.

24. Ibid., 207.

25. Ibid., 155.

26. Ibid., 264.

27. Ibid., 252.

28. Friedrich Nietzsche, *Gay Science* (New York: Random House, 1974), no. 182, p. 125.

29. Jean-Jacques Rousseau, *Emile* (New York: Basic Books, 1979), 39.

30. Hannah Arendt, *The Life of the Mind. Part II: Willing* (New York: Harcourt, Brace, Jovanovich, 1978), 19–20.

31. Friedrich Nietzsche, *Gay Science*, no. 329, p. 62; Leslie Thiele, *Friedrich Nietzsche and the Politics of the Soul* (Princeton, N.J.: Princeton University Press, 1990), 57; Lancelot Whyte, *The Unconscious Before Freud* (New York: Basic, 1960), 176.

32. Jean-Paul Sartre, *Being and Nothingness* (New York: Washington Square, 1966), 707.

33. Ibid., 710.

34. Jean-Paul Sartre, *The Flies*, (London: Hamish House, 1946), 120.

35. Albert Schweitzer, *Ethics and Civilization* (London: A & C Black, 1923), 2. 259.

36. Friedrich Nietzsche, *Beyond Good and Evil*, no. 32, p. 45.

37. See Larry May, *Sharing Responsibility* (Chicago: University of Chicago Press, 1992), 173.

38. Hannah Arendt, *Willing*, 377–78.

39. Martin Heidegger, *Nietzsche* (San Francisco: Harper, 1991).

40. Martin Heidegger, *Discourse on Thinking* (New York: Harper, 1969), 62; see also the interview in *Der Spiegel*, May 31, 1976.

41. See Hugo Ott, *Martin Heidegger: A Political Life* (New York: Basic Books, 1993); Thomas Sheehan, "Heidegger and the Nazis," *New York Review of Books*, June 16, 1988, 38–47.

42. Larry May, *Sharing Responsibility*, 173.

43. Max Weber, "Politics as a Vocation," in *On Being Responsible*, ed. James Gustafson and James Laney (New York: Harper and Row, 1968), 301.

44. Ibid., 301.

45. Ibid., 309.

46. Ibid., 308.

47. Pinchas Lapide, *The Sermon on the Mount* (New York: Orbis Press, 1982).

48. Max Weber, "Politics as a Vocation," 301.

49. Ibid., 308.

50. *The Autobiography of Malcolm X* (New York: Ballantine, 1973), 459.

51. José Miguez Bonino, *Doing Theology in a Revolutionary Situation* (Philadelphia: Fortress Press, 1975), 29; for the report of the meeting, see J. H. Oldham, "A Responsible Society," in *Man's Disorder and God's Design* (New York: Harper, 1948).

52. The man who was most influential in the use of the term was not unaware of the criticism. W. A. Visser 't Hooft, *The Ten Formative Years 1938–48* (Geneva: World Council of Churches, 1948), 9: "A responsible society is one where freedom is the freedom of men who acknowledge responsibility to justice and public order, and where those who hold political authority or economic power are responsible for its exercise to God and the people whose welfare is affected by it." Visser 't Hooft continued in *The Evanston Report* (New York: Harper and Brothers, 1955) to try to refine the meaning of "responsible" ("a criterion to judge existing social orders") and he had not given up in the 1960s when rebellion against the term became obvious.

53. Jose Bonino, *Doing Theology in a Revolutionary Situation*, 31; see also Ernest Lefever, *Amsterdam to Nairobi* (Washington: Ethics and Public Policy Center, 1979).

54. John Howard Yoder, *The Politics of Jesus* (Grand Rapids: Eerdmans, 1972), 98, 136, 131, 155.

55. Ibid., 158.

56. Martin Buber, *I and Thou* (New York: Scribner, 1970), 57, 62.

57. Emmanuel Levinas, *The Levinas Reader* (New York: Basil Blackwell, 1989); Franz Rosenzweig, *The Star of Redemption* (Boston: Beacon Press, 1971); Emmanuel Mounier, *Personalism* (London: Routledge and Kegan Paul, 1952); Gabriel Marcel, *Homo Viator* (New York: Harper Torch, 1962).

58. Karl Rahner, *Hearers of the Word* (New York: Herder and Herder, 1969).

59. See Yves Congar, *The Mystery of the Church* (Baltimore: Helicon, 1960); Edward Schillebeeckx, *Christ the Sacrament of Encounter with God* (New York: Sheed and Ward, 1963); Bernard Haring, *The Law of Christ*; Gabriel Moran *Theology of Revelation* (New York: Herder and Herder, 1966).

60. Dietrich Bonhoffer, *Ethics* (New York: Macmillan, 1965).

61. See Wayne Floyd and Charles Marsh, eds., *Theology and the Practice of Responsibility: Essays on Dietrich Bonhoefer* (Valley Forge, Penn.: Trinity Press, 1994).

62. H. Richard Niebuhr, *The Responsible Self* (New York: Harper and Row, 1978).

63. Ibid., 68.

64. See H. Richard Niebuhr, *The Meaning of Revelation* (New York: Macmillan, 1962) and *Radical Monotheism and Western Culture* (New York: Harper, 1970).

65. Ibid., 57.

66. "A being not only knows itself in relation to other selves but exists as self only in that relation." Ibid., 71.

67. Vaclav Havel, *Living in Truth* (London: Faber and Faber, 1987), 155.

68. See Carol Gilligan, "Justice and Responsibility: Thinking about the Real Dilemmas of Moral Choice," *Toward Moral and Religious Maturity*, ed. Christiane Brusselmans (Morristown, Penn.: Silver Burdett, 1980), 228, 245–47.

69. Carol Gilligan, *In a Different Voice*, chapter 2, 24–63.

70. See Nona Plessner Lyons, "On Self, Relationships and Morality," *Mapping the Moral Domain*, ed. Carol Gilligan and others (Cambridge: Harvard University Press, 1988), 21–48; Nel Noddings, *Caring: A Feminist Approach to Ethics and Moral Education* (Berkeley: University of California Press, 1984).

71. Carol Gilligan, "Do the Social Sciences Have an Adequate Theory of Moral Development?" in *Social Science as Moral Inquiry*, ed. Norma Haan and Robert Bellah (New York: Columbia University Press, 1983), 40.

72. Carol Gilligan, *In a Different Voice*, 101.

73. Walter Brueggeman, "Voices of the Night—Against Justice," *To Act Justly, Love Tenderly, Walk Humbly* (New York: Paulist Press, 1986), 5.

Chapter Three

1. J. L. Austin, *Philosophical Papers* (Oxford: Clarendon Press, 1961), 149.

2. John Martin Fischer and Mark Ravizza, eds., *Perspectives on Moral Responsibility* (Ithaca, N.Y.: Cornell University Press, 1993), 5.

3. Bruce Waller, *Freedom without Responsibility* (Philadelphia: Temple University Press, 1990), 65 (italics are mine). As for what moral responsibility means, Waller writes on p. 73 that "'moral responsibility' justifies or even requires special treatment or special deserts."

4. Ibid., 73. In this distinction "moral-judgment responsible focuses on the process by which responsibility is assigned" (p. 74).

5. Waller's book is thus a variation on a theme that runs from Jeremy Bentham to B. F. Skinner, that is, the unfairness and ineffectiveness of blame and punishment. But Skinner's position is that the way to get rid of responsibility is to deny its premise: freedom. See B. F. Skinner, *Beyond Freedom and Dignity* (Hammondsworth: Penguin Books, 1973), 25, 206.

6. Ludwig Wittgenstein, *Blue and Brown Books* (New York: Barnes and Noble, 1969), 16.

7. See E. P. Evans, *The Criminal Prosecution and Capital Punishment of Animals* (London: Faber and Faber, 1906).

8. Mary Midgley, *Beast and Man* (Ithaca, N.Y.: Cornell University Press, 1978), 235.

9. The report is entitled "The Unspoken Tragedy: Firearm Suicide in the

United States." It was issued on June 3, 1995 by the Educational Fund to End Handgun Violence and the Coalition to Stop Gun Violence.

10. Melody Allen in *New York Times*, December 21, 1993, CI.

11. Christopher Stone, *Should Trees Have Standing?* (New York: Avon, 1975).

12. Victor Frankl, *Man's Search for Meaning* (New York: Washington Square, 1985), 90.

13. Brian Walsh and others, "Trees, Forestry and the Responsiveness of Creation," *Cross Currents* 44(Summer, 1994), 149–62.

14. Martin Buber, *I and Thou*, 57.

15. Ibid., 146.

16. T. S. Eliot, *Old Possum's Book of Practical Cats* (New York: Harcourt, Brace, 1939), 54.

17. Elizabeth Marshall Thomas, *The Tribe of Tiger* (New York: Simon and Schuster, 1994), 101.

18. Elizabeth Marshall Thomas, *The Hidden Life of Dogs* (Boston: Houghton Mifflin, 1993), 111–21.

19. See Hannah Pitkin, *Wittgenstein and Justice* (Berkeley: University of California Press, 1972), 225.

20. Gail Sheehy, *Passages* (New York: Dutton, 1976).

21. As in the documentary films by Frederick Wiseman or in Robert Coles's books that stay close to the interviewee's words.

22. Elisabeth Kubler-Ross, *On Death and Dying* (New York: Macmillan, 1969).

23. Ibid., 114.

24. See Ludwig Wittgenstein's description of giving reasons as leading up to whether it will "appeal to the judge." As cited by G. E. Moore, in *Classics of Analytic Philosophy*, ed. R. Amerrman (New York: McGraw-Hill, 1965), 278.

25. Martin Buber, *The Knowledge of Man* (New York: Harper and Row, 1965), 115.

26. Hans Jonas, *The Imperative of Responsibility*, 90.

27. Hannah Arendt, *The Human Condition* (Chicago: University of Chicago Press, 1958), 40.

28. Thomas Moore, *Care of the Soul* (San Francisco: HarperCollins, 1992), 5.

29. Kenneth Eble, *A Perfect Education* (New York: Collier Books, 1966), 15.

30. John Stuart Mill, *On Liberty* (Indianapolis: Hackett, 1978), 5.

31. William James, *Varieties of Religious Experience* (New York: New American Library, 1958), 49; see also Gerd Theissen, *A Critical Faith* (Philadelphia: Fortress, 1979), 63.

32. Robert Bellah and others, *Habits of the Heart* (Berkeley: University of California Press, 1985), 304.

33. Ibid., 16.

34. Fyodor Dostoyevsky, *Brothers Karamazov*, 537.

35. Dietrich Bonhoeffer, *Ethics*, 235.

36. Eugene Levinas, *Nine Talmudic Readings*, (Bloomington: Indiana University Press, 1990), 87, 85.

37. *Washington Post*, March 30, 1993.

38. Mark Danner, "The Truth of El Mozote," *New Yorker*, December 6, 1993, 50–133.

39. Hans Jonas, *The Imperative of Responsibility*, 93.

40. Dallin Oaks, "Rights and Responsibilities," *The Responsive Community* 1 (Winter, 1990–91): 40.

41. Amatai Etzioni, *The Spirit of Community* (New York: Crown, 1993), 251–67.

42. Ibid., 26; see also Christopher Lasch, *The Revolt of the Elites* (New York: Norton, 1995), 89: "We are so busy defending our rights (rights conferred for the most part by judicial decree) that we give little thought to our responsibilities"; see also the "Bill of Rights and Responsibilities for Learning," drawn up by the American Federation of Teachers: *New York Times*, September 10, 1995, E8.

43. Henry de Vries and Nina Galston, *Materials for the French Legal System* (New York: Parker School, 1969), 3–4.

44. See Robert Seltzer, *Jewish People, Jewish Thought* (New York: Macmillan, 1980), 298; for the biblical texts summarizing the law, see Micah 6:8: "Do justly, love mercy, walk humbly"; Amos 5:6: "Seek me and live"; Habakkuk 2:4: "The righteous shall live by faith."

45. Quoted in Philip Howard, *The Death of Common Sense* (New York: Random House, 1994), 122.

46. Isaiah Berlin, *The Crooked Timber of Humanity* (New York: Knopf, 1990).

47. *Universal Declaration of Human Rights* (New York: United Nations, 1947).

48. Edmund Pincoffs, *Revisions*, ed. Alasdair MacIntyre and Stanley Hauerwas (Notre Dame, Ind.: University of Notre Dame Press, 1983), 153.

49. Mary Ann Glendon, *Abortion and Divorce in Western Law*, 39.

50. John Stuart Mill, *On Liberty*, 10–11.

51. H. L. A. Hart, *Punishment and Responsibility* (London: Oxford University Press, 1968), 44.

Chapter Four

1. In Newt Gingrich, Dick Armey, and others, *Contract with America*, 9–10, it is noteworthy that the proposal for welfare reform starts with a heading of "personal responsibility" but ends with the aim "to promote individual responsibility."

2. "The problems of the human heart in conflict with itself . . . alone can

make good writing." William Faulkner as quoted in Bruno Bettelheim, *Freud and Man's Soul* (New York: Knopf, 1983), 111.

3. See Tibor Scitovsky, *The Joyless Economy* (New York: Oxford University Press, 1976).

4. Michael Sandel, *Liberalism and the Limits of Justice* (Cambridge: Cambridge University Press, 1982); John Rawls tries in a subsequent book to find a place for what he calls "comprehensive doctrines," such as religious motivation; see *Political Liberalism* (New York: Columbia University Press, 1994).

5. Mary Midgley, *Wickedness* (London: Kegan Paul, 1984), 174.

6. Ibid., 63.

7. Herbert Fingarette, *Self-Deception* (New York: Humanities Press, 1969), 47.

8. D. H. Lawrence, "Apropos of Lady Chatterly's Lover," *Lady Chatterly's Lover* (London: Penguin, 1994), 320.

9. William Doherty, *Soul Searching: Why Psychotherapy Must Promote Moral Responsibility* (New York: Basic Books, 1995), 8. Despite the subtitle of the book, "responsibility" is not discussed after the introduction, where it is assumed that today there is a "flight from responsibility."

10. Howard Greenstein, *Judaism—An Eternal Covenant* (Philadelphia: Fortress Press, 1983), 30.

11. Euripides, *Medea* 1078–80.

12. A. E. Taylor, *The Mind of Plato* (Ann Arbor: University of Michigan Press, 1964), 97. Plato has often been understood to have a simplistic notion of one good and one bad element. One of his most famous images is of a charioteer trying to control two horses going in opposite directions (*Phaedrus* 246–57). That image can have varying interpretations. But in the above paragraph I am referring to Plato's description in the *Republic* of two conflicting elements and a mediating third.

13. Romans 7:15.

14. Quoted in Reinhold Niebuhr, *Man's Nature and His Communities* (New York: Scribner, 1965), 24.

15. See Sebastian Moore, *The Inner Loneliness* (New York: Crossroad, 1982), 48.

16. Hannah Arendt, *Essays in Understanding*, ed. Jerome Kohn (New York: Harcourt Brace, 1995); Conor Cruise O'Brien defends "an Enlightenment that is aware that there is far more evidence extant in favor of the Christian doctrine of Original Sin than of Rousseau's doctrine of Original Virtue"; see *On the Eve of the Millennium* (New York: Anansi, 1995).

17. Etienne Gilson, *God and Philosophy* (New Haven, Conn.: Yale University Press, 1941).

18. Timothy Cooney, *Telling Right from Wrong* (Buffalo, N.Y.: Prometheus Books, 1985), 25.

19. Sigmund Freud, *The Psychopathology of Everyday Life* (New York: Norton, 1901); *The Ego and the Id* (New York: Norton, 1923).

20. John Stuart Mill, *On Liberty*, 58.

21. Erich Neumann, *Depth Psychology and A New Ethic* (London: Hodder and Stoughton, 1969), 14.

22. William Butler Yeats, *Responsibilities and Other Poems* (New York: Macmillan, 1916).

23. *New York Times*, February 3, 1995.

24. Greg Louganis, *Breaking the Surface* (New York: Random House, 1995), 141.

25. Michael Zimmerman, *An Essay on Moral Responsibility* (Totowa, N.J.: Rowan and Littlefield, 1988), 2: "Our language much more readily sanctions 'the lifeguard is *morally* responsible for the swimmers' deaths' than it does 'the anonymous donor is *morally* responsible for the charity's success', the reason for which escapes me."

26. Larry May, *Sharing Responsibility*, 34.

27. Martin Heidegger, *Being and Time* (London: SCM Press, 1962), #58, p. 326; Hannah Arendt, *Willing*, 184.

28. Karl Jaspers, *The Question of German Guilt* (New York: Dial, 1947).

29. Quoted in Jonathan Glover, *Responsibility* (New York: Humanities Press, 1970), 20.

30. Aristotle, *Nicomachean Ethics* 1110a.

31. Bruce Waller, *Freedom without Responsibility*, 183.

32. Gregory Vlastos, *Socrates, Ironist and Moral Philosopher* (Ithaca, N.Y.: Cornell University Press, 1991), 189.

33. Protagoras 324a–c

34. James Kunen, "Teaching Prisoners a Lesson," *New Yorker*, July 10, 1995, 34–39.

35. H. L. A. Hart, *Punishment and Responsibility*, 159.

36. Quoted in James Kunen, "Teaching Prisoners a Lesson," 37.

37. Ironically, the Constitutional Court of South Africa, in abolishing capital punishment, quoted judges and authors from the United States. These included William Brennan from the 1972 case of Furman vs. Georgia: "a society that wishes to prevent crime . . . not to kill criminals simply to get even with them." *Newsday*, June 29, 1995, 41.

38. Robert Morganthau, " What Prosecutors Won't Tell You," *New York Times*, February 7, 1995, p. A25. See also Alexis de Tocqueville, *Democracy in America* (New York: Knopf, 1948), 2. 166: "While the English seem disposed to retain the bloody traces of the Middle Ages in their penal legislation, the Americans have almost expunged capital punishment from their codes."

39. David Dennett, *Elbow Room* (Cambridge, Mass.: MIT Press, 1984), 65.

40. Bruce Waller, *Freedom without Responsibility*, 184.

41. Surely one of the best books ever written on the immorality of capital punishment is Helen Prejean, *Dead Man Walking* (New York: Vintage, 1993).

42. Aristotle, *Nicomachean Ethics* 1109b30–1111b5; see also Hannah Arendt, *Willing*, 16–19.

43. Quoted in Bernard Weisberger, *They Gathered at the River* (Boston: Little, Brown, 1958), 211; see also Richard Hofstadter, *Anti-Intellectualism in America* (New York: Vintage Books, 1963), 111.

44. In British English one more often "takes" a decision, although "makes" has made inroads.

45. Stanley Hauerwas, *The Peaceable Kingdom* (Notre Dame, Ind.: University of Notre Dame Press, 1983), 124.

46. David Dennett, *Elbow Room*, 135.

47. Michael Polanyi, *Personal Knowledge* (New York: Harper Torch, 1964), 309.

48. David Dennett, *Elbow Room*, 157, referring to Thomas Aquinas *De Ver.* q. 23, a. 4; see also Augustine, *The Enchiridion: On Faith, Hope and Love* (Chicago: Regnery, 1961), 123: "Now, it was expedient that man should be at first so created, as to have it in his power to will what was right and to will what was wrong. . . . But in the future life it shall not be in his power to will evil; and yet this will constitute no restriction on the freedom of his will. On the contrary, his will shall be much freer when it shall be wholly impossible for him to be the slave of sin." For the history of the attempt in Christianity to reconcile freedom and necessity, see Leszek Kolakowski, *God Owes Us Nothing* (Chicago: University of Chicago Press, 1995).

49. William Schweiker, *Responsibility and Christian Ethics* (Cambridge: Cambridge University Press, 1995), 146; see also Charles Taylor, "Responsibility for Self," in *Free Will*, ed. Gary Watson (New York: Oxford University Press, 1982), 111–26; Mary Midgley, *The Ethical Primate* (New York: Routledge, 1994), 84.

50. Buber, *I and Thou*, 59.

51. Mary Midgley, *Beast and Man*, 267.

52. Ibid., 265.

53. William Lynch, *Images of Hope* (New York: Mentor Books, 1966), 185.

54. Michel Foucault, *Madness and Civilization* (New York: Vintage Books, 1973).

55. Glenn Loury, *One by One from the Inside Out: Essays and Reviews on Race and Responsibility* (New York: Free Press, 1995), 37.

56. Aristotle, *Nicomachean Ethics* 1113b.

57. Andrew Delbanco and Thomas Delbanco, "Annals of Addiction," *New Yorker*, March 20, 1995, 50–63.

58. Leon Kass, *The Hungry Soul* (New York: Free Press, 1994).

59. See Ellen Bass and Laura Davis, *The Courage to Heal*, 3rd ed. (New York:

Harper, 1994); Richard Ofshe and Ethan Watters, *Making Monsters: False Memories, Psychotherapy and Sexual Hysteria* (New York: Scribner, 1994).

60. Vaclav Havel, *Living in Truth*, 153.

61. Michael Walzer, *Thick and Thin: Moral Arguments at Home and Abroad* (Notre Dame, Ind.: University of Notre Dame Press, 1994), 97.

62. Hannah Arendt, *The Life of the Mind: Thinking* (New York: Harcourt, Brace, Jovanovich, 1978), 5.

63. Murray Kempton, *Newsday*, Dec. 22, 1994.

64. John Stuart Mill, *On Liberty*, 74.

Chapter Five

1. Peter French, *Collective and Corporate Responsibility* (New York: Columbia University Press, 1984), vii.

2. Elizabeth Wolgast, *Ethics of an Artificial Person* (Stanford, Calif.: Stanford University Press, 1992).

3. Peter French, *Collective and Corporate Responsibility*, viii.

4. Caroline Walker Bynum, *The Resurrection of the Body in Western Christianity 200–1336* (New York: Columbia University Press, 1995).

5. Jean Piaget, *The Moral Judgment of the Child* (New York: Free Press, 1965), 331: summarizing the work of Paul Fauconnet.

6. Peter French, *Collective and Corporate Responsibility*, xi.

7. Peter French, *Responsibility Matters* (Lawrence: University of Kansas Press, 1992), 143.

8. Bernard Meltzer, *Symbolic Interactionism* (Boston: Routledge and Kegan Paul, 1975), 121.

9. Erving Goffman, *Interaction Ritual: Essays in Face to Face Behavior* (Garden City, N.Y.: Anchor Books, 1967); *Relations in Public* (New York: Basic Books, 1971).

10. Emile Durkheim, *Education and Sociology* (Glencoe, N.Y.: Free Press, 1956), 123; not surprisingly, Durkheim places sociology in charge of education: "The role of sociology is predominant in the determination of the ends that education should follow (p. 129).

11. Glenn Loury, *One by One from the Inside Out*, 29. Christopher Lasch (*Revolt of the Elites*, 106) criticizes the communitarians by saying "that they seem to be more interested in the responsibility of the community as a whole—its responsibility, say, to its least fortunate members—than in the responsibility of individuals." In this statement Lasch mistakenly sees this contrast as whole to part, but what his own language reveals is two different

meanings of responsibility, namely, the responsibility of the community *to* the least fortunate and the responsibility of individuals *for* their actions.

12. For the history of "society" from the Greeks down to the present, see Hannah Arendt, *The Human Condition*, 38–49.

13. P. W. Duff, *Personality in Roman Private Law* (Cambridge: Cambridge University Press, 1938).

14. James Coleman, *The Asymmetric Society* (Syracuse, N.Y.: Syracuse University Press, 1982), 7.

15. Jean-Jacques Rousseau, *The Social Contract* and *Discourse on the Origin of Inequality* (New York: Washington Square, 1967), 169.

16. Jean-Jacques Rousseau, *Emile*, Book 5.

17. Jean-Jacques Rousseau, *Les Solitaires*; see Susan Okin, *Women in Western Political Thought* (Princeton, N.J.: Princeton University Press, 1979), 169–70.

18. John Dewey *Democracy and Education* (New York: Free Press, 1966), 112–18; "The Need for a Philosophy of Education," in *Dewey on Education* (New York: Modern Library, 1964), 4.

19. John Dewey, *School and Society* (Chicago: University of Chicago Press, 1990), 81.

20. Peter French, *Responsibility Matters*, 137.

21. Alexis de Tocqueville, *Democracy in America*, 2. 106.

22. Ralph Nader, *Taming the Giant Corporation* (New York: Norton, 1976), 43–61.

23. Frederick Taylor, *The Principles of Scientific Management* (New York: Harper and Brothers, 1911); on the application of this theory to the school, see Alan Tom, *Teaching as a Moral Craft* (New York: Longman, 1984), 16–19.

24. Cited in David Tyack, *The One Best System* (Cambridge: Harvard University Press, 1974), 41.

25. John Westbrook, *John Dewey and American Democracy* (Ithaca, N.Y.: Cornell University Press, 1991).

26. James Fallows, *More Like Us* (Boston: Houghton Mifflin, 1989), 193.

27. Reinhold Niebuhr *Moral Man and Immoral Society* (New York: Scribner, 1960), 95.

28. Ibid., xi.

29. Dietrich Bonhoeffer, *Ethics*, 191–92: "The distinction of individual and society is too abstract and leads to that complete ethical aporia which nowadays goes by the name of 'social ethics'"; see also Edward Leroy Long, "The Social Roles of the Moral Self," in *Private and Public Ethics*, ed. Donald Jones (New York: Edward Mellen, 1978), 158–79.

30. A. S. Neill, *Summerhill School* (New York: St. Martin's Press, 1992), 5.

31. *New York Times*, March 3, 1994.

32. Allan Bloom, *The Closing of the American Mind* (New York: Simon and Schuster, 1987), 67.

33. Victor Frankl, *Man's Search for Meaning*, 174.

34. Jürgen Habermas, "A Talk between Jürgen Habermas and Adam Michnik," *New York Review of Books*, March 24, 1994, 25.

35. P. F. Strawson, "Freedom and Resentment," in *Freedom and Resentment and Other Essays* (London: Methuen, 1962), 1–25.

36. For a study of small groups and their functioning today, see Robert Wuthnow, *Sharing the Journey* (New York: Free Press, 1994), especially 158–61; 317–40.

37. Ferdinand Tönnies, *Community and Society* (New York: Harper and Row, 1963).

38. Michael Walzer, *The Revolution of the Saints* (Cambridge: Harvard University Press, 1965), 196: "The Puritan transformation of the family remained incomplete; so long as children were born, instead of appearing voluntarily like colonists in a new country, the family could not become a purely political society."

39. Edmund Morgan, *The Puritan Family* (New York: Harper and Row, 1944), 149; for the text of the Synod, see Perry Miller, *Errand into the Wilderness* (New York: Harper, 1956), 7–8.

40. John Demos, *A Little Commonwealth: Family Life in the Plymouth Colony* (New York: Oxford University Press, 1970).

41. Shoshana Alexander, *In Praise of Single Parents: Mothers and Fathers Embracing the Challenge* (New York: Houghton Mifflin, 1994). Judith Stacey, reviewing this book, notes: "Communitarians above all should recognize that just as no one can be a single parent, neither can two parents rear responsible members of our communities by themselves." See *The Responsive Community* 5 (Spring, 1995): 67.

42. Mary Ann Glendon, *Abortion and Divorce in Western Law*.

43. Susan Moller Okin, *Justice, Gender and the Family* (New York: Basic Books, 1989).

44 Ronald Beiner, *Political Judgment* (Chicago: University of Chicago Press, 1983), 122.

45. Richard Sennett, *Flesh and Stone* (New York: Norton, 1994), 56; on the city as a teacher of responsibility, see Jane Jacobs, *The Death and Life of Great American Cities* (New York: Macmillan, 1961).

46. William Bradford, *History of Plymouth Plantations 1606–46* (New York: Modern Library, 1952).

47. Richard Hofstadter, *Anti-Intellectualism in America* (New York: Harper, 1967).

48. Newt Gingrich's *To Renew America* is an all too typical case of this confusion. Early in the book (p. 37), he writes that "America must be described in romantic terms. . . . To me America is a romance in which we all participate." That would be a fine sentiment if in the rest of the book Gingrich did not use

"America" to refer to an existing nation state. The eight-page introduction uses "America(n)" thirty-nine times; never once does the Speaker of the U.S. House of Representatives refer to the United States. In the page and a half chapter, Individual versus Group Rights, "America" appears fifteen times, the "United States" not at all.

49. Colin Powell, *My American Journey* (New York: Random House, 1995), 612.

50. *Shabbat* 54b.

51. Pope John Paul II, *Crossing the Threshold of Hope*, (New York: Knopf, 1994), 208.

52. Migali Larson, *The Rise of Professionalism* (Berkeley: University of California Press, 1977).

53. Rena Gorlin, *Codes of Professional Responsibility* (Washington: Bureau of National Affairs, 1986).

54. Richard Sennett, *Authority* (New York: Knopf, 1980), 62–87.

55. *New York Times*, Business Section, Sept. 18, 1994.

56. James Coleman, *Asymmetric Society*, 101.

57. Christopher Stone has proposed reforms that would require greater flow of information within companies, thus reducing the plea of ignorance; see *Where the Law Ends: The Social Control of Corporate Behavior* (New York: Harper and Row, 1975).

58. Peter French, *Responsibility Matters*, 97.

59. Aristotle, *Nicomachean Ethics* 114a; Peter French, *Collective and Corporate Responsibility*, 164.

60. James Coleman, *Asymmetric Society*, 104–11.

Chapter Six

1. Stephen Toulmin, *Return to Cosmology* (Berkeley: University of California Press, 1982), 172.

2. It should be noted that some early humanists, including Montaigne, did argue that animals should be treated humanely; see Montaigne's "Essay on Cruelty" in *The Essays of Michel De Montaigne* (New York: Knopf, 1935), 2. 92–93.

3. Martin Heidegger, "Letter on Humanism," in *Basic Writings* (San Francisco: Harper, 1993), 213–66.

4. C. S. Lewis, *The Abolition of Man* (New York: Macmillan, 1947), 82–83.

5. Christopher Chapple, "Noninjury to Animals: Jaina and Buddhist Perspectives," in *Animal Sacrifices*, ed. Tom Regan (Philadelphia: Temple University Press, 1986), 213–36.

6. Friedrich Schweitzer, *Ethics and Civilization*, 2. 255.

7. Ibid., 250.

8. Ibid., 254.

9. R. H. Tawney, *Equality*, 3d ed. (New York: George Allen and Unwin, 1964), 49.

10. Jean Bethke Elshtain, *Democracy on Trial* (New York: Basic Books, 1995), 68.

11. Ibid., 71, 69.

12. Ibid., 73.

13. *The Compact Edition of the Oxford English Dictionary*, 2. 436.

14. Ann Douglas, *Terrible Honesty* (New York: Farrar, Straus, Giroux, 1995), 254–66; Aileen Kraditor, *The Ideas of the Woman Suffrage Movement* (New York: Norton, 1965).

15. Carl Degler, *In Search of Human Nature* (New York: Oxford, 1991).

16. Katha Pollitt, *Reasonable Creatures* (New York: Vintage, Books, 1995), 42–62.

17. Plato, *Republic* 454e.

18. Jean-Jacques Rousseau, *Emile*, 357–58.

19. Plato, *Symposium* 189e–190d.

20. *New York Times*, April, 23, 1970, editorial page.

21. For an optimistic outlook on Earth Day and the successes since then, see Gregg Easterbrook, *A Moment on the Earth* (New York: Viking Books, 1995); for a more balanced outlook, see "Earth Day at 25: How Has Nature Fared?" *New York Times*, April 18, pp. C1–C5; on a more negative note, see "Earth Day's Birthday," *New York Times*, editorial page, April 22, 1995: "All is not well. It is too soon for anyone to declare victory, too soon for complacency, too soon for Congress to abdicate its responsibility for national stewardship."

22. Roderick Nash, *The Rights of Nature* (Madison: University of Wisconsin Press, 1989), 70.

23. Genevieve Lloyd, *The Man of Reason: Male and Female in Western Philosophy* (Minneapolis: University of Minnesota Press, 1984), 11–15.

24. Carolyn Merchant, *The Death of Nature* (San Francisco: Harper and Row, 1980), 68.

25. Lynn White, Jr., *Machina Ex Deo: Essays in the Dynamism of Western Culture* (Cambridge: MIT Press, 1968), 93.

26. See Dietrich Bonhoeffer, *Ethics*, 226–27.

27. John Passmore (*Man's Responsibility for Nature* [New York: Scribner's, 1974], 7) notes that the Christian attitude toward (nonhuman) nature is much more dependent on the Greeks than the Hebrews.

28. Genesis 1:28; see Ian McHarg, "The Place of Nature in the City of Man," in *Western Man and Environmental Ethics*, ed. Ian Barbour (Reading, Penn.: Addison-Wesley, 1973), 174: "The literal interpretation of the creation in Genesis is the tacit text for Jews and Christian alike—man exclusively divine, man

given dominion over all life and nonlife, enjoined to subdue the earth. The cosmos is thought to be a pyramid erected to support man upon its pinnacle. . . . "

29. Roger Sorrell, *Saint Francis of Assisi and Nature* (New York: Oxford University Press, 1988), 8.

30. G. K. Chesterton, *St. Francis of Assisi* (Garden City, N.Y.: Image Books, 1957), 87.

31. Roger Sorrell, *Saint Francis of Assisi and Nature*, 47; see also Edward Armstrong, *Saint Francis: Nature Mystic* (Berkeley: University of California Press, 1973), 98.

32. René Dubos, "Franciscan Conservation versus Benedictine Stewardship," in *A God Within* (New York: Scribner, 1972), 169.

33. Ibid., 174.

34. Peter Singer, *Animal Liberation* (New York: New York Review of Books, 1975).

35. Mary Midgley, "Review of 'Rights of Nature' by Roderick Nash," *Commonweal*, June 16, 1989, 376.

36. Edward O. Wilson (*The Diversity of Life* [Cambridge: Harvard University Press, 1992], 280) makes a conservative estimate that the rate of extinction worldwide is 27,000 species a year.

37. Charles Mann and Mark Plummer, *Noah's Choice: The Future of Endangered Species* (New York: Knopf, 1995), 215.

38. James Serpell, *In the Company of Animals: A Study of Human–Animal Relationships* (New York: Basil Blackwell, 1986).

39. Natalie Angier (*The Beauty of the Beastly* [Boston: Houghton Mifflin, 1995], 118) notes that "cockroach researchers need never fear that animal rights activists will break into their lab at midnight to liberate their experimental subjects."

40. Christopher Stone, *Earth and Other Ethics* (San Francisco: Harper and Row, 1987), 217.

41. Elizabeth Marshall Thomas, *The Tribe of Tiger*, 133; Lewis Thomas, *Late Night Thoughts on Listening to Mahler's Ninth Symphony* (New York: Viking Books, 1983), 36: Concerning the horse, Clever Hans, who it was discovered could not really count but was watching his experimenter's behavior for clues, Lewis reflects: "He was considerably better at observing human beings and interpreting their behavior than humans are at comprehending animals or, for that matter, other humans."

42. (New York: Oxford University Press, 1966), 203.

43. Peter French, *Responsibility Matters*, 97.

44. Wendell Berry, *The Unsettling of America* (San Francisco: Sierra Club, 1977), 85.

45. Cited in Maurice Friedman, *Martin Buber: The Middle Years 1923–45* (New York: Dutton, 1983), 192.

46. G. K. Chesterton, *Orthodoxy* (Garden City, N.Y.: Image Books, 1959), 61.

47. Frederick Turner, "Escape from Modernism in Science, Religion, Politics and Art," in *Sacred Interconnections*, ed. David Ray Griffin (Albany, N.Y.: SUNY Press, 1990), 147.

48 Alfred North Whitehead, *Aims of Education* (New York: Free Press, 1967), 27, 26.

49. Lawrence Kohlberg, *The Philosophy of Moral Development* (San Francisco: Harper and Row, 1981).

50. An exception would be Robert Nisbet, *Twilight of Authority* (New York: Oxford University Press, 1975), 238–39, where hierarchy is presented as "an ineradicable element of the social bond."

51. Ken Auletta, "Opening up the Times," *New Yorker*, June 28, 1993, 56.

52. Ibid., 60.

53. Elizabeth Drew, *On the Edge*, 98–99: "The unhierarchical structure and the collegial style of the Clinton White House seemed, at first, wonderful." Drew does mention (p. 240) the existence of "circles" in the White House.

54. Michael Walzer (*Thick and Thin*, 98) says "there is no linearity, then, and no hierarchy. The order of the self is better imagined as a thickly populated circle, with me in the center surrounded by my self-entities who stand at different temporal and spatial removes." A circle still has "linearity" and, I would also claim, hierarchy. But for such a hierarchy of a "thickly populated" self, a sphere would be a better image than a circle.

55. Pseudo-Dionysius, "Celestial Hierarchy," in *The Complete Works* (New York: Paulist Press, 1987), 143–91.

56. John Passmore, *Man's Responsibility for Nature*, 187, is right in saying that ethics has "to be justified by reference to human interests." That is not necessarily a "utilitarian" position. It simply acknowledges that unless a reality is related to human interest it cannot be spoken of ethically. "Inter-est" means to be related to us. To say "a being has intrinsic worth apart from humans" is still a human judgment.

57. Peter Medawar, *The Uniqueness of the Individual* (New York: Methuen, 1957).

58. Many writers on ecology are oblivious of this meaning of uniqueness. For example, Eric Freyfogle, *Justice and the Earth* (New York: Free Press, 1995), 72: "We should be quick to note that many modern ethicists believe that humans are *sui generis*—unique—and that moral worth does not extend beyond humans. We can refer to these philosophers as the exclusivists." One has only to consult the use of "unique" in writers such as Lewis Thomas, Wendell Berry, or Loren Eiseley to show that Freyfogle has completely misunderstood the word.

59. Jane Flax, *Thinking Fragments*, 216–21.

60. Ibid., 232.

Chapter Seven

1. Edward Hall, *Beyond Culture* (Garden City, N.Y.: Doubleday, 1976), 14.

2. Saint Augustine, *The Confessions of St. Augustine* (Garden City, N.Y.: Image Books, 1960), book XI.

3. H. Richard Niebuhr, *The Responsible Self*, 93.

4. Henri Bergson, *Creative Evolution* (New York: Modern Library, 1944), 5.

5. George Eliot, *Middlemarch* (New York: Oxford University Press, 1986), 825.

6. Martin Buber, *I and Thou*, 12–13.

7. Samuel Beckett, *Endgame* (New York: Grove Press, 1958), 49, 70.

8. James Hillman, *Suicide and the Soul* (New York: Harper, 1975), 168.

9. Michael Sandel, *Liberalism*, 179.

10. Alasdair McIntyre, *After Virtue* (Notre Dame, Ind.: University of Notre Dame Press, 1980), 206.

11. Jaroslav Pelikan, *Reformation of Church and Dogma* (Chicago: University of Chicago Press, 1984).

12. See Albert Camus, *The Rebel* (New York: Vintage Books, 1956), 246–52; on the emergence of oral tradition in Jewish history, see Ellis Rivkin, *The Shaping of Jewish History* (New York: Scribner, 1971), 42–52.

13. G. K. Chesterton, *Orthodoxy*, 48.

14. Jaroslav Pelikan, *The Vindication of Tradition* (New Haven, Conn.: Yale University Press, 1984).

15. As in Marx: "The tradition of all dead generations weighs like a nightmare on the brain of the living."

16. John Dewey, *Experience and Education* (New York: Collier Books, 1963).

17. Yosef Yerushalmi, *Zakhor: Jewish History and Jewish Memory* (Seattle: University of Washington Press, 1982), 82.

18. Adam Michnik, "A Talk Between Jürgen Habermas and Adam Michnik," *New York Review of Books*, March 24, 1994, 29.

19. J. R. Lucas, *Responsibility*, 77.

20. *New York Times*, August 31, 1994.

21. *New York Times*, February 23, 1995.

22. Ian Buruma, *The Wages of Guilt*, 176.

23. Gordon Craig, "An Inability to Mourn," *New York Review of Books*, July 14, 1994, 43–45.

24. Ian Buruma, *The Wages of Guilt*, 258.

25. Ibid., 170; for a study of the whole era, see Daikichi Irokawa, *The Age of Hirohito* (New York: Free Press, 1995).

26. *New York Times*, August 16, 1995, p. A24. An earlier statement by the Parliament had drawn criticism for avoiding the words responsibility, apology, and guilt. See *New York Times*, June 7, 1995, 1.

27. *New York Times*, March 15, 1995.

28. Among the many books published near the fiftieth anniversary of the bombings, the most detailed and controversial is Gar Alperovitz, *The Decision to Use the Atomic Bomb* (New York: Knopf, 1995); see also Ronald Takaki, *Hiroshima* (Boston: Little, Brown, 1995); Robert Jay Lifton and Greg Mitchell, *Hiroshima in America* (New York: G. P. Putnam's Sons, 1995).

29. The United States never considered using the atomic bomb against Germany. However, historians have not found racist reasons for the decision; at least at a conscious level, the reasons were military. See Martin Sherwin, *The World Destroyed: The Atomic Bomb and the Grand Alliance* (New York: Vintage Books, 1975).

30. Michael Walzer, *Just and Unjust Wars* (New York: Basic Books, 1977); James Johnson, *Just War Traditions and the Restraint of War* (Princeton, N.J.: Princeton University Press, 1981); when the United States government acceded to Japanese requests not to use "V-J Day," the *London Times*, March 8, 1995, pronounced: "The fact that Japan was defeated in a just war is inescapable; it cannot be buried in polite euphemism." That Japan was defeated is an inescapable fact; that World War II was a "just war" is a claim based on theory.

31. *Aboth* 4:2; see Judah Goldin, ed. *The Living Talmud* (Chicago: University of Chicago Press, 1957), 155.

32. *New York Times*, March 1, 1995, p. A19.

33. Ian Buruma, *The Wages of Guilt*, 94.

34. Robert McNamara, *In Retrospect: The Tragedy and Lessons of Vietnam* (New York: Times Books, 1995).

35. Ibid., 314.

36. Theodore Draper ("The Abuse of McNamara," *New York Review of Books*, May 25, 1995, 16–17) makes the legitimate point that McNamara's opposition to the war was made known by the publication of The Pentagon Papers in 1971. Very few people, however, mastered the contents of that document. Draper also objects to the "vitriolic" editorial of the *New York Times* and similar attacks. However inadequate the apology may be, official acknowledgment of failure should not be met with contempt.

37. *New York Times*, April 30, 1985.

38. Cited in Telford Taylor, *The Anatomy of the Nuremberg Trials* (New York: Knopf, 1992), 167.

39. *New York Times*, November 12, 1988.

40. See Ray Monk, *Ludwig Wittgenstein: His Life and Work* (New York: Penguin Books, 1991), 481.

41. For a bibliography of this extensive literature, see Michael Shermis and Arthur Zannoni, *Introduction to Jewish-Christian Relations* (New York: Paulist Press, 1992).

42. Solomon Zeitlin, *Who Killed Jesus?* (New York: Harper, 1942); Ellis Rivkin, *What Killed Jesus?* (Nashville: Abingdon Press, 1984); John Dominic Crossan, *Who Killed Jesus? Exposing the Roots of Anti-Semitism in the Gospel Story of the Death of Jesus* (San Francisco: Harper, 1995).

43. *Catechism of the Catholic Church*, (Washington: United States Catholic Conference, 1994), 154.

44. The Council of Trent, for example, said that "The purpose of the Passion and Death of the Son of God our Saviour was to redeem the sins of all time.... The sinners were the authors, the instruments, as it were, of all the sorrows he endures." The contemporary catechism in referring to "Jesus" rather than "the Son of God our Saviour" makes it more difficult for Jews to recognize the statement as theological.

45. Jules Isaac (*The Teaching of Contempt* [New York: Holt, Rinehart and Winston, 1964], 122–23) cites Charles Peguy's statement that "it was not the Jews who crucified Jesus Christ, but all our sins; and the Jews, who were only the instrument, partake with the others at the font of salvation." Isaac is appreciative of the evident good intention of Peguy's, but the Jews still end up as the instrument.

46. See Philip Hallie, *Lest Innocent Blood Be Shed* (San Francisco: Harper and Row, 1979); Eva Fogelman, *Conscience and Courage: Rescuers of Jews during the Holocaust* (New York: Anchor Books, 1995); André Trocmé, *Jesus and the Nonviolent Movement* (Scottsdale, Ariz.: Herald Press, 1973); Vera Laska, *Nazism, Resistance and Holocaust in World War II: A Bibliography* (Metuchen, N.J.: Scarecrow Press, 1985).

47. Conor Cruise O'Brien, "A Lost Chance to Save the Jews," *New York Review of Books*, April 27, 1989, 27–35.

48. Yosef Yerushalmi, "Response to R. Ruether," in *Auschwitz: Beginning of a New Era?* ed. Eva Fleischner (New York: ICTAV, 1977), 104; for the persecution in Spain, see Robert Seltzer, *Jewish People, Jewish Thought* (New York: Macmillan, 1980), 366–68; for the history of the papacy and the Jews, see Edward Synan, *The Popes and the Jews in the Middle Ages* (New York: Macmillan, 1965).

49. Albert Borgmann, *Crossing the Postmodern Divide* (Chicago: University of Chicago Press, 1972), 2–3.

50. Hannah Arendt, *The Human Condition*, 237.

51. Albert Hirschmann, "Morality and the Social Sciences: A Durable Tension," in *Social Science as Moral Inquiry*, 27.

52. Robert Heilbroner, "What Has the Future Ever Done for Me?" *New York Times Magazine*, January 19, 1974, 14–15.

53. Hans Jonas, *The Imperative of Responsibility*, 18.

54. Ibid., 10.

55. Peter French, *Responsibility Matters*, 101.

56. Ibid., 145.

57. Marina Warner, *Six Myths of Our Time* (New York: Vintage Books, 1995), 47.

58. Hans Jonas, *The Imperative of Responsibility*, 39.

59. Dietrich Bonhoeffer, *Ethics*, 234.

60. Richard Farson, *Birthrights* (New York: Macmillan, 1974).

61. Edmund Morgan, *The Puritan Family* (New York: Harper Torch, 1966), 75–79; Morgan notes that girls were also included in this process although they were not learning a trade (p. 76).

62. Robert Bly, *Iron John: A Book about Men* (Reading, Penn.: Addison-Wesley, 1990).

63. Robert Coles, *The Moral Life of Children* (Boston: Atlantic Monthly, 1986), 77.

64. David Elkind, *Children and Adolescents* (New York: Oxford University Press, 1970), 99.

65. Wayne Booth, *The Company We Keep* (Berkeley: University of California Press, 1988), 253.

66. PBS, February 14, 1992.

67. Sisela Bok, *Lying* (New York: Vintage Books, 1978), 217.

68. Barbara Myerhoff, *Number Our Days* (New York: Dutton, 1978), 267; see also Hannah Arendt, *The Human Condition*, 233.

69. In a disputed Supreme Court decision allowing a high school to test athletes for drugs, Justice Antonin Scalia cited "the schools' custodial and tutelary responsibility for the children." *New York Times*, June 27, 1995, p. B6. This claim is not surprising, given the history of the court's attitude to schoolchildren's rights. Nevertheless, it seems to me a terrible violation of the right to privacy when there is no reasonable cause.

70. William Kilpatrick, *Why Johnny Can't Tell Right from Wrong* (New York: Simon and Schuster, 1994), 34.

71. John Dewey, "My Pedagogical Creed," in *John Dewey on Education*, ed. Reginald Archambault (Chicago: University of Chicago Press, 1974), 427–39.

72. John Westbrook, *John Dewey and American Democracy*, 506–08.

73. G. Langford, *Philosophy and Education* (London: Macmillan, 1968), 114.

74. Eleanor Duckworth, *The Having of Wonderful Ideas* (New York: Teachers College Press, 1987), 113.

75. Alan Tom, *Teaching as a Moral Craft*, 80.

76. An influential book in the 1960s and republished in 1978 is entitled

Values and Teaching (Columbus, Ohio: Merrill), but the authors Louis Raths, Merrill Harmin, and Sidney Simon are about advising "teachers" not to teach. They assume children will develop their own "values." But "it is entirely possible that children will choose not to develop values. It is the teacher's responsibility to support this choice also." (p. 47). On adult education, see Malcolm Knowles, *Self-Directed Learning* (New York: Association), 1975); William Reinsmith, *Archetypal Forms in Teaching* (Westport, Conn.: Greenwood, 1992), 158–59: "However the case may be, the fact remains that once students take responsibility for their own learning teaching sooner or later will come to an end. . . . To put it another way: In the last analysis there is no teaching, only learning. And all learning is self-taught." The last sentence would seem to contradict the next to last.

77. Carl Rogers, *Freedom to Learn for the 80s* (Columbus, Ohio: Merrill, 1983), 137.

78. Newt Gingrich's *To Renew America* joins this literature attacking teaching. In the second wave of history, the teacher was active, the student passive. In the coming third wave, "responsibility is placed on the learner rather than on the teacher" (p. 143).

Chapter Eight

1. Cited in Jeffrey Stout, *Ethics after Babel* (Boston: Beacon, 1988), 166.

2. See Stephen Toulmin, *Cosmopolis: The Hidden Agenda of Modernity* (New York: Macmillan, 1990), 100.

3. Northrop Frye, *The Educated Imagination* (Bloomington: Indiana University Press, 1964), 64. Sidney Lumet makes the point in criticizing Hollywood's confusing of generality and universality; in contrast, he writes of Carl Dreyer's "Passion of Joan of Arc": "The more confined and the specific the choices were, the more universal the results became." See Sidney Lumet, *Making Movies* (New York: Knopf, 1995).

4. Jean Leclercq, *The Love of Learning and the Desire for God* (New York: Fordham University Press, 1974), 128.

5. Wayne Meeks, *The Moral World of the First Christians* (Philadelphia: Westminster, 1986); Gerd Theissen, *The Social Setting of Pauline Christianity* (Philadelphia: Fortress, 1982).

6. Bernard Williams, *Morality: An Introduction to Ethics* (New York: Harper and Row, 1972), 25.

7. Paul Johnson, *Modern Times*, 11.

8. Carl Degler, *In Search of Human Nature*, 187–211.

9. Matthew Arnold, *Literature and Dogma* (New York: Macmillan, 1883), xxvii; compare the first sentence of Alfred North Whitehead's *Aims of Educa-*

tion, 1: "Culture is activity of thought, and receptiveness to beauty and humane feeling." The essay was first published in 1917.

10. Theodore Adorno as cited in Russell Jacoby, *Social Amnesia* (Boston: Beacon Press, 1975), 34.

11. Quoted in Thomas Merton, *Conjectures of a Guilty Bystander* (Garden City, N.Y.: Image Books, 1968), 44.

12. Boris Pasternak, *Doctor Zhivago*, cited in James Douglass, *The Non-Violent Cross* (New York: Macmillan, 1962), 9.

13. Larry May, *Sharing Responsibility*, 174–75.

14. Ludwig Wittgenstein, *On Certainty* (New York: Harper Torch, 1972), no. 612, 81.

15. F. S. C. Northrop, *The Meeting of East and West* (New York: Collier Books, 1966), 439.

16. R. G. Mulgar, *Maori, Pakeha and Democracy* (New York: Oxford University Press, 1989).

17. E. E. Evans-Pritchard, *Nuer Religion* (London: Oxford University Press, 1956), 84: A deformed baby was declared to be a hippopotamus and could therefore be drowned.

18. Christopher Chapple, "Noninjury to Animals: Jaina and Buddhist Perspectives," *Animal Sacrifices*, 213–36.

19. Jomo Kenyatta, *Facing Mount Kenya* (London: Martin Secker and Warburg, 1938).

20. See her novel *Possessing the Secret of Joy* (New York: Harcourt Brace Jovanovich, 1992).

21. Seble Dawit and Salem Mekuria, "The West Just Doesn't Get It," *New York Times*, December 8, 1993; see the comments of Clifford Gertz in David Berreby, "The Unabsolute Truths of Clifford Gertz, *New York Times Magazine*, April 9, 1995, 46: "Look, I think clitoridectomy is a horrible business. . . . But what we are going to do? Invade the horn of Africa and arrest everybody. If you're serious about addressing this, you ask people there about the practice and you listen to them. You listen to women from there who justify the practice. You want to change things, you don't start by proclaiming that you possess the truth. That's not very helpful."

22. See G. Werner Jeanrond, *Call and Response* (New York: Continuum, 1995), 8–9.

23. Gershom Scholem, *Major Trends in Jewish Mysticism* (New York: Schocken, 1961), 10–14.

24. James Bury, *A History of Freedom of Thought* (New York: Holt, 1913), 247–48.

25. Hannah Arendt, *On Violence* (New York: Harcourt, Brace and World, 1970), 56.

26. Ian Buruma, *The Wages of Guilt*, 255.

27. Ibid., 253.

28. Ibid., 253.

29. *New York Times*, May 7, 1995, IV, 3.

30. *New York Times*, February 19,1995, business section.

31. John Locke, *Some Thoughts Concerning Education* (Cambridge: Cambridge University Press, 1927); Erik Erikson, *Childhood and Society*, 2d ed. (New York: Norton, 1963), 251–55.

32. Willard Waller, *The Sociology of Teaching* (New York: John Wiley, 1932), 336: the author describes intimidation of a child by having the child strip naked.

33. On the question of shame, see Christopher Lasch, *The Revolt of the Elites*, 197–212.

34. See David Remnick, *Lenin's Tomb* (New York: Random House, 1993), 279–89.

35. Frederick Binder and David Reimers, *All the Nations Under Heaven: An Ethnic and Racial History of New York City.* (New York: Columbia University Press, 1995). In the 1640s, when there were one thousand people, there were already eighteen languages. A letter from Minister Megapolensis to the Synod of Amsterdam in 1655 says that there is already too much diversity on Manhattan Island and "it would create a still greater confusion if the obstinate and immovable Jews came to settle here." See Edwin Gaustad, *A Documentary History of Religion in America* (Grand Rapids, Mich.: Eerdmans, 1982), 86.

36. *One Nation, Many Peoples: A Declaration of Cultural Interdependence* (Albany: New York State Department of Education, 1991); for a dissenting voice, see Arthur Schlesinger, Jr., *The Disuniting of America* (New York: Norton, 1991).

INDEX